SYSTEMOLOGY
180

*Thank you for supporting independent publishing
and the work of the Systemology Society*

mardukite.com

MARDUKITE ACADEMY PREMIERE PAPERBACK

SYSTEMOLOGY
180

THE FAST-TRACK TO ASCENSION
⟨A HANDBOOK FOR PILOTS⟩

THE BASIC THEORY AND PRACTICE OF
SYSTEMOLOGY AS COMMUNICATED BY

JOSHUA FREE

THE JOSHUA FREE IMPRINT
JFI PUBLICATIONS

© 2023, JOSHUA FREE

ISBN : 978-1-961509-14-6

Also available in hardcover.

A MARDUKITE SYSTEMOLOGY PUBLICATION
Mardukite Research Library Catalogue No. "Liber-180"
Developed for Mardukite Academy & Systemology Society
cum superiorum privilegio veniaque
FIRST PAPERBACK EDITION
September 2023
Published from
Joshua Free Imprint – JFI Publications
Mardukite Borsippa HQ, San Luis Valley, Colorado

A Flight Manual for Spiritual Ascension!

A perfected "metahuman" state for the Human Condition awaits; free of emotional turbulence, societal programming and an ability to be truly Self-Determined from the clear perspective of the actual Self, the Eternal Spirit or "I-AM" Awareness that is back of and beyond this existence—an "Angel" or "god" that has fallen only by its own considerations, by being convinced that it resides locally here on earth within a perishable human shell.

"Systemology 180: The Fast-Track to Ascension" by Joshua Free presents newly revised instruction from the Mardukite Academy to deliver the fastest results in climbing the ladder of Ascension.

Hundreds of exercises and techniques that progressively free you from bonds of the Human Condition and increase your spiritual horsepower enough to break the chains and attachments to the material world and an existence confined to a physical body.

The premiere Systemology Society Technical Volume revealing the entire Pathway to Self-Honesty, concise training for all the "routes" from six different courses and a complete collection of Defragmentation procedures published from 2019 through 2022.

The ultimate manual for Professional Systemology Pilots, Zuists, Mardukite Ministers, and all those Seeker's who are flying solo. Priceless to anyone with even a basic Systemology background.

As a bonus to this volume, this reference edition also includes: "The Complete Systemology Technical Dictionary (Version 5.0)"

Destination: INFINITY!

*Based on the professional
piloting procedure lectures
given by Joshua Free to
the Systemology Society
from 2019 through 2022*

TABLET OF CONTENTS

∞

EDITOR'S NOTE

"The Self does not actualize Awareness
past a point not understood."
—*Tablets of Destiny*

While preparing this book for publication, the editors
have made every effort to present this material in a
straightforward manner—using clear, easy to read and
understand language.

Wherever a word that is defined in the glossary
first appears in the text, it will be **bold**.

A clear understanding of this material is critical for
achieving actual realizations and personal benefit
from applying philosophies of *Mardukite Zuism* and
NexGen Systemology spiritual technology.

The *Seeker* should be especially certain not to simply
"read through" this book without attaining proper
comprehension as "knowledge." Even when the
information continues to be "interesting"—if at any
point you find yourself feeling lost or confused while
reading, trace your steps back. Return to the point of
misunderstanding and go through it again.

It is expected that a *Seeker* will work through this
material multiple times to achieve optimum results.

And *now* responsibility for this power and its
actualization is passed on to you, the *Seeker*.

Take nothing within this book on faith.
Apply the information directly to your life.

Decide for yourself.

∞

"Becoming a person means that the individual moves, knowingly and acceptingly, toward being the process which he inwardly and actually is. He moves away from being what he is not – away from being a facade. He is not trying to be more than he is, with attendant feelings of insecurity or bombastic defensiveness. He is not trying to be less than he is, with the attendant feelings of guilt and self-deprecation.
He is increasingly listening to the deepest recesses of his psychological and emotional being, and finds himself increasingly willing to *be*, with greater accuracy and depth, the *Self* which he most truly is."

—CARL ROGERS
Founder of Humanistic Psychology
in his book "On Becoming a Person"

SYSTEMOLOGY
180

THE FAST-TRACK TO ASCENSION

SYSTEMOLOGY GRADE-V SUMMARY AND OVERVIEW [THE BACKTRACK & A NEW DAWN OF IMMORTALITY]

Greetings *Seekers*—

Welcome to *Systemology Grade-V*!

Let us take a moment here to catch up and get on the same page before delving further along on the *Pathway*.

Many *Seekers* crossing paths with our Systemology actually do so by routes of "magic" and "mysticism"—and what is *magic* really, but an attempted **codification** of *mysticism*. "**Religion**" is, of course, yet another way in which to make attempts to understand *spiritual systems*. But here in this physical universe, here on planet Earth at the very least, these *routes* have only offered glimpses and hints to what is otherwise never understood perfectly. And whenever truths are actually gleaned, they are done so through an **individual**'s own filters of understanding—seeming to be very real for themselves, who are in **agreement** with it— but it is never even perfectly communicated thereafter. The perfect duplication of an "originating" experience is never really able to be passed to another—and even if it were, that other individual would still perceive it within the confines of their own filters of understanding. In essence, this mode has led us to a system or Universe comprised of agreements from the 'lowest common denominator' so to speak.

When we consider *magic* as a "codified" or "systematized" understanding of *mysticism,* or what is otherwise *spiritual* phenomenon, what we are really seeing is a progressive or **gradient** course of breaking agreements with the Physical Universe—to rise above the **imprints** and **implants** that fix our **attention** and considerations to the low-level reality of this **Beta-Existence**. This is the *Great Work*, in effect, what **esoteric** circles have whispered of for thousands of years concerning a "Great Magical Arcanum"—an incommunicable understanding, an awareness of **realization**, that all of the facets have pointed to collectively but which is never generally found from any one avenue of pursuit

14

exclusively. Nor does an individual benefit from perpetually spinning the dial on an intellectual combination lock with the hope that they will randomly and miraculously crack the safe and open the vault cover to the perfected true **knowledge** and supreme understanding.

The present author's development of "Systemology" resulted from a quarter-of-a-century dedicated to "practical occultism" and "esoteric avenues" of exploration and experimentation in the 'New Age' underground. In all that time, dozens of literary discourses (books) were given on those subjects directly, chronicling the *Pathway* taken specifically by the present author. Is this the only way in which answers could be gleaned? Perhaps not. But such an outline *was* refined and presented along the way—and when completed, when a bird's eye overview was finally accessible, it revealed a strong parallel to the *actual* "Gates" separating this Universe (and its participants) from the ALL. Consequently, in 2019, the "Grades" (now used to represent the "Mardukite Academy") were distinguished—not only for intellectual purposes, but specifically to define very tangible and finite *gradients* or *ledges* of **actualized** **"realizations"** and increased Awareness; what some individuals might classify as *states* of Beingness.

THE GRADES OF MARDUKITE ACADEMY

Systemology begins with Grade-III, partly based on earlier research developments. Pursuits into the theory and practical **methodology** of "Systemology" occurred consecutive with the original work of the Mardukite Chamberlains (Mardukite Org.) starting as early as 2008. Of course, the actual emphasis at the time is what we now consider "Grade-II" for our system. Our complete educational system is presently as follows (defined for the "Mardukite Academy"):

Grade-I	Route of Mysticism (and Magic)
Grade-II	Mardukite Mesopotamia (Religion)
Grade-III	Mardukite Systemology [Master]
Grade-IV	Metahuman Systemology [Wizard Lvl-0]
Grade-V	Spiritual Systemology [Wizard Lvl-1]

SYSTEMOLOGY TECHNIQUES

The "systematic processing" techniques for what is now "Class-1 Piloting" originally developed as an advanced methodology for "Mardukite Ministers" to practice spiritual advisement and religious counseling from within our unique tradition. This is, perhaps, most evident in the primary "Class-1" textbook, *The Tablets of Destiny (Revelation)*" [*Liber-One*]. Unquestionably, it paved the way for solid developments of "Grade-III" work (and above) in an innovative, new and relevant way not elsewhere explored in the commercial 'New Age' or even the 'esoteric underground'. Additionally, as relayed in *"The Power of Zu"* lectures, an increased urgency on its behind-the-scenes development resulted from efforts toward personal rehabilitation following an incident in October 2015, when the present author was struck by a large truck while walking. Were it not for our Systemology, there would have been no additional work by Joshua Free from then onward. This is not stated to give some 'wild' testimonial to our work; but the facts remain as they are.

A complete collection of "Grade-III" work developed for nearly a decade behind-the-scenes before its back-to-back release in late 2019. By the end of 2021, the Systemology Society completed an additional tier of developments —"Grade-IV"—which ended with a proverbial 'Wall of Fire' that we must now cross in order to achieve any higher vistas with additional *Grades*. But certainly, no one actively involved or participating in this program can dispute the positive gains and tremendous accomplishments demonstrated by the solid work performed thus far—a collection of knowledge and techniques that we are now able to reflect on in its entirety with the new Grade-V volume, "*Systemology-180: The Ascension Manual (A Handbook for Pilots)*."

PILOTING AND PROCESSING

There are two coinciding "lanes" of the *Pathway* leading toward the same basic gradients (or "states" if you prefer): *Piloting* and *Processing*. The first is traveled primarily by

"training" (particularly from books and lectures) with supplemental applications of "systematic processing"; whereas the second is accomplished by an untrained *Seeker* that
is "processed" with the guidance and direction of a trained
Pilot. A *Seeker* working alone has only the first option—to
be their own *Solo Pilot*. As such, they are responsible for all
the training as a *Pilot* and also the processing as a *Seeker*.
Determination must be high in order to successfully "Fly
Solo" since there is no one else to help maintain a *Seeker's*
"**presence**" in "session" or to keep them from "free-spin-
ning" in thought if they stray from a technique.

"Flying Solo" for the entire *Pathway* may require a longer
more intensive journey, but it can still yield stable results.
There is, however, a common misconception among our
readers, that books and training for *Pilots* only apply to
processing *others*. This is most certainly not the case. *Piloting* is the proper handling of "systematic processing"
whether it is applied alone to *Self* or applied to *Self* under
the direction of someone else. In either case, to be effective, the same systematic knowledge must be applied; it
must be *Piloted*—even when the *Pilot* and *Seeker* are the
same individual.

Whether a *Seeker* is operating alone or not, all techniques
of "systematic processing" are *Self-processed*; they all must
be processed by *Self*. A *Pilot* is only directing attention, but
the "**command-lines**" are not a magic spell delivered by a
magic wand. The *Pilot* is not "doing" anything *to* the *Seeker*;
the *Seeker* must apply the "command lines" of the technique to *Self* as *Self*. This systematic application of communication and **intention** is what makes "processing" possible or effective. It is the same principle that allows all
other metaphysical and spiritual techniques any effectiveness; however, our Systemology Grades simply employ the
most direct applications of the underlying fundamentals
that yield significant results without a lot of excessive
mystical or religious themes draped on top unnecessarily.

GRADE PROCESSING AND PILOT CLASSIFICATIONS

The basic gradients and presently existing classifications—as well as our publications representing them for the "Mardukite Academy"—are:

—*Grade-III*—

Class-1 Systemology: The Original Thesis [*Liber-S1X*]
　　　　"The Power of Zu" Lecture Series [*Liber-S1Z*]
　　　　The Tablets of Destiny (Revelation) [*Liber-One*]
Class-2* Crystal Clear: Handbook for Seekers [*Liber-2B*]
　　　　"Mardukite Systemology" Academy Lectures‡

—*Grade-IV*—

Class-2C Metahuman Destinations Course [*Liber-2C,2D,3C*]†
Class-3 Imaginomicon [*Liber-3D*]
Class-3E The Way of the Wizard [*Liber-3E*]

Each systematic processing "Route" along the *Pathway* **correlates** to specific technical documents (or "flight manuals") containing basic information and instructions for a *Pilot* to operate specific techniques toward a finite result or end-point. "Route-1" and "Route-2" are described in Grade-III; while "Route-3" and "Route-0" pertain to Grade-IV. The complete training is contained within half-a-dozen books that introduce the theory and practice of various exercises. The actual techniques themselves are now collected in an upper-level reference volume, "*Systemology-180: The Fast-Track to Ascension (A Handbook for Pilots)*," which is of high-power value to those individuals that have completed the full Grade-III and Grade-IV education on its proper "systematic processing" and application to everyday life. This information is not only critical to *Professional Pilots*, but to all *Seekers*, especially those "*Flying Solo*" as solitary practitioners.

---

*　Each *Class* is a prerequisite for a "higher" *Class*. The material subsequently builds upon itself to form a greater and more complete understanding of the "big picture" being communicated overall.

‡　Available in "*The Complete Mardukite Master Course*" (anthology) and "*Mardukite Systemology: Mardukite Master Course Academy Lectures (Volume 4).*"

†　Reissued as two volumes in 2022.

PERSONAL DEFRAGMENTATION

The emphasis and goal of the portion of the *Pathway* given above is a preliminary to **"Ascension,"** a stable point of elevated realization and Awareness, which we define as **"Beta-Defragmentation."** —And by *"Beta"* we, of course, mean *this* Physical Universe; and where it applies to the Human Condition (in Grade-III and Grade-IV), we mean *this* present 'incarnation' or **association** of an **'Identity'** with a specific physical meat-body life-cycle of a *'genetic vehicle'*. As it is comprised of all Grade-III and Grade-IV material, "Class-3E" training is the only level of completion that covers enough detail to ensure a total "Beta-Defragmentation" regimen properly.

> The **Alpha Spirit** has one singular continuous life-track or *'Spiritual Timeline'* that is experienced in *Beta-Existence* as the separate life-times of a *'Genetic Vehicle'* or some other *body*.

"Defragmentation" is the personal processing of the **conditions** and upsets that impinge on an individual's ability, attention and/or Awareness to fully Self-determine and Self-direct a high quality of experience **(existence)**. In Grade-III and Grade-IV, the emphasis of 'systematic processing' remains on what is most accessible to an individual regarding experience during *this* "life"—but as we have discovered, much of the incidental imprinting taking place during *this* "lifetime" is really only detrimental because it is compounded onto a long "string" or "chain" of earlier similar and comparatively more significant imprints (and implants) on the *Backtrack*. And this is where we inevitably run up against what many refer to as *"past-lives."*

EXPLORING THE BACKTRACK (PAST-LIVES)

This "spiritual timeline" is a primary focus and emphasis of the higher level "Wizard Grades" in our Systemology—and when referring to that part of the timeline which is 'past', we began to refer to it as the *"Backtrack"*—and thus the first new core volume of our Grade-V material is concisely titled: *"Systemology: Backtrack."*

"Past-Lives" are only **semantically** described as such from the perspective of the birth-growth-death-cycle inherent in the incarnation of a physical body, that we refer to as a *'Genetic Vehicle'*, because it is independent of the actual *Self*, though an individual (*Alpha-Spirit*) may certainly be fragmented enough to wholly *consider* "itself" *as* the physical body in totality. This mentality is what prompts the desires for material greed or the 'fight' for survival in a physical universe, when in actuality, the *Alpha-Spirit*, the actual *Awareness* of *Self*, is "eternal" and cannot help but to go on "spiritually" existing and surviving. When a 'genetic vehicle' "dies" the *Alpha-Spirit* most certainly goes on to "live another day" as another form. Virtually every religion and spiritual philosophy suggests so, though the general understanding of this is not based in truths and therefore not carried with certainty by folk in their everyday life on Earth.

Our interest in the *Backtrack* is unique to our Systemology. Although for thousands of years, "past-lives" are frequently the subject of discussion in theosophical and metaphysical circles, there has been little codification or systematic understanding associated with it. For example, our interests are primarily on the "spiritual timeline" of the *Alpha-Spirit.* Such data is too often confused with the *cellular* or **genetic memory** of the physical organism 'used' by an *Alpha-Spirit.* "Genetic memory" *can* affect the Human experience—and operation of a 'genetic vehicle'—but the implications are only as significant as the *Alpha-Spirit* considers themselves to be 'Identified' *as* that 'genetic vehicle' (and no longer themselves as an 'Individual'). The *Self* takes on that "record" when it confuses the "I" with the "my" (in regards to a "body" as a separate entity). And of course, when the "body" is injured or **pinged**, the **sensation** forces attention and *Awareness* of the *Alpha-Spirit* to "snap-in" on the "body."

SPIRITUAL TECHNOLOGY OF ASCENSION

On the surface, there are very few practical differences between the technical theory behind "Beta-Defragmentattion" and what we consider "Alpha-Defragmentation" techniques (or else the proverbial "A.T." work we have been pursuing at the Systemology Society for many years). For the most part, only the **consideration** of significance and importance differs in regards to where 'systematic processing' is directed—and, of course, the associated *Pilot* training necessary to systematically handle the *Backtrack*. In some cases, it is also quite possible that imprinting and implanting from the *Backtrack* could effectively 'stall' or inhibit successful Beta-Defragmentation if it is actively triggered or in stimulation. This, of course, must be handled—which means a *Pilot* must be prepared to do so. We are not directly exploring "past-lives" in Grade-III and Grade-IV, but should such data emerge during these early processes, the matter cannot be ignored. Such training falls under the classification of Grade-V, and again, that proverbial "A.T." work.

Much of Grade-IV (such as "*Imaginomicon*") is considered "pre-A.T." work, also called Wizard Level-0; whereas Grade-V is the first true "A.T." gradient, and Wizard Level-1. The term "A.T." came about during semantic debates concerning how to precisely categorize the "Wizard-Level" work of our Systemology. But, in the end, the basic list seemed to surround the same general ideas—and fortunately, the same alphabetic letters:

—A—	—T—
Alpha	*Techniques*
Actualization	*Technology*
Ascension	*Technician*
Advanced	

SYSTEMATIC PROCESSING ROUTES 0-3

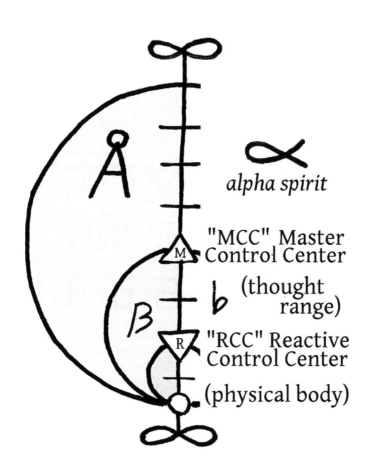

alpha spirit

"MCC" Master Control Center

(thought range)

"RCC" Reactive Control Center

(physical body)

ROUTE-1 REVISED (R1R)
CATHARTIC PROCESSING INSTRUCTIONS
"RR-SP-1" EXCERPT FROM LIBER-ONE

"Systemology Procedure RR-SP-1" (as based on **cuneiform** signs) debuted in the premiere edition of *"Tablets of Destiny"* (*Liber-One*)—and is reprinted in the original *Grade-III* mega-anthology *"The Systemology Handbook"* (to which a serious *Seeker* or *Pilot* may still refer to for reference). Although must of the original instruction has been retained, its practice was updated and revised in 2022, after three years of continued experimental research by the *Mardukite Academy of Systemology*, completion of *Grade-III* and *Grade-IV* material, and new developments of *Grade-V*. The first efforts toward revising RR-SP-1 appear as "Systemology Operating Procedure 2-C" (*SOP-2C*) as given in *"Metahuman Destinations"* (*Liber-Two*) for *Grade-IV*. The original steps for RR-SP-1 (based on cuneiform signs[*]) given in the premiere edition are as follows:

1. **US** — "to lead off; accompany; impose a process or path."
2. **TAB** — "to begin; start; fasten/hold level; commence."
3. **GI** — "to return; to go around a corner and back to."
4. **BA** — "to divide; allot; deduce; deduct; reduce."
5. **RA** — "to purify; cleanse; give release or be clear."
6. **DU** — "beingness; to become; to arrive at or ascend."
7. **TEN** — "to stop; end; extinguish or cool down."

The first step is to establish a good communicative energy between *Seeker* and *Pilot*. When "processing" begins, the *Seeker* should be seated comfortably, in a distraction-free environment, across from the *Pilot*, essentially face-to-face, but not touching—at a distance of three feet, since when used professionally there is often a table or desk in between.

---

[*]   Cuneiform sign translations are derived from Mardukite Research Library *"Sumerian Language"* volumes edited by Joshua Free.

Communication is more quickly and easily established with familiarity. A relationship develops between the *Seeker* and *Pilot*. It is favorable if the same *Pilot* continues to assist a *Seeker*, because **affinity** levels increase. We communicate better with those we feel "close" to and "like." By working with the same *Pilot*, a *Seeker* is assured that the assisting *Pilot* increases their understanding of the *Seeker's* "background." In spite of any records of former processing retained,[‡] the *Pilot* should begin each session simply by establishing communication about the *Seeker's* journey on the *Path*. Session time is not for casual conversation.

The *Pilot* is not to editorialize or educate during these periods. The *Pilot* is simply meant to provide "processing," selectively directing the *Seeker's* attention, completely awake in a state of focused concentration. Any discussion before the session should relate specifically to the *Seeker* and situations that may be currently bothering them at the time. The *Seeker* may even request that a particular **incident** or *Imprint* be processed during that session. Anything of this nature should be discussed before proceeding; mainly because anything spoken during "processing" should be specific to the "process." "Processing" is not an exploration of the *Seeker's* associative free thought or an opportunity for *Pilots* to relate anecdotal experiences from their own *Life*.

Once a few minutes of initial communication has occurred, it is important for the *Seeker* and *Pilot* to establish an agreement (or validation about Reality) for this session. Aside from this, there is no validation or **invalidation** to

---

[‡] All flight records (of processes) are confidential. Any information from the session should be recorded while it is taking place and retained by the *Pilot* in a *Flight-Log* for that specific *Seeker*. The *Pilot* may record, for training purposes and verification, their personal experience of the session in a separate *Flight-Log* designed to simply keep track of processing-hours ("air time") and critical details. The *Seeker* may also wish to retain record of their own personal experience and realizations in a specially designed *Adventure Journal*. As of 2020, this publication is available from the Systemology Society.

anything that the *Seeker* relates as an experience. There is prompting and redirection if necessary, but no **evaluation** is expressed; only an **acknowledgment** of receipt of communication. If during the session, a *Seeker* suddenly comes to some elated **realization** or asks questions that seek interpretation, the *Pilot* should always put the focus of *Awareness* back on the *Seeker* to examine, such as: "well, what do you think?" or "anything is possible" and then continue the processing steps.

It is assumed that when entering into these processing steps, a *Seeker* has read the "*Tablets of Destiny Revelation*" book (and/or "*Crystal Clear: Handbook for Seekers*") and, for example, knows what an *Imprint* is. Extending a copy of the book to a *Seeker* is the first act by a *Pilot* toward "education." It is assumed that *Seekers* you are first in contact with, those in close proximity to you, are already experienced in some type of visualization and concentration exercises such as demonstrated in previous Grades. If not, then there is some preliminary work that should be done prior to Systemology Processing. A *Pilot* should not engage in assisting Grade instruction unless they have completed *The Complete Mardukite Master* program. A *Master* is entrusted with tools to provide such instruction, but a *Pilot* should not be using "flight time" for education in this way. Formal course materials and Grade instruction are handled separately from Processing Sessions—*or* combined with books used on the *Seeker's* own time and initiative.

The *Pilot* assures the *Seeker*—in a few words—that they are safe; that they will remain awake and *Aware*; that Systemology "processing" is in no way hypnotherapy. To establish additional trust and agreements, the last statements made by the *Pilot* during this step will be along the lines of: "Now, I'm going to assist you in a process. Would that be fine with you?" Explain the process and defragment any unclear (or unknown) words used for the Processing Command Line. Then: "So, I was thinking of beginning the Processing now. Is that okay?" Every time the *Seeker* provides a response, the *Pilot* acknowledges receipt of the communication: "Okay." "Mm-hmm." "All right." The subject of communication in *Piloting* is covered further in "*Metahuman Destinations (Volume One).*"

The combined ZU *Awareness* active in both the *Pilot* and *Seeker* simultaneously should be a high enough frequency to handle, surface and reduce *Imprints* safely. When a *Seeker's Awareness* is reduced by *Imprints* during everyday life, their handling of ZU force (energy) is not enough for them to overcome *Imprints*. As a result, we tend to be subdued by them and make poor decisions, which reinforce them with more of our energy and **attention**. During "processing," they may be **intentionally** "*resurfaced*" and exhausted without incident by combining *Awareness* of the *Seeker* and the *Pilot*.

The journey is always upward. Any *Imprints* resurfaced during **cathartic processing** are likely to be already resurfacing in the *Seeker's* daily life from time to time, so there is no danger in simply stimulating them for actual reduction and a sense of release.

Δ Δ Δ Δ Δ Δ Δ

The *Pilot* must wait until the *Seeker* is "present" and "Aware"—securely "buckled in"—before "take-off." This original method of *cathartic processing* begins by entering a state of focused concentration, which for most people experienced with meditation and thought discipline from former Grades, is as simple as closing their eyes. However, it may be that the *Seeker's* current *Awareness* level (on the ZU-line) is providing too much restlessness or withdrawal to use processes requiring elevated levels of *Awareness*. This happens with "subjective processing" all of the time and may be remedied with "**objective** processing" without breaking the session.*

---

* See "*Crystal Clear*" (*Liber-2B*) for an introduction to "objective" exercises; and "*Metahuman Destinations*" (*Liber-Two*) introduces "Presence in Space-Time" for SOP-2C.

A common exercise to refocus attention before starting a "process" is for the *Pilot* to have a *Seeker* look around, spot and identify basic objects in the room. This helps orient the *Seeker* to be "**in-phase.**" It is very possible during *cathartic processing* that a *Seeker* will move out of phase with *Self* and relive a **traumatic experience** from the perspective of an alternative **Identity Phase** someone else involved in the original *Imprint*, such as the dominating force (individual) that inflicts the painful experience. This Phase-shift is part of what must be reduced and exhausted as an *Imprint*. It is part of the behavior patterns exhibited when an *Imprint* is stimulated. We often respond as one of the "phases" or "personalities" exhibited in the *Imprint*—and it may be the victim; it may be the domineer; or it may switch between the two. But we must start and end sessions as "Self."

The present author was fortunate, some years back, to find a professional **Abreactive** *Therapist* to help develop Route-1 properly. For example, at the start of the session, the *Seeker* is instructed to "close their eyes" to establish a state of focused concentration. [The instruction to count down from *seven* has been omitted.] It is important that the *Seeker* respond to the *Pilot's* "Processing Command Lines" to make "processing" work. It is important the the *Pilot* only speaks to the *Seeker* in line with the formula of the "process" and includes no other discussion or "command." A *Pilot* is not commanding the *Seeker* to *do* anything—the *Pilot* is entering input commands to run a "process" that the *Seeker* is **responsible** for "running" themselves to produce a desired result. Otherwise, we are back to casual conversation, which is not nearly as effective. When the *Seeker's* eyes are closed, the *Pilot* acknowledges that the command has been received and executed ("very good").

The *Pilot's* next statements are very important, to: "start the session," making certain the *Seeker* is presently "in phase" and in good communication. We don't always know where someone is likely to *go* when they close their eyes (for subjective processing), so a *Pilot* needs to be certain the *Seeker* is still consciously "with them" and "in phase" in present **space**-time.

Then, the *Pilot* assures the *Seeker* that: "At some future point, when I say the phrase *'End of Session'*, anything and everything that has been said and any emotion experienced during this session will have no influence on you, and the session will be ended." Statements like this should end with "Do you understand?" This maintains a clear communication **flow**.

Δ Δ Δ Δ Δ Δ Δ

The main substance of the Route-1 "process" begins with identification and resurfacing of an *Imprint*: any source of emotional **turbulence** and fragmentation. [**GSR-Biofeedback** may be used to indicate a "**charged**" item for processing; as indicated in *Grade-IV*, "*Way of the Wizard*" or "*Metahuman Systemology Handbook.*"] This could be a painful experience or some other instance when "shock" encoded an *Imprint* with a sensation, thought (attitude, **postulate**, belief) or emotional charge. It is likely that the original *Imprint* on a chain of related incidents will not be immediately identified. It may be that the most recent similar instance of difficulty is troubling the *Seeker* and tying up their *Awareness* and attention, but it is linked to older or earlier *Imprinting*.

A *Pilot* is dedicated to assist the *Seeker* in releasing any reactive **associations** to *Imprints* by *resurfacing* these experiences where the *Imprints* occur. The *Pilot* should not prompt for overly specific data when processing incidents. Simply acknowledge what the *Seeker* says and **incite** movement through an incident. "Okay. Continue." A *Pilot* should not act doubtful or direct a *Seeker* to validate what they say with "how do you know..." or "what makes you think..." &tc.

The *Pilot's* goal is to bring the *Seeker's* attention back to the earliest instance of similar *facets* or environmental stimulation. The ultimate goal *is* to find the first instance when the *Imprint* was encoded. Each time the *Pilot* is not seeing a reduction in a given *resurfacing*, there is an even earlier time when the **facets** appear. So, you keep moving the **Backtrack** earlier in time to get the most basic. You can "process" out all instances of restimulation, when the *Seeker* demonstrated some type of irrational response to their environment as part of the *Imprint*—but this is not nearly as effective as "processing" the original or earliest point when the *Imprint* was formed. The most commonly processed *Imprints* are related to fear, loss, pain, rejection and self-worth.

If there was a discussion prior to the session start concerning a recent issue or *Imprint* that restimulated a reactive-response, then the *Pilot* directs the *Seeker's* attention to that **channel** with: "Locate a time when you ___." Once located, the *Pilot* asks "When" it was and directs the *Seeker* to: "Move to that incident." Wait for an indication that this has happened. If the *Seeker* needs more direction, the *Pilot* may change the command to: "Locate a time when you were first feeling ___" or "Recall the first instance when you experienced ___."

When an instance is finally *located* (or showing "charge" if using *GSR-Biofeedback*), and the *Seeker* has *moved* to it, the *Pilot* asks for the "duration" of the incident—or "How long" the **Imprinting Incident** took place. With this data in hand, the *Pilot* directs (the *Seeker* to close their eyes if they have not and) to: "Move to the beginning of that incident. Tell me when you are there." Once the *Pilot* acknowledges that they have ("Okay") they query: "Tell me what you see." The *Pilot* should acknowledge anything the *Seeker* says and prompt them to "Move through the incident to ___" using the *duration* indicated.

If at any point the *Seeker* appears to be demonstrating physical stress or somatic **pings**, the *Pilot* simply assures them they: "are doing fine. Continue. Tell me what you are seeing." Any physical discomfort or pain stimulated most likely relates to the location where *Imprint* energy has localized on the *genetic vehicle*. It *will* be experienced until it is reduced. Physical sensations are very strong *facets* of an *Imprint*. Any **perception** in an *Imprint* is a *facet*, which means any associated *facet* may trigger them. It is a *Pilot's* responsibility to assist the *Seeker* in identifying the *facets* holding the energy of an *Imprint* in place. The *Seeker* may be prompted to identify any generalized *facets* in the experience: "what do you see?" or "what do you hear?" or "what do you smell" and so forth. "Move through to the end point." And when the *Seeker* affirms they have, the *Pilot* asks: "What happened?"

Δ Δ Δ Δ Δ Δ Δ

Acknowledging the *Seeker's* narrative is the completion of the first processing cycle. Original instructions for RR-SP-1 prompt a *Seeker* to return to the experience repeatedly in order to discharge it by *catharsis*. There is no predetermined number of times necessary to run out the charge in this way. Each additional time the incident is run through, the *Pilot* performs the same steps as before, except that the *time* and *duration* are not **treated** again.

A *Pilot* should record all facets and facts, details and statements that the *Seeker* communicates. The RR-SP-1 instructions indicated that an incident should continue to be run if new information comes through each time; meaning more of the *Imprint* is discharging. This *one* method for applying *Route-1*, selected for the ease of its instruction and application. *Procedure R-1R* recognizes additional *Piloting* knowledge earned during the three years since *Route-1* was first published for open-experimentation by the Systemology Society.

During intensive sessions, *language facets* associated with the *Imprint* are sometimes vocalized by the *Seeker*—demonstrating the extent of *Imprint* blockage. They may even speak in the "phase" of someone else from the *Imprint* (incident). Negative language *Imprints* are often held in place by similar statements said at the time of the *Imprint*. Statements such as "I can't do this" or "this isn't working" or "this is never going to work" or "just forget it" or "I'm never going to get out of this"—these may actually be a part of what was said during the *Imprint* and not simply a statement made by the *Seeker* "in phase" as themselves regarding their attitude about the current "process" taking place. The *Pilot* should recognize this, reducing the *language facet* of the *Imprint* by having the *Seeker* "go over it again"—repeating the statement many times until it turns on more *facets* and/or they realize what "phase" or "facade" they are wearing when this statement runs on a **circuit** as an *Imprint* response.

Δ Δ Δ Δ Δ Δ Δ

"*Route-1*" techniques require running (processing) an *Imprint* until the "emotional charge" is reduced and the *Seeker* experiences a release from the *Imprint* and its fragmentation. Emotional release is a critical component of the "process." Any *facets* described from each run through should be recorded. They may assist the *Pilot* in returning the *Seeker* to earlier instances in life where a similar situation (or even a similar *facet*) is present. Understand that we are targeting *Imprints*, not situations. The same *Imprint* is likely to have resurfaced in many instances of day-to-day life, under varying circumstances. This is another reason why only one *Imprint* should be the target of an individual session—because in the course of chasing down the *first* Imprinting Incident, a *Seeker* may have to "return to the beginning of the incident and move through to the end" several times where it is finally **confronted**.

After one or two runs through an incident, the *Pilot* needs to determine if the "charge" on the line is *rising* or *falling*—which can be determined by a "*rise*" or "*fall*" of electrical resistance (*Ohms*) when using *GSR-Biofeedback.** The *Pilot* may also ask if the *Imprint* is "reducing or getting more solid." If the charge is reducing, then continue to run through it. If the incident is *not* reducing, then the incident begins earlier—*or* the incident is connected on a chan-

---

*   Refer to *Grade-IV* "*The Way of the Wizard.*"

nel-line of related *Imprinting*, meaning the actual incident that is necessary to resolve the "charge" on this channel takes place at an earlier time (sometimes even prior to the present incarnation). The earliest similar event is the *Imprinting Incident* that unravels the fragmentation on the entire channel.

"Process time" may be reduced by finding the earliest instance of an *Imprint*, clear and simple. An incident is usually run through twice. Not only does this take some charge off the line, but it allows a *Seeker* to more easily locate earlier incidents on the channel. Once located, any perceived *facet* should be processed—sights; smells; tastes; feelings; humidity; even brightness. The *Imprint* is consciously and intentionally given full attention to reduce the entire charge of fragmentation.

Emotional levels of *Awareness* can initially dip quite low during *Route-1* Imprint Processing—then the ability to cope increases and finally moves up the *ZU-line* to the MCC (range) when *Imprinted* fragmentation is reduced and emotional release is experienced. Don't be surprised if this release is in the form of laughter, vibrancy and enthusiasm. We are not invalidating what has happened to an individual; we are extinguishing its emotional pull on us. If possible, the exact **Alpha Thought** or "postulate" that the *Imprint* inspired (or incited) should be identified in order to also properly free up intellectual considerations directly associated with the *Imprint.*

We can be *imprinted*, for example, with an idea that we are "not any good" and we may go into a *phase* of being the thing that is "not any good." Alternatively we display hostility in times when the *Imprint* is stimulated by shifting to another "phase"—telling others that they are "no good." If statements such as "it's no good" come up in Processing, they should be exhausted as part of the *Imprint*—they are not actually statements *about* the "process."

Δ Δ Δ Δ Δ Δ Δ

Successful *catharsis* occurs when the *Seeker* is able to arrive at the highest level of being in their ability to confront the *Imprint*. The *Seeker* may experience sighs, yawns, tear-swells, chuckling, and eventually a higher "realization" or "actualization" point. This is the critical "destination" that the *Pilot* is assisting the *Seeker* to arrive at. The *Seeker* arrives at a new **degree** (or state) of realization about themselves, actualization (as *Awareness*) of their previous response-reactions—they have "arrived" or "ascended" to a new state of *Beingness*. This point of "ascension" or "becoming" is critical in order to complete the "process."

Procedure R-1R takes *Route-2* and *Route-3* developments into consideration.‡ In view of this fact, and in view of our first revision of Standard Procedure—*SOP-2C*—there are additional tools a *Pilot* may incorporate with *R-1R* in order to fully "clear the channel" (particularly if the earliest *Imprinting Incident* is difficult to contact or is not reducing). The most appropriate is processing analytical recall of all "three **circuits**" on a channel—prompting a *Seeker* to also locate incidents when they "caused another ___" or when they observed "others causing others ___." Upper-route methods also include times when they "causing yourself ___." These methods are particularly useful when there are sensations (pains and pings) triggered by *Imprints* on a fragmented channel. When incidents are not readily located, *imagined* ones may be substituted to simply "run out" considerations on that channel and potentially resurface related memories.

A *Pilot* should not mistake being "stuck" with "deep processing" where a *Seeker* may go silent for long periods of time. When a *Seeker* is stuck, the *Pilot's* skills may assist pushing through; but sometimes it is not a matter of skill or technique. It may be that an individual's *Awareness* level is up high enough to resurface and reduce a complete *Imp-*

‡   *Route-2* is introduced in "*Crystal Clear*" (also reprinted in "*The Systemology Handbook*"); *Route-3* is introduced in "*Metahuman Destinations* (also reprinted in "*The Metahuman Systemology Handbook*").

rint in one session. Sometimes the information necessary to resolve the *Imprint* is not surfacing, even with repetitive returns and scanning the *Backtrack*. Some things can get buried deeply. In this instance, restimulation due to Processing will usually cause what was not uncovered during the session to emerge within a few days *after* the session. Therefore, the same *Imprint* should be "processed" two or three days later.

A heightened state of beingness must be established for the Processing to be successful. Sessions should never be "flown" in such a way as to simply strengthen or reinforce an *Imprint*. The previous steps to returning and reducing should be "flown" so long as new attention is being discharged. Statements may be "flown" so long as they are leading to a phase shift or to uncover a new *facet* or earlier similar incident, but otherwise the general ZU-state of the *Seeker* should increase once the entire *Imprint* is laid out and "flown over" a few times.

Δ Δ Δ Δ Δ Δ Δ

Assuming the *Seeker* has reached a critical point of *Imprint* reduction or End-Point, the *Pilot's* final steps are considered Landing Procedures. If the *Seeker* has reached this point on this leg of their journey, they should be informed that: "Okay then, we are going to pick this up at a later time. Is that okay with you?" They may agree readily to this or they may be hesitant. This suggestion by the *Pilot* is not made in haste (or impatience); it is a decision that requires wisdom. If the *Seeker* is hesitant, the *Pilot* may restate: "I understand, more may come to the surface later." And then the *Pilot* should elevate the *Seeker's* Zu-levels (*Awareness*) with light analytical recall (*Route-2*): "a time when you felt vibrant"; "a time when you were enjoying life"; "a time you were winning"; &tc. Finally the *Pilot* solidifies trust (established during opening procedures) by stating: "End of session."

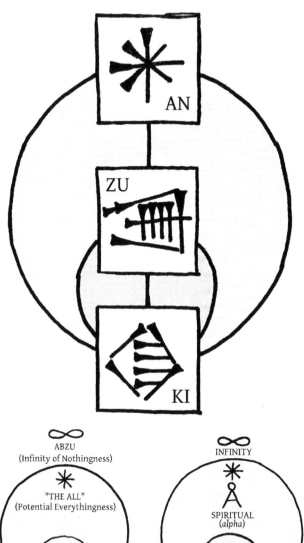

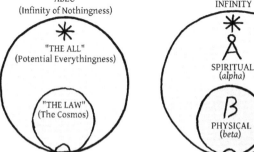

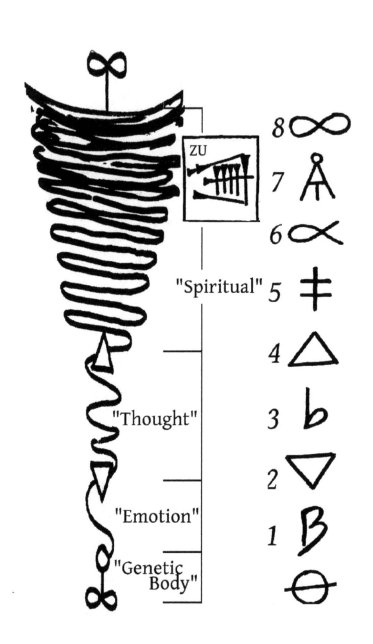

ZU

8 ∞

7

6

"Spiritual" 5

4 △

"Thought" 3 b

2 ▽

"Emotion" 1 B

"Genetic
Body" ⊖

ROUTE-2
ANALYTICAL PROCESSING INSTRUCTIONS
"AR-SP-2" EXCERPT FROM LIBER-2B

"Route-1" methods of "*RR-SP-1*" (or "R-1R" in the new 2022 revised edition of "*The Tablets of Destiny Secrets Revealed*") are not necessarily the most appropriate for solo *Self-Processing*. "Route-1" *catharsis* requires an individual to fully successfully relive or "**resurface**" emotional drama intensely to effectively discharge **entangled** emotional energy and analyze content of an *encoded imprint*. Without focusing interest to properly confront what surfaces, all a *Seeker* has done is successfully "restimulate" the *imprint*.

In this book, our attention now turns away from *Catharsis* and toward another ambiguous ancient spiritual practice that the Greeks called "*Kenosis*," thereby lending the name to our "Route-2" method: "*Kenostic Processing.*"

"*Keno*"—otherwise "*Kenos*" (Greek)—ties to the old **Proto-Indo-European** root: "*ken-*" meaning "empty." There is no real need to **codify** or systematize a whole series of "emptyings" or "emptiness" *processes*. But of course, since this *is Systemology* we are talking about; so, naturally we end up doing that anyways—in *Self-Honesty*.

"Spiritual emptying" (as *Kenosis*) was applied in the past to two directions of travel for *Self*. In Christian mysticism, Jesus *empties out* his "divinity" in order to "become human." The true identity of his *Self* remains unchanged in the *Spiritual Universe* (AN),[‡] as does our own—but according to their definitions, this transition is a form of *Kenosis*. Approach it from the other direction, and you are changing states toward "**Ascension**." *Kenosis* must now take place for *Self* to purge the Human Condition it took on. This is

---

[‡] He most likely descended from a former realization of *beta-existence*—referred to as the "*Magic Kingdom*" in our *Systemology*—which occurs just prior to this mechanical one we currently identify with and occupy attention and trapped Awareness as the Human Condition.

how we return to the Spirit. Without this high level *Self-Actualization*, "body death" does not guarantee actualized "Ascension."

Kenostic Processing relates to "analytical recall." The better a *Seeker* handles "analytical recall," the more effective other *Systemology Processes* will be in progressing them on the *Pathway to Self-Honesty*. *Cathartic* and *Kenostic* methods are both "subjective." Other *Processes* may be *objective*, with eyes wide open, dealing with the space around us.

Routes of *defragmentation* all involve some measure of "emptying out" whatever is *not* "*Self*." When running *Cathartic* or *Kenostic* techniques we are always "emptying out" stored charges of emotional energy entangled with *imprints* and the **thought-formed** "*beliefs*" we feed personal energy into. To reclaim the energy—the *ZU*, the *Knowingness*—and freedom of the *Spirit*, it is obvious that we must "purge" everything that is not **Alpha Self**. These methods ultimately return *Awareness* back toward the "spiritual." The only reason any sense of "wonder" and "discovery" is attached to this, is because we apparently forgot that we have tread upon this very same *Pathway* at least once before... on our descent.

We refer to individuals on the *Pathway to Self-Honesty* as "*Seekers*" because such individuals set out to recover something that has been lost or forgotten. Apparently our "sense of *Self*" got misplaced along the way as we took on these shells. The very fact that we have descended this *Pathway* is of benefit to us—in recognizing truth of our *Self*, the Reality around us and all of Existence. This inner sense allows us to recognize it when we achieve it or find it. That recognition—that sense when reading or working through *Systemology* that we somehow *already know* this information and find it strange that it should have taken so long for someone to systematize the knowledge—it is that very recognition that validates the Reality of this *Path* for the *Seeker*.

∞   Some of these are described later in this book.

"Analytical Recall" (*Route-2*) is actually a preferred method —and "Route-1" is used only when necessary, such as when an *imprint* is in restimulation. An individual likely has kept much of their *Awareness* entangled with their *imprints* (and what some refer to as **conditioning**). A lower Route is taken only to free up enough to actually achieve higher *analytical* levels of *Awareness*.

Kenostic Processing methods in this "self-help" book are just as effective as when *piloted*. Although we focus our attention on analytical levels of *Thought-frequency*, this *Tech* contacts emotional energy held suspended and entangled in low frequency **bands** of **emotional encoding** and *conditioning* just like *Cathartic Processing*. This new *Tech* is quite effective in doing that—but more importantly, it is effective in progressing *Seekers* toward target goals of Grade-III, which is to restore personal ZU-energy or *Awareness* of the Human Condition.

"Analytical Recall" methods provide a direct increase in conscious *Awareness*—**faculties** inherent in our *beta-existence*, such as perception or memory recall. Such attributes directly affect intelligence—and not only "analytical" intelligence but increased *beta*-perceptiveness that accompanies "emotional intelligence."

Systematic *Self-Processing* may be performed with the same effectiveness as experienced *Piloted* processing so long as the *Seeker* is capable of maintaining the same strength, integrity and education level as a successful *Pilot*. This is one additional reason why we simultaneously provide these "Extended Courses" aimed at *Pilot Training* for *Systemology Air Command*—our "*Flight School*." At the same time we focus on general education of materials and personal processing.

A tradition fails when it no longer duplicates the effective results of its originator. I do not wish to see a repeat of history with something carrying such great potential thrust and a futurist orientation as Our Cause: *Systemology*.

Education not only increases a *Seeker's* understanding of *NexGen Systemology* or *Mardukite Zuism*, but it increases personal effectiveness of *Tech* when applied to *Self* or others. It is interesting that a person, simply by learning to effectively use the Tech, can assist progress for another on the *Pathway* even when they, themselves, have perhaps not fully actualized. *That's interesting.* Perhaps it is because of the *combined Awareness* of the two people involved.

Previously we targeted hidden suppressed energy stores using intensive *"Resurface and Reduce"* methods, these other light *"Analytical Recall"* methods—that lend themselves perfectly to *Self-Processing*—focus on "conscious events" stored in our memory. These methods may stimulate suppressed memories once the various *facets* are brought to full conscious *Awareness*, but as a person increases in their *Awareness*—which we demonstrate systematically with a gradient scale—the ability to effectively manage personal memory and energy stores also increases.

Systemology Procedure "AR-SP-2" ("Route-2") is intended to raise an individual's general *beta-Awareness* level visibly on the **BAT** test and its evaluations. This automatically generates conditions for a *Seeker* promoting increased certainty in personal *Life-Management*. And isn't that what everyone is here for anyways? We don't need a revolt in order to upgrade evolution to *Homo Novus*. A *defragmented* individual simply applies their Alpha-Thought and has but only *decide* to *be* more than Human.

And that is all we are doing when *piloting* our *Seekers*—is freeing up their ability to decide and for the first time in perhaps thousands of years, returning to them the power of *clear choice.*

Δ Δ Δ Δ Δ Δ Δ

Basic *defragmentation* techniques of *Systemology* target freeing personal energy tied up, or entangled, in *imprints* and *thought-forms*. It is usually wound up in what we have lost **control** of, or **responsibility** of, and therefore are not being treated as our own. In *Self-Processing* methods, we are using *analytical* faculties to reduce **erroneously** cemented personal stores of *ZU*. This *ZU* we speak of is the essence of *Life* itself, but we are **treating** the parts of it we can experience or measure—which for our purposes is *Awareness*.

We introduce the **Standard Model** and *ZU-line* and *Awareness Charts* and *Scales* prior to instructing "Route-2" techniques for a good reason: they provide orientation of *Self*, for which we have few other valid landmarks or benchmarks or signposts on which to evaluate.

If you can imagine the orientation of *Self* in a space and time without measure, one can understand just how difficult it might be to chart any definitive "pathway" of movement within it. An "I" floating out in the wide open spaces has no concept of direction until it *creates* one, fixes upon one, and orients all other certainty and knowledge to it. Are you beginning to see? If not, you will by the end of this book.

When we say to "use a process so long as it is effecting change," this means utilizing the *Awareness Scale*—or one of its derivatives—as a gauge. A *Seeker* can expect that when they hit an erroneous solid ("ridge") on the *ZU-line* that they will dip down in levels of emotion and fragmented thought in order to first bring memories up to the surface and onto the screen for analysis. "Route-1" *Cathartic Processing* methods targeted the deepest emotional turbulence, which is mostly nonsensical other than pain and **enforcement** felt. This is simply burned off *via* repetition, but it is not necessarily brought to a scrutiny at analytical levels; it's just being burned off as fuel—fuel to transmute or transform the *imprint* or *belief* into free **flowing** ZU potential again. We aren't stripping away anything that is the "true" *Alpha Self*; we are simply shedding layers of skin that aren't *Self*, which seem only to keep us bound and wrapped in the convolution of *beta-existence*. The irony is that when you get into higher levels of *Awareness*, none of this seems confusing and mysterious. To a common man it is actually quite complicated.

A *Seeker* is only able to experience realizations at their level of *Awareness* or below it. This means that experiences resurfaced directly in "Route-1" are only effectively *analyzed* when a *Seeker* is above the level of which those *imprints* are wound up, fixed or cemented. For example, a person who is afraid—suspended somewhere around (1.5) on the *Emotimeter*—is able to easily recall and revisit experiences scaled as "fear" or lower on the *Scale*. But, they won't be able to process anything rationally in the range of Thought above the mechanisms of the "RCC" **Reactive Control Center** at (2.0).

Although revisiting and resurfacing memories may bring a person temporarily below the **threshold** while experiencing them, *systematic processing* then carries the energy back up to *Analytical* degrees of *Awareness* and discharges it there by simply using a higher **vibration** of Thought—as opposed to **succumbing** to it. Therefore, you want to "run" something emotional until you feel elated, extroverted—or at the least, enthusiastic about your own future and potential in life *in spite* of the fact that such-and-such has happened at some point. You've survived. You're here now. That situation is no longer present—no longer a **presence** influencing you now. So, you run it through, experience it, analyze every *facet* and then decide if there is anything still worth adding to the files. But it should be analyzed; not simply piled up.

While on the *Pathway to Self-Honesty*, it is important to analyze and account for all past **considerations**. It is important for to actually take these things out and look at them, because they do affect an individual. It is too easy to simply store them up and carry them around as though they are arbitrary. But, they *do* affect us—and *especially* when they are hidden away, folded up and put in our pocket. That's a sure way *not* to be ever rid of something.

We are on a mission to recover our true potential; not add something artificial that wasn't already there. A superior truth is attained on the *Pathway to Self-Honesty*, otherwise an individual is practicing Self-hypnosis, adding layers of programming without sorting out all of what lies beneath. We put considerable energy into telling ourselves that things are not as they are, instead of analyzing the original belief we agreed to in making things as they are. This is one reason why personal ZU *Lifeforce* and energy has the appearance of being depleted over time—with age and experience. The actual energy of *Life* is always supplied as a constant from Source; no different at the end of an individual's physical lifetime than its beginning. Something else has changed—but not the energy *fed into* the system.

Over time and with more accumulation of experience, *emotionally encoded imprints* and libraries worth of *thought-formed beliefs* are all like stacks of important books that we have agreed to, taken responsibility for, even dabbled with a bit—but never really get around to "owning" the knowledge of for ourselves. They pile up like walls and barriers to seeing anything more—because we have already agreed to the *Reality* that these stacks exist. They aren't going to just *go away* on their own. You can try wishful thinking—and most of you probably have already.

By bringing efforts of our past up to the surface—including those efforts of others applied toward us—we are able to bring the *moves* and *counter-moves* of this **Game** to a scrutiny. This is the only way we could possibly earn any knowledge or actual information from our experience. Otherwise, experience is a rather *fragmenting* aspect of *Life* with no real use. If its purpose is so that we can learn, than we must be bring it out and learn—thus being *Aware* or increasing our *Awareness* as a result. Otherwise we lose our *Awareness* to personal databases and libraries chock-full of all the *Lifeforce* we have chosen to file away entangled. Basic *Systemology Processing* and *Self-Processing* is applied to change this. It puts the *Seeker* on a track where they are able to unravel and free up the vitality that is already theirs—just hidden away and forgotten. It is about time that we *remind* people just how beautiful and amazing the true *Alpha Spirit*—the *Self*—really is; how beautiful and amazing *Life* can *really* be.

Δ Δ Δ Δ Δ Δ Δ

The first procedural outline or formula for basic *Systemology Processing* was demonstrated in the original edition of the book and conference for "*Tablets of Destiny*" in August 2019. That seven-step procedure was defined by a list of ancient Sumerian "**cuneiform signs**" representing words, concepts or phrases. That basic underlying formula is very powerful and effective—clearly devised by priests and priestesses of the ancient Temples. The steps are easily applied to other forms and formulae of *Piloted Processing*.

"Route-2" *Systemology Processing** may be conducted as basic two-step *Self-Processing* (while using this "self-help" book). If used to modify instructions for existing *Piloted* procedure, these "two steps" would effectively replace "step three" and "step four" of the original sevenfold formula. This means that instead of using those two steps from "Route-1" the previous version of *processing* aimed directly at "resurfacing and reducing" *encoded emotional imprints*, we replace with instructions for "Analytical Recall" ("Route-2" *Tech*).

The two steps, as defined by Sumerian cuneiform, are:

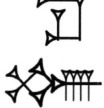

3. *SI* — "to recall; remember; be conscious of in Mind."

4. *SUG* — "to empty out; to clear; strip away; make naked or bare."

Former spiritual leaders have referred to *Kenostic* methods as, very literally, an "emptying out." When we think of the similarities between *Cathartic* and *Kenostic* methods, both seem to involve a basic "emptying" or "discharge" or "clearing" of some energetic restriction that once diminished *Awareness* maintained as *Self*.

---

*   Original designation given as "*AR-SP-2*" in the first edition text.

In order to provide some greater sense of distinction, the *Seeker* should consider the "Analytical Route" to be a systematized process of "releasing the hold" *of-and-from* such and such. Systematic analytical processing work emphasizes a recall and analysis of *facets* more than the *subject* of the incidents and events themselves. When scanning personal experience some aspects are going to be more pleasant or unpleasant than others. It should be understood that the first "response" or "reaction" is a good indicator of a "hold" that needs to be "released."

> Any type of discomfort or emotional reaction
> to a *memory* is *fragmentation* showing its face—
> some degree of emotional attachment
> and its reinforcement as Reality.

By recalling as many *facets* in our memory of an event that we consciously can, we release energetic stores entangled with **superfluous** information beneath the surface of conscious memory. Actualized **consciousness** is really the only place that memory serves any analytical function. Therefore, there is no **logical** reason to keep energy bound up in *imprints* and *beliefs* that we aren't making conscious use of, but of which affects us.

It would seem that the **standard-issue** Human Condition has limited space or attention or resources in which to maintain these energetic *solids* during a single lifetime in *beta-existence*. Because:—

> once sufficient non-survival *imprinting* is accumulated,
> and the person succumbs to be its effect,
> they fall into apathy and consider themselves dying.

As a *Seeker* progresses on the *Pathway to Self-Honesty*, the level of *Self-Actualization* is **proportional** to the degree of certainty maintained concerning *Self* and its causal role in the universe.

-It is when we are at *cause* that we are most *actualized*.

-When we are surrounded by *effect*, our *Awareness* is lowered.

Effective "*Analytical Recall*" requires identifying and analyzing any *facets* associated with recalled events and incidents. Only after we are able to bring our *Life*-experience to a scrutiny; analyzing the information; evaluating validity or truth; evaluating effectiveness or rightness of our beliefs; and everything we have accepted or agreed to as Reality—only after all of this can we say with any certainty that we have yielded some kind of knowledge, something real.

Even if we do, in the end, determine that *Life*-experience accumulated in this Physical Universe *is* actually mostly erroneous, then we still have learned something *real*.

Recall of events must be firmly rooted in our actual memory as we believe things are or have experienced them—not simply a result of how we are told things are. When we take a look at memory kept all balled up in a corner—when we take it out and look at it once and for all —we clear out the clutter and find what, if anything, there is to appreciate about experiences we attach our beta-personalities to. Because that is what we do. So, let's do everything we can do to clear out the clutter from this world—because its getting pretty murky. So, let's getting going on clearing it all up. It starts with *Self*.

ROUTE-2B
EXISTENTIAL PROCESSING INSTRUCTIONS
"SP-2B-8/A" EXCERPT FROM LIBER-2B

A *Seeker* familiar with our *Standard Model*, the *ZU-line* of "*Mardukite Zuism*"—or a clear and true understanding of ancient Mardukite-**Babylonian** "seven-plus-one models"—finds our "*Spheres*" Model is a visual aid to what is known. We want to use what we know to *realize* from this is our ability to *Be*; to project *Awareness* as a *realization* of every point on the map of potential existence between here and *Infinity*.

The greater the *realization* of interconnection (and influence) with these other *Spheres*, the more certain we are of *Self-directed* ability to *Be* the *Cause*—to "*Be Your Own Reason*" to the extent you can conceptualize that. For most of us, this would be just outside *Infinity*, once you get that far. This prepares a *Seeker* to start thinking from higher realms of Alpha Thought related to **Games** and *Universe* **Logics**. All you have to do here—and our *Pathway* map lets you off easy on this one—is essentially: "*fake it 'til you make it.*"

The eight *Spheres* are represented in *Absolute Totality,* with positive and negative values for all *space-time energy-matter*. On the subjective scale of *Self*—where we operate experience of *beta-existence* from *Awareness* of *Self* and *Self-determinism* as "*Cause*"—*Self* is placed at the center of the model. This is *Self-Mastery* of *Self* actualized in *beta-existence* —meaning: to the extent that *Self* is actualized in the Physical Universe (KI). This pertains to the difference between *Self-Honesty* actualized in *beta-existence* and *Total Self-Actualization*, which is an **Alpha** state actualized **exterior** to the Physical Universe and "Physical Body."

When higher frequencies are *realized* with more than intellectual or "mental" consciousness it is easier to simply dissolve lower-range energies **inhibiting** and *fragmenting* expression of personal management. This is one reason why *Standard Processing* alternates between resurfacing the

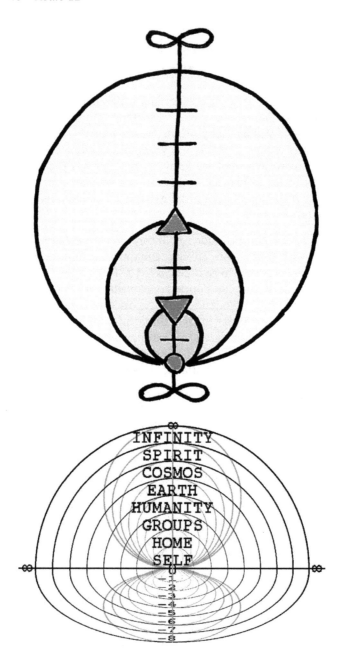

INFINITY
SPIRIT
COSMOS
EARTH
HUMANITY
GROUPS
HOME
SELF

past and managing an individual's present concerns—basically handling the most accessible facets of life; then afterward processing higher spiritual lessons and exercises to allow for a greater state of *Beingness*—not simply the *Knowingness*.

The *Self* at ("1") on the *"Spheres"* model, which also includes ("-1"), is not directly the same as the emotional level of (1.0) on the *ZU-line*, but rather in relation to (1.0) as vibrations of physical energy-matter in action. *Self* is critical in our equations, because if you take that off this *chart*, then you don't have a *chart*. Consider *Self* at ("1") as *Awareness* of *Self* and efforts toward a continued existence *for-and-as* *"Self"* in the Physical Universe.

> The greater (or higher) we actualize *Self*, the greater our "reach"—and *that* is what is meant by *"Circles of Influence."*√ *Self* remains in place. All we are doing in *Life* is extending the *reach* (or not) of our *Awareness*—but we are not displacing *Self*.

Think about what you have seen charted as *Alpha Spirit Self* at (7.0) in former models. Now imagine that instead of moving up into *Infinity*, you direct that whole scale of personal existence into an alternate reality in the position of ("1"). *Self* is still (7.0) in *Alpha* state—the individuated I-AM of the *Spiritual Universe*. It now projects its *Awareness* into *beta-existence* of a physical "dimension" in position ("1"). It may raise its level of consciousness in regards to this new *playing field*, but whatever happens to it, however it decided to direct *Awareness*, the true "core" or "Eternal Self"—back on the *Standard Model*—remains at (7.0) unchanged. Therefore, the *Spheres* are specifically related to our *experience* as *Self* in *beta-existence* or some Universe.

The entire *Identity* then—the entire personal ZU-line as *Self*—is **manifest** in a Physical Universe at ("1"). It represents an individual's personal ability, actualized *Self-Realization* and *Self-Control* for personal management. We are

√ More details on this appear in the *Grade-IV* personal integrity and ethics-processing manual, *"The Way of the Wizard"* (*Liber-3E*).

dealing with "control" from the point of view of a very powerful force called the *Alpha Spirit;* a *force* that can effectively direct or impinge its *Will-Intention* onto existence. Many have passed off *control* of this *force* to some other *source.* However, personal progress on the *Pathway* is dependent on the quality of your own *Self-control.*

It should be clearly evident that the fundamental aspect behind this work is CONTROL; *how* CONTROL is operated and *who* is doing it. When you—or when you *Pilot* your *Seeker* to —direct attention to things, or select things to give attention to, and change your attitudes about things, *at Will:* this is "control." Our methods allow you to choose how to control and direct attention. This increases a *Seeker's* certainty of *control* and personal management of *Self.*

Moving along to the next *Sphere,* we create or manifest and maintain some type of *shell* for our *shell,* calling this ("2") the domain of *Home and Family.* Such domestic security is what *Maslow* tried to say with his "Pyramid of Self-Actualization." Once we realize we are *Self* or "enshrouding" or "controlling" this body in *beta-existence,* our field of influence immediately manifests toward conditions best suited for perpetuating existence—and that requires a *Family* or a "domestic" situation of some sort; a home-base.

Just as *Awareness* can "identify" with a *genetic body* for *beta-existence,* so too might one take on an *Identity* of "family" at ("2") as the next layer enshrouding *Self.* But, if we maintain full *Self-Determinism* at ("2")—as in the same analytical efficiency we achieve for *Self* at ("1")—without *losing* control of our *Awareness* in the second sphere, then it may be used as an effective survival tool for a physical level of existence.

This idea of *Identifying* with anything other than *Self* from its highest point of independent spiritual *Self-directed* existence is a primary source of *fragmentation.* Just as you can over-*Identify* and "lose yourself"—as they used to say—at ("2") in the *Family-Home-Domestic* band of existence, it obviously doesn't stop there. Rippling out from this **epicenter** of *Self*: after *Home* we have the entire domain of *Organiza-tions*, *Societies* and any "identification with a group" at ("3"). For the average individual, this is probably com-posed of a series of various "rings" or "social circles" that may be independent from one another, yet still overlap in various ways. These are indicators of a "group mentality" as an *Identity*, which will naturally hold its own *Awareness* level—even its own numeric value from the *Emotimeter* and so forth. Basically, any which way we might treat *Self* as an "individual" on the *Pathway*, we can equally evaluate one or another of these *Spheres* as an "entity." The remaining "Spheres of Existence" correspond to greater and greater circles of inclusion and influence.

Process-out any programmed *fragmentation* associated with the concept of CONTROL. This means the word itself; any time its been used as an effort toward you; any time you've attempted it and were successful; unsuccessful; anything that shows up in *Processing* that would inhibit you from ex-ercising utmost potential regarding true *Self-Honest* "Con-trol." You can actually do this with any concept that you want to release programming on. **Process-out** agreements and statements that allowed the concept to suddenly be considered "wrong"—much like what contemporary soci-ety holds negatively in regards to the concept of RESPONS-IBILITY. These key words represent the power that is in-herently yours, but of which has been disguised as "bad."

We can directly align or synchronize the *Spheres* with our other *models* and *scales* only at ("0"), ("4") and ("8"). The states given as **continuity**-*zero*, *(4.0) beta-Actualization* and *Infinity* are **anchor**-points by which we keep our graphic demonstrations consistent. At ("4") we have the "Ring-Pass-Not" of the Human Condition—or more correctly, the boundary else *Humanity*, the *Homo Sapien* creatures, or **Homo Sapiens Sapiens**.

Our goal in *Systemology* is to elevate the state known as *Homo Sapien* to its next spiritual evolution on the Pathway —what we call "*Homo Novus*." This is apparently a name that some in the *Systemology Society* are using to officially classify the achieved state of *Self-Honesty*. As an *Organization/Group* ("3"), *Systemology* applies efforts to influence the Sphere of Humanity.

Beyond the inclusive Sphere of the Human Condition ("4"), we arrive at the zone of *All-Life* on planet *Earth*—including all *bodies* or *identities* carrying *Awareness* of *Self*. This means *All Animals*—but we can extend a precise definition to *All-Cellular Life*, because any **extant** form of *Life* on planet Earth with individuated form or body-structure that has a perspective—POV or "point-of-view"—from itself qualifies at ("5"). The entire *Earth-planet* is a living body; just one of the many bodies composing structure of the entire **Cosmos** or *universe* at ("6"). At the level of ("6") we have reached a structure for *All Physical Existences*, followed by *All Spiritual Existences* at ("7"). And then of course, ("8") is *always* "Infinity" or the "*Absolute Supreme.*"

Δ Δ Δ Δ Δ Δ Δ

When reaching outward from *Self*, these *Spheres* represent levels of *Mastery*, meaning "true leadership" in *Self-Honesty*. This is rare in our society, because everyone is bred to be a "follower"—to simply perform a task of copying-and-pasting any programming that are given. Look what that mentality is doing to our planet.

At this time, however, Humanity as a whole is not being actualized by the population at ("1")—No. ("–1") instead. Not remotely *Self-Actualized*—still a reactive effect of some other cause. Have you met a lot of *really Aware* people out there walking around lately? Or, are they spiraling down... An individual operating at ("–1") gives control over to their RCC. They may be even more worse off than that.

> You find less *leadership* and *individuality*
> —more *automation* and *hive-mind*—
> as you move downward
> An individual becomes an invert of a leader;
> an invert of causes; an invert of individuality
> and away from *Identification* with "*Self*."

At ("–2") the lack of *individuality* or *Self-identification* leads to lack of actualized ability or certainty to properly manage a domestic situation. That **"personality"** quickly becomes antagonistic to them. They have sentiments of "married people are trapped" and "people are better off alone" at ("-2"). They make many "generalizations" about "people." What cannot be comprehensibly *realized* must be *negated* to be manageable—or *rejected,* which inhibits reaching or expanding *Self* outward in the other direction.

Imagining the *Beingness* at each subsequent "Sphere of Existence" is a type of *Creative Processing.* While you perform basic exercises, manipulating various visualizations or "thought-forms" at *Will*, significant *emotional encoding* or event-based *imprints* may *resurface.*

"Traversing the Spheres" is similar to how *'ye olde occult mentors'* had their initiates using the *Kabbalah*—and they called it *"Pathworking."* Some modern revivals of Mesopotamian tradition do this using Babylonian Star-Gate lore. They call the rituals *"Gatewalking"* or *"Starwalking."* It doesn't really matter what you call it—these old techniques are very useful.

As you get a sense or "feel" for each *Sphere*, you are tracing out a route to it using a thought-form you can interact with. This is progressive work. You *realize* them faster and more clearly each time—reaching further; ascending higher. With a little practice, you *could* travel all through the *Spheres* without effort. In time, you should be able to achieve any state—and *realize* the full range—of potential *Self-generated facets* in existence to experience between here and *Infinity*. This is what opens the **internal** *Gates* that holdback entire stores of **potentiality** wound up and entangled within and behind all *beta-existence.* You are—in effect—increasing all certainty regarding **parameters** of what is considered possible. This is *how* you increase your "reach" as *Self;* by increasing the extent of certainty to which there is *something* considerable to reach for.

Δ Δ Δ Δ Δ Δ Δ

We call this portion of *Grade III*, "*Crystal Clear*," because we are cleaning up our "reality lenses"—clearing away *fragmentation* and looking through the lens at this thing we call *Life, Reality* and *Existence*—this thing we call "ZU." It's not always pretty at first, but it's the truth of things, and it's what we are here to clear up. It would be difficult to *Self-Actualize* further unless we successfully isolate the most occult and esoteric thing between here and *Infinity*— this thing called "Self."

A *Self-Honest* individual realizing
full potential of *Will-Intention* at (5.0)
is "Tarot Card Number One"—*The Magician*.

If that is an esoteric aspiration of yours at all, than this *Pathway* illustrated in *Systemology* effectively works to your ends as well. *Systemology* is *universal*.

WILL **encompasses** the first order of understanding in spiritual existence. Everything you associate with the ZU-line moves up and expands as a "*Universe*." There is so much more wave-action happening there.

WILL is—**relatively**—the spiritual equivalent
of *emotional energy*,
but in a frequency band of spiritual existence.

Around (5.0) WILL and *Intention*, the ideals of *Systemology* and "magic" *do* actually meet. The difference is that aside from "Mardukite Academy," no "magical paths" out there lead directly to a point of *Self-Honesty*. They may be able to produce effects or results following basic principles of **Cosmic Law**, but we take things to the *next level*.

—The point of WILL at (5.0) is potential actualization
by a first order of understanding in *beta-existence*.

This is only potential—not realized the same for everyone. On this same logic:

—The point *Games, Logics* and other *Universes* are
realized into being (6.0) is potential for the second

order of understanding, regarding *wisdom* and "true
,knowledge" actualized from from the second point
of realization in *beta*; and finally,

—The point of *Alpha Spirit* at (7.0), which is an *Alpha*
state of *Total Self-Actualization;* the third and highest
order of realization and understanding achievable
from "communicable knowledge" and use of language. This is achieved with *Self-direction* by an
individuated *Self* with all channels of communication *defragmented* to this point.

The *Liber-2B* exercise where answers to the "I-AM" phrase
are listed on paper is best realized not by simply leaving
the page with "I-AM" blank. That would not be *Self-Honest*.
You can do it, but you aren't impressing anyone if it's not
true for you. We are not ignoring *facets* attached to *Self* as a
"personality"—we are *Dissolving them*. Consider adding another page to this. Take your list of I-AMs and then take
this other piece of paper and put "NOT-I" at the top.

This new method basically requires you take your list and
just start *Processing-out* the "I-AMs" one right after another. Simply take all that which you have accumulated and
associated with each, and *process* it "out." You are able to
run your mental "eraser" over each word or association a
single time—physically too, if you use a pencil.

Every time you "run that out" a little more in session, you
erase it a little more. When you have no reactive-re-
sponses or programming inherently attached, erase it
completely and add it to the "NOT-I" list. In *Systematic Processing*, you are shedding perceived layers of "My-Self"
that have accumulated and continue eclipsing the "I" to a
point where it is often no longer even recognizable.

SYSTEMOLOGY PROCESS "SP-2B-8A"

The following esoteric exercise is derived from "*Arcane
Tablets*" as a practice toward *realization* of merging "*individual consciousness*" with "*Cosmic Consciousness*," which is

to say the highest state of being as an Ocean of Infinity (8.0)—AB.ZU in *Sumerian* cuneiform. The purpose of such "high level" exercises in mystical schools and spiritual traditions is not necessarily *to be* the Ocean of Infinity (8.0), but to actualize *Self* (7.0) as a *Total Awareness* of the *Alpha Spirit* "I" amidst a focal center or wave-peak of that Ocean. To fully actualize this from *beta-existence*, one would necessarily have to clear *Awareness* (*ZU-channels*) up to the point of (7.0). Mystical teachings contain very specific focus-directing creative exercises that often seem trivial at face value which actually achieve results if conducted as a continuous regimen of personal practice over time.

—IMAGINE your physical body is enshrouded in a *sphere of light.*

—FOCUS your *Awareness* on the *Eighth Sphere* of *Infinity.*

—IMAGINE the *Infinity* of *Nothingness* extending out "infinitely" on all sides as a great Ocean of Cosmic Consciousness.

—FOCUS your *Awareness* from *Self* as a singular focal point of individuated consciousness in the center of the *Infinite Ocean.*

—SENSE that the *Nothingness-Space* all around you is rising up as tides and wave-actions of invisible motion; its abyssal stillness broken by the singular point that is *You.*

—SENSE that as you press your *Awareness* against the *Nothingness*, there is no resistance, there is no sensation; no feeling of any kind.

—IMAGINE your totality of *Awareness* as the singular focal point of *Infinity*—then REALIZE that the waves you see crashing up against you and rippling into *Infinity* are an extension of your every thought, will and action.

—REALIZE that you are the *Alpha Spirit*; that "wave peak" in an otherwise *Infinity of Nothingness* stretching out within and back off all that was, is and ever WILL.

—REALIZE that your conscious *Awareness* as "I", your direction of WILL as *Alpha Spirit*, and the "central wave

peak" born out of *Infinity* are all the same pure individuated ZU—are all *One; None; Infinity.*

—WILL yourself to project *Awareness* ahead of you and
see an extension of this ZU as your projection of Identity extending infinitely in front of you—all the way to
the *zero-point-**continuity*** of existence—and back to *Infinity.*

—REPEAT this several times, IMAGINING this ZU as a
Clear Light radiant extension from *Self*, directed across
Infinity to *Zero-point* and back to *Infinity*; then REALIZE
that you are dissolving and wiping out all *fragmentation*
from the channel as you direct the *Clear Light.*

—REPEAT this several times, until you feel confidant in
your current results for this cycle of work.

—RECALL the moment you last imagined your physical
body enshrouded in a *sphere of light.*

—RECALL the instance you decided to start this present
session—get a sense of the Intention you *Willed* to begin
the session.

—REALIZE that your *beta-Awareness* and the true WILL
of the Alpha Spirit are One; End the session.

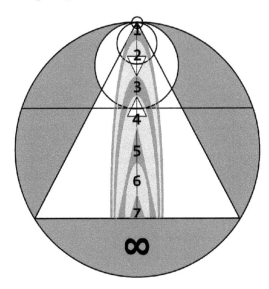

ROUTE-3
COMMUNICATION PROC. INSTRUCTIONS "SOP-2C" EXCERPT FROM LIBER-2D

Preliminary steps for a piloted systematic processing session correlate with the original RR-SP-1 Version of piloted procedure: 1) "to lead off; accompany; to impose a process or path"; and 2) "to begin; start; fasten/hold level."

Step-1 : **"Presence"**
\ first point of contact
\ basic communication

Step-2 : "Communication and Control"
\ increased communication
\ beingness in session as Self

These steps being met, the next two steps would represent whatever actual "processing" technique or "Route" is being used, but we may generalize it as a "STEM" formula:

Step-3 : "Systematic Processing" (Maneuvers Part-A)
\ orientation point in space-time (ST)
\ attention on the line

Step-4 : "Systematic Processing" (Maneuvers Part-B)
\ management of energy and matter (EM)
\ intention on the line

These two steps apply to each effective Route of systematic processing. The basic pattern is the same: 3) getting attention on the line; 4) putting intention on the line. Each of the Routes follows this formula, and each is emphasized in one of the manuals. The first two routes are established in former texts as follows:

	Route-1 "RR" (*Liber-One*)	Route-2 "AR" (*Liber-2B*)
Step-3 :	\ Resurface	\ Recall
Step-4 :	\ Reduce Charge	\ Analyze

In each of the Routes, there is a direction of attention by the *Pilot*, which is a query to bring something about or cause the effect of getting the Seeker in touch with a particular current. Once a "subject" is the focus of attention—or a point/spot/object in space has been identified—then the action or Will-intention may be put on that line of attention and the communication or energetic flow ensues.

A *Pilot* assists the *Seeker* in processing systematically applying communication. The *Pilot* puts out a query on the line (even if it is in the form of a command) and the *Seeker* generates an answer and responds (even if it is only the physical act of completing a basic command). A *Pilot* is not supposed to be "answering questions" for the *Seeker*. This is not a game of "tell me what's wrong with me." A *Pilot* directs the *Seeker's* attention and puts intention on the line in lieu of the *Seeker* directing the command. In either case the command is put forth and a process cycle ensues. It is still up to the *Seeker* to identify the content of their own "Mind" and respond to questions/commands.

The flow necessary for a *Seeker* to generate new/higher realizations in effective systemological work is as follows:

a) the Pilot selectively directs attention with a "what is it __"-type query flow; and

b) the Seeker processes to generate the "it is a __"-type resulting answer.

If at any time the direction of flow on this basic fundamental is reversed, the entire benefit of systematic processing is easily nullified. The opposite flow of directed attention is called "education"—and it is not a technique used in a systematic processing session. If an individual is confused about vocabulary or **semantics**, they should be directed to discover the answer in our books (and/or a dictionary) that is kept available in the room and retrieve the information from a glossary. If a *Seeker* says they don't understand a particular word (and we are referring to specifically the meaning of a "word" and not necessarily "the point of a process"), then the *Pilot* can say, "okay, let's look that up and find out together." The point here is to always work with whatever the *Seeker* is able to do, making sure not to invalidate their potential gains by pushing them past a tolerance threshold or reinforcing what they are unable to do or reach for in their current state.

Once willingness and determinism has been returned to a *Seeker* through processing, actualized ability to "change the mind" and its considerations at will increases, and incorporation of new information or education is actually of some benefit, because the *Seeker* is in a position to actually *do* something with the information. To do otherwise or follow a different course of actions is to place something that is already misunderstood even further out of reach.

Introducing heavy education onto someone lowers their levels of *Awareness* when improperly handled. If someone is constantly telling you "it is __; this is __; that is __" a lot of your attention is being directed or determined outside of your Will-Intention. And significances of the *is* always belongs to someone else; on their word or **authority**. However, when someone asks you "what is __," you are able to engage personal processes to generate answers and you are able to Self-determine agreements of a reality.

Of course, in the world-at-large we find a lot of give-and-take concerning these types of flows; though it will be noticed that certain individuals are predominantly projecting an outflow and certain individuals are predominantly receiving inflows; and the key to balancing this acrobatic act is to return control of attention and intention back to the Seeker—allowing them to determine where to place their attention and what intention to put on the line. The Seeker is determining the significances of things for themselves; and that is the essence of a **consideration**. Systematic processing at *Grade-IV* concerns questions that have "open answers" or wide ranges of consideration as opposed to simply prompting for "yes/no." There is a time and purpose for such "yes"/"no" types of **assessment**, but *Systemology Operating Procedure 2-C* for "Route-3" does not incorporate these methods directly.

Remaining steps of SOP-2C are listed below, to complete a session (regardless of the Routes taken).

Step-5 : "Clearing the Channel"
\ purify; cleanse; clear away
\ handling the energy flow or circuit

Step-6 : "Realizations"
\ beingness; to become; to arrive at; to ascend
\ spiritual rehabilitation; increase in Self-determinism

Step-7 : "Landing Procedures"
\ attainment of destination; actualization of more ideal state
\ End of Session

Where "Route-1" is referred to as "emotional cathartic processing" or "imprint processing" and "Route-2" is often treated as "thought processing" or "deprogramming," it is actually quite difficult to limit the function of any route to only one or another type of defragmentation results. The irony continues if we view "Route-3" as "**communication processing**" or "control processing" when such must always be present in a session for any Route to function. It should thus be considered that these descriptions are merely the "emphasis" of a particular Route.

Internal communication between Self and Self, and those between Self and the "Mind-Systems" linking Self to *beta-existence* and control of a genetic vehicle, is an actualization of the first "Sphere of Existence" and the reach of the Alpha-Spirit to communicate as Self. Self is always the spiritual energy source for whatever is communicated and experienced as its universe or reality. The Mind assigns considerations to particles and waves as forms and these are thereafter treated with some significance and meaning for experience as beta existence.

Communication with others in our immediate proximity constitutes the solidity of the second "sphere of existence" and the first circle of reach or influence that expands from a consideration of Self as an epicenter of potential reach. This expands through various spheres, levels, veils or thresholds, all the way back to the *Gateways of Infinity*. The second systematic "sphere of existence" that we communicate an energetic exchange with is primarily our "home" and domestic life; perhaps also our immediate family and friends—essentially whatever an individual keeps closest in "reach" or "around the house" to maintain the sense of Self as a physical being incarnate and connected. But we are also members of other "groups" and **participate** and give witness to many forms of communication.

"Route-3" as "communication processing," means specifically processing imprinting and fragmentation encoded or programmed as "*communication.*" This is not, of course, restricted only to spoken or written communications, but any activity or motion or event or exchange that may be observed or experienced. In theory, the same events or channels could be treated by any one or another of the Routes. All the Routes are equally effective when operated for their ideal level or purpose of use.

	Route-3 (*Liber-2C+2D*)	Route-0 (*Liber-3D*)[‡]
Step-3 :	\ Contact	\ Imagine
Step-4 :	\ Communicate	\ Make it solid

There are then a total of four possible "Routes" composing an infinite number of potential techniques that may be applied within the structure of *Systemology Operating Procedure 2-C*. Some **terminals** and circuits that seem inaccessible at one level of processing or actualization are suddenly within reach from a higher level of realization. For this reason many of the processes are used regularly as "standard" procedure; they effectively apply to whatever level a Seeker is at in their progress. Processes systematically work by providing the most effective general increase in actualization and when a process is applied again on a new terminal from a new POV and range of considerations, it will not be just the same process being run again.

---

‡ The designation for "*Imaginomicon.*"

Once control and communication are established in a session with preliminary processes, it is customary to use basic recall commands to refocus and concentrate the *Seeker's* attention onto the session and onto the communication line with Pilot. It requires the ability to "recall" imagery in the mind—at least what the *Seeker* is willing to reach for at their level of development. This also requires contacting the "terminals" of our experience and ability to "confront" or "face-up to" the **mental-images** attached to the other ends of the circuits running in our Mind.

With "communication processing" a *Seeker* is given the opportunity to confront and face up to the interactions with individuals and the environment without being in direct emotional restimulation and without making effects on the *Seeker* (from contact with the line) more solid. The *Seeker* gradually regains ability to face these terminals without inhibition or experiencing distortion/turbulence on the line.

Whatever a person is not willing to handle or reach for; whatever they are not willing to know or what has not been answered or responded to; whatever blackness and distortions appear in what is seen or treated in the mind— all of this could be said to be facets of "the primary thing we cannot see beyond." Whatever that "thing" is, it has become a mystery and it has been enshrouded by layers and layers of other erroneous fragmentation.

To run "Route-3" processes, a *Seeker* must be willing and able to face the terminal at the end of the channel; see it clearly and recall activities that took place—the energy flows concerning that terminal at that instance. Another "Route-0" version of these processes involves "imagining" events and interactions that have not actually taken place between terminals, but of which by running through them as a mental exercise, provides greater considerations on events that *have* actually taken place.

We generally consider the blackness of a mystery or the backside of an individual as the opposite of knowing something or getting a response (or a question answered). When attention is directed onto the mystery, the unknown, the unanswered question and the beingness that is not acknowledged, we are often looking at blackness, emptiness and in the case of live terminals, we tend to "look away from" or divert our attention in lieu of actually facing or treating them in the physical universe. In one "Route-0" conceptual exercise, the backside of someone is imagined a mystery and the front side is an answer.

The original purpose of "Route-1" was to handle various **"physiological** pings" or "**somatic** responses" that emerge automatically if wired as a reactive mechanism in a circuit. These naturally affect thought-flow and may generate into thought-forms that go beyond control of their creator (the *Seeker*). A *Pilot* can generally determine a *Seeker's* charges on a line or their level of communication and control with any terminal based on their willingness or ability to literally be responsible for the reactive-response "pings" that kick up when "facing that direction." How can an individual be "free" when their considerations and willingness to reach are so thoroughly tied to how this, that and the other is "*making* them feel"? Or if they are to only agree with what they "like"—how easily could this be controlled.

An individual is then as well off mentally and spiritually as they are able to properly manage and handle the energy and matter of present space-time by knowingly maintaining true relationships or communication with these "things" in present space-time. Most fragmented individuals are "hung up on the past"—treating the energy and matter in present space-time as though it is still happening at some other point on the **timeline**. This is a direct contradiction to the state of *Self-Honesty*.

Whenever the Self reaches—whether in the natural state of the Alpha-Spirit extending its consciousness as arms in front of it to feel around in the emptiness, or whether putting out a line of attention to contact another individual just to know they exist—the individual is putting out a query or request for answers, and awaits the response.

The human condition may be said to be the result of a ceaseless "quest for answers" that has resulted in the experience of the most lowest-level **condensation** of consideration for potentiality of existence. It is quite clear that the Mind-Systems are occupied with resolving the inflowing information with the considerations otherwise programmed and encoded. And when approached with an experience or the confrontation of some object or mental image, communication ensues.

When an individual puts out their attention—extends their reach—information is returned on a circuit as a communication flow. To make sense of this, an individual:

1.) searches their own databanks of experience for an answer/response;

-and- (*failing to receive this...*)

2.) inquires or requests answer/response (communication) from another;

-and- (*failing to receive this...*)

3.) observes others and/or the environment for other cues/information;

-or- (*the first method used by an Actualized Technician...*)

0.) experiences direct "**gnosis**" or other actualized realizations internally.

Of course, true gnosis would require having cleared the channels (used to receive such data) of fragmentary debris or erroneously programmed limitations on consideration or any other reactive 'pings' that would otherwise inhibit the reception of total understanding. This is the component—the practice of defragmentation—that is too often missed by other forms of "enlightenment," which can in themselves become just another type of trapping for the more intellectual or mystically inclined when operated outside of Self-Honesty. We have found that those who are formerly so ingrained into these methods and doctrines as an end-point have actually had difficulty in extending their reach to any higher *Grades* in our Systemology.

While there is *no* reason for us *not* to encourage the study of ancient esoterica and the work developed over the past 6,000 years—which is revealed quite adamantly in *Grade-I* and *Grade-II* material—it should be noted in Self-Honesty that magicians and priestesses, however much enlightened they may be within their own **paradigms**, run the risk of being entrapped in their systems by actively imposing higher-level barriers on themselves than the average human would even understand. In this respect, lower *Grades* always seem more dangerous than the upper-level work, due to the likelihood of misuse of such material—whereas most upper-level work is so refined and esoteric that it protects itself by being essentially "not useful" to those unprepared to understand it; it's functional meaning is not properly communicated to an individual that has no reality on a particular channel.

"Circuit-0" is an energy flow treated as *Alpha Defragmentation*, which is to say the condition of Self as "Actualized Technician" (A.T.) or "Wizard" consciously operating from "exterior" to *beta-existence*. This does not mean that the individual is "out of touch" with the Physical Universe—on the contrary, they are operating the human condition from a point that is outside the consideration that they are stuck *inside* "being" *human.*

We limit added discussion and commentary in a processing session because of how "fragmenting" and **aberrative** most human communication is. This is the very type of fragmentation **processed-out** in Route-3. All of the "got to" "ought to" "should" "shouldn't" "must" "must not" statements compound into a certain pattern of thoughts, associative 'pings' and empty communications with a Mystery. All of these communications that have been stored up as "experience" over the course of our lives are imprinted and will become challenges against our ability to experience free range of consideration, conception, thought and creation.

ROUTE-3C
CIRCUIT PROCESSING INSTRUCTIONS
"SOP-2C" EXCERPT FROM LIBER-2D

Can you recall a time when you told someone something? Can you recall a time when someone told you something? How about when someone else was talking to another or a group? Can you recall a time when you told yourself something with intention? In each of these instances—What was said? How did the communication make you feel? What did you see around you at the time? How does that communication cause you to see the world differently? How do you feel about that communication now?

All forms of contact with the world outside is a form of communication; and systematically these communications are linked to the energy and circuits taking place "within us"—*interior* to the Mind-System. All the **external** sensory data must be received and processed as Self to have any kind of registry as real—and how clear are these channels dictating the relay and reality of this "experience"?

The same rules of communication taking place in session between the *Pilot* and *Seeker* (as terminals) are the same fundamentals of "communication processing" when a Seeker has set up lines of communication (or been **enforced** to put attention on a line) in their life and been subject to an inflow or outflow that they are now responsible for "carrying around as experience."

The function of systematic processing is not actual erasure or elimination of a *Seeker's* memory. In fact, it has been demonstrated that the type of exercises we employ may actually contribute to improved abilities of recall and analytical memory. This actually happens because an individual's willingness to reach even within themselves (and the circuits already existent) increases; they find themselves with more free range access to their own "Mind-System" than they did before.

We can assume that the development of an RCC or *Reactive Control Center* (inherently part of the ZU-line communicated between Self and a genetic body) is likely the product of survival experiences early on the cellular line and of which collected its own energies and information centers to communicate between various nerves and systems that later developed as an organism extended its reach further and further from one cell.

An organism develops response-reaction mechanistic systems during encounters with various barriers and other material interactions of the Physical Universe. These mechanisms begin to define the very **parameters** of what the organism is willing to *be*, *know* or *do*. Some mechanisms of the genetic vehicle are not only the result of *this* lifetime, but of which have been inherited along the "genetic line" on which the physical body evolved from an **organic** being. This is, of course, separate from "past lives" that Self would associate with its own personal identity, since it is not likely to have controlled a body in the past that is on the exact same genetic line as the current one; but we have encountered some cases where, for example, a woman's daughter born in this lifetime was actually her own mother in a former lifetime—in that they shared an opposite role to one another in a former period on the timeline.[*]

The machinery set up along the evolutionary line—which we refer to as the RCC at (2.0) on the Standard Model/Zu-Line—is still very active in the human condition. The issue is not that it exists; but that Awareness as Self is too often reduced to the consideration that the Self is operating as a "body" and not even as a "Mind" and especially not in realization of being a "Spirit" commanding the other two systems. Information is stored below the surface of the RCC and given heavy emotional charges to keep it there, therefore barring an individual with free access to the energy it contains. It is not the energy within the imprint or

---

[*]   In our structured paradigm of systemology, "past lives" start
       being handled in upper-level *Grade-V* processing work.

mass that an individual is seeking to reclaim, because inflow from source is unlimited; it is actually the "blockage" that needs to be freed so new incoming energy is in full circulation—and a lifeform can actually reach toward its own continuation.

Objective processing is also "communication," providing increase of *Awareness* and presence by establishing a realization that in the physical universe—concerning matter and "need to know about" **compulsions**—the answer *is* simply the answer, or rather that the question *is* the answer, but its sometimes treated as the "other side of" because it must be "hidden." Yet, things are not hidden; individuals hide—they hide themselves from the truth and reinforce everything they "don't want to know about" as opposed to that which they are willing to reach toward—and quite literally, "know about."

Humans—by programming or agreement—are convinced that continued existence from one day to the next is something to *do*, meaning: a "problem" to be solved—because life has to serve a purpose and to serve as purpose is to solve a problem. So, we have resolved ourselves to the fact that in order for Self to have its own purpose and be its own reason, it must have "problems" to solve. But there are many orders or levels of problems that could be solved. The only issue is when the Alpha-Spirit is so enamored with the Physical Universe and fixed on the association of a physical body that the primary "problem of life" remains at a lower order of reasoning. Since every day is a new problem to solve, new reasoning and new answers are constantly being sought to erroneous questions and the repeated quest for a truth that has all been beaten over their head time and time again and yet still they feel it is something that they must "go looking" for. There is a small semantic irony in referring to a systemologist as a *"Seeker"* until they reassign enough of their consideration to be an Actualized Technician (A.T. /*"Wizard"*).

The lower an individual is considered on the emotional range of the *Beta-Awareness Scale*, the more literal or solid we would expect them to take words. Below (1.0) on the Standard Model, words have the ability to inflow on someone as solidly as throwing a ball at them. Yet, they are only words—and here we mean specifically "words" and "language" and "images" and any basic form of communication regardless of the intention behind it. At (1.0) on the Standard Model, "association" includes "all things as all things" as all "things" reach closer a state of inert continuity (0.0)—and where everything is as equally solid and as equally significant as everything else, which is exactly the way in which the RCC processes data.

One of the primary qualities of personal fragmentation is the **misappropriation** of associated identification; we are talking about *facets* of *imprints*, where dissimilar aspects of existence are suddenly encoded together. At one level, this happens with painful and traumatic experiences with others and the environment—and again, potentially even with ourselves. At another level, this happens when we feel experiences of loss or strong invalidation—the sense that others have taken something from us, or that the cycles-of-action taking place in the environment are somehow "unfair." This all leads to greater and greater misunderstanding—and if we have no solid *ledge* to stand on to *know*, where does that leave us?

Symbols are often used in the place of actual "things" during communication. Everything we can treat as a "thing" is a symbol at its own level or gradient. This creates an entire scale, then, concerning what a symbol can actually be —since it appears that it is the symbol that is being communicated as an energy pattern and not actual "things." These symbols are simply treated as "real things."

A "symbol" is also the pattern form by which we recognize an energy for what it is. How else can we determine the nature of one type of wave-flow from another? We must be inherently able to identify differences in the energy flows and then assign significance and meaning to it by our consideration. The end result is "our concept" or "reality" *on* whatever line we are treating. But the meaning of symbols may be altered or programmed. And in the absence of true *knowing*, a "symbol" is a poor substitute.

Objective processing techniques are intended to resolve past considerations in memory that restrict a Seeker. This includes implants that inform that the present is too un-safe to confront and manage, and that the future is some unknown Mystery that is inherently dangerous. It may or may not be surprising to some individuals just how many of their programmed and encoded considerations of *Life, the Universe and Everything* have essentially led them to be trapped within these very conclusions.

Creative ability is an *Alpha* quality. The willingness to cre-ate is to make something real and solid as an absence of nothingness—including points in space. The willingness to create also means the ability to freely create again and again. When a *Seeker* realizes that they are not "losing" anything by giving up the hold on heavily charged images and fragments—because they can recreate anything at Will —than they will feel more certain in maintaining control and responsibility of the mental images.[*]

An individual is responsible for the creation of and reac-tion to all activity taking place on the Zu-line (**personal identity continuum**). Emotional charge present on the line of any circuit is in many ways reinforced by a resist-ance to loss; the idea that another consideration would somehow dissolve our existing "beliefs" is treated as a loss. This only comes from a consideration that *Self* is somehow unable to duplicate creation of any such things again. Willingness for an individual to create and commu-nicate (and even control a piloted session) is dependent on the responsibility, *Awareness* and ability to carry a source particle, bit or thought to its receipt-effect point.

The Alpha-Spirit learns very early in its existence that to be a source of creation or communication is to be the gen-erator of an energetic effect. Then we learn, in the pres-ence of others, that our creations and communications

---

[*]   Refer to "*Imaginomicon*" (*Liber-3D*).

have an effect on others and the solidity of these things somehow increases. These are exactly the type of energy flows treated as "circuits" for "Route-3" techniques.

When the Nothingness does not appear to communicate (any more than than the walls and solids of inert physical existence do), the Alpha-Spirit develops its reach, willingness and communications in the direction of "somethingness." Of course as more and more of these "somethings" develop and as more beings begin to create "somethings" to show off to others, the energy becomes more and more compressed and solid and the remnants of these creations filter down into the lower-energy environments and existences of shared agreement. These considerations all become more and more solid as they are concentrated at these lower-levels of existence. They begin to act as walls to considerations at those lower-levels and if the sense of *Self* is placed within them as a POV, those considerations actually do become as solid as walls are experienced at the continuity level of the Physical Universe.

The final steps of *SOP-2C*, regardless of the Route taken, regard clearing the channel (or line-circuit of communication) and allowing the *Seeker* an opportunity to arrive at new levels of realization.

Whatever you wish to call them: realizations, awakenings, cognitions, true gnosis, deep insights, or increased actualization—these are all indicators of a fully completed process or that a communication line-circuit is defragmented. It is important for the *Pilot* to acknowledge the forward progress a *Seeker* makes on the *Pathway* without invalidating what they have not yet realized and without conditioning the *Seeker* to become dependent on validation from others to determine their successes or achievement of a new realization. The realization is for them to make—and whatever is true for them at that moment *is* what is true for them at that moment, and any other impression or enforcement of another POV (*point-of-view*) is going to be received as an invalidation.

There are two main categories of intention that exist on the flow of a circuit with a terminal:

  a) the **insistence** of; a reach toward; and

  b) to **protest** against; a withdrawal from.

It is these two categories that tend to form into functions of an automated mechanism, especially if not acknowledged. Response-reactions can be automated because a system works in the direction of greatest efficiency. Of course, as soon as these functions become automatic, and the individual has forgotten this agreement, responsibility and control are misplaced.

Basic processing commands may apply to a **dichotomy** on the circuits, differentiating considerations of what a *Seeker* would reject/protest or accept. For example, the *Seeker* has experienced communications where they were "enforced" or "had to have *x*" or were "prevented from having *x*" or has "had *x* imposed" on them or an "outright denial of *x*" &tc. &tc. This will come out of considerations concerning:

  a) With what might you protest?

  -*or*- With what might you reject?

  b) With what might you agree?

  -*or*- With what might you find acceptable?

  -*or*- What would you accept?

In processing, these specific commands would be used alternately from (a) to (b) to see if there is a heavily charged emotional reaction with any terminal, or if the analytical treatment of this will essentially free up the ideas that they are holding on strongly to, and if necessary—once a terminal has been identified—worked on via multiple Routes to make certain that the emotional charge on the line (sadness, anger, frustration, pains, pings, &tc.) have been properly desensitized (or literally "discharged").

Rejecting, blocking or persisting—anything other than a free-flow of energy—on channel is the first steps toward making something undesirable more "real" or "solid" on that line unknowingly. The masses that build up continue to receive a steady flow of energy, but since it is not passing through, it creates turbulence on that channel and creates a disturbance in the Self-Honest experience of existence for the Alpha-Spirit. When barriers and restrictions are encountered—including no response—you can actually see an individual's "mood" or *beta-Awareness* level decline as they enter increasingly lower states of consideration as Self. We would expect a person to be very hung up on any circuit that it has had this kind of relationship with for a long period of time.

Primary considerations regarding any turbulent circuit— or which a communication has not been properly acknowledged or answered:

> What were you intending to create/effect/communicate?
>
> Who were you intending the communication for as a receipt-point?
>
> What mechanisms are you now operating in order to continue this communication so **compulsively**?

A Pilot may not be able to ask a Seeker the third question directly. Therefore, the last part is simply a consideration of what the resulting realization should be once relevant information or facets of specific events are accounted for and run through in "recall" a few times. Some additional ways in which we may pose considerations in language:

> What are you rejecting/protesting against/insisting on?
>
> How did you communicate that in the past?
>
> How are you still communicating that now?
>
> Who/what are you waiting on acknowledgment/ response from?

"Route-3" is named so for two reasons: it is the third Route established (**chronologically** speaking) for *Professional Piloting Procedure*, and it involves identification of terminals and processing of *three circuits* of energy-flow related to that terminal. The purpose of this is to process *all* three energy flows that are related to a terminal, concept, event, idea, emotion, &tc.

Processing all three circuits to a terminal is far more effective than emphasizing, for example, *only* "what has happened *to* the Seeker." The other side of this is "what has the Seeker done?" But even that is only two circuits of energy; so, we balance this with another circuit—and that is "what the Seeker has observed another doing to others"; therein we have the third. Example:

   Step-3 : Contact Terminal
     \ example terminal : "*communication*"

   Step-4 : Communications on Circuits to Terminal
     \ Circuit-1 : "what could you *communicate* with?"
     \ Circuit-2 : "what could *communicate* with you?"
     \ Circuit-3 : "what could others *communicate* with?"

Although our example is a perfectly legitimate model, and one that it *is* actually effectively workable, this is a slightly confusing way to learn Route-3. "Communication Processing" is used for processing "*communication*" with a terminal. "Communication" is not a mass itself and therefore is not technically a terminal.

The same example might be restated for example as: "what would be acceptable to communicate with?" or "what would you be willing to communicate with?" In this sense, "willingness" is essentially synonymous with what would be "considered acceptable"—meaning no heavy emotional charges or response-reactivity on that line. It does not necessarily mean that a Seeker must then "agree" with any other significance or sentiment attached to it.

"**Willingness**"—the word is used quite frequently to describe the range of consideration and personal ability that an individual has achieved—and we mean literally the willingness to confront or face some terminal, subject, live-form, &tc.; increasing the willingness to hold a reality —and even create reality—without becoming the effect of it, or subject to some mechanistic reactivity or associative conditions that restrict any other consideration.

Accumulated "experiences" and "agreements" along some channel are a cause of many lingering automatic "problems" and "pings" that may be restimulated into action by various facets and conditions. These begin to define and restrict a very specific range of what an individual will find acceptable to confront in their lives. How many times has an individual said that they "don't want to know" or "don't want to deal with" &tc. &tc. And over time they begin to give up their determinism and control of knowing and dealing or managing the energy flows on various channels of information and experience.

As an individual finds difficulty with maintaining control on certain parts of the body as they become more and more "out of communication" with them—meaning that they are rejecting or blocking a flow between the Self and that part of the body. It is easy to understand, systematically, how such improper handling of personal energy (attention and intention) can actually result in having energetic blockages on the channels with the body.

Communications of Self with Self is also a circuit, but do we not treat it as part of the "three" and therefore refer to it as Circuit-0. This information is treated specifically in later work regarding "Actualized Technician" (Wizard Grades) for which *Grade-IV* is a "bridge" to. In the case of "Route-3" practice, Circuit-0 would be "what has Self communicated to Self?" This is not absolutely necessary for *Grade-IV* processing work and should only be introduced if it will always be applied thereafter. Essentially, once a Pilot is using "Route-3" to treat systematic processes, than "Route-1" and "Route-2" would also require incorporating all three circuits in order to get the same effective results.

The following outlines standard practices of using "Route-3" (also logged as "SP-2C") for *Systemology Operating Procedure 2-C*.

Step-3 : Contact Terminal

\ terminal, live-form, belief/attitude, emotions/
  sensations

Step-4 : Communications on Circuits to Terminal

\ Circuit-1 : Self *to* others/terminal (*out-flow*)

\ Circuit-2 : others/terminal *to* Self (*in-flow*)

\ Circuit-3 : others/terminal *to* others/terminal
  (*cross-flow*)

\ Circuit-0 : Self *to* Self (*Alpha-flow* or "postulate")

It is a common mistake to focus only on events rather than the consideration, emotion or feelings attached to that channel. Isolated event should be run with "Route-3" only if it has just recently taken place, as a means to manage it better. Otherwise, trying to use SOP-2C to process "every time a tree branch hit you in the face" is not very productive; however, processing out energetic flows regarding times you experienced stinging pains in the face, times you caused others to experience stinging pains in the face and then also times when others caused another to experience stinging pains in the face... suddenly the idea of being at cause again over the sensations felt in the face becomes stronger. This applies to those incidents which later continue to carry heavy emotional charges that *make* us "*feel*" a certain way when a terminal or channel is active. These matters treated "outside of our control" are what require systematic processing to bring back under controlled communication by and as Self.

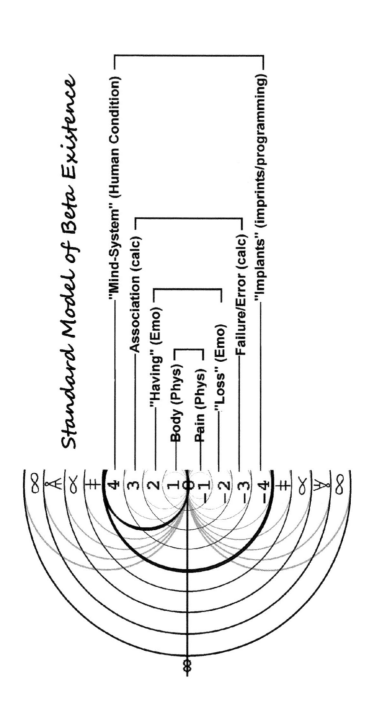

Standard Model of Beta Existence

ROUTE-3D
UNIVERSE PROCESSING INSTRUCTIONS
REVISED FROM LIBER-3D

IMAGINATION is the vehicle or **catalyst** for an individual's *Creative Ability.* Such abilities originate at the level of the "Spirit" or "*Alpha Spirit.*" They are "*Alpha*" qualities originating within one's own "Personal Universe" apart from any programmed or encoded "reality agreements" concerning *Beta-Existence*, which is to say, the "Physical Universe." The two "Universes" are separate—and it is only when an individual confuses the Reality of *one* with the *other* that they tend to find their experience of Life and Existence especially difficult... and *fragmented.*

Being an Alpha quality, Imagination is above or *senior* to "Associative Thought" of the Mind-System as it applies to experience of *Beta-Existence.* Where the common denominator of personal thought and effort in *Beta-Existence* is toward the **Existential "Prime Directive"**: "*To Survive*"— the "name of the **game**" in all upper-level Universes and truer Alpha **echelons** of spiritual existence is: "*To Create.*"

The Spirit is able to create, essentially, from *Nothingness*— and does not require fragmentation or **condensation** of *other* "energy-matter" *parts* in which *to be* creative. In this wise, an Alpha Spirit exists and operates in an unlimited Home Universe that defies some of the hardest-held beliefs about the Physical Universe.

Most individuals are taught to put personal value in "experience." In order to get a sense of worth—to feel as if they can show something for it; or *have* something as the ultimate goal—the information is stored for "future" use. It's only valid function is evaluation of "effort" necessary to "act" in the Physical Universe (*Beta-Existence*) using a "body" that exists to communicate with a similar material **continuity** level. But unfortunately, as an individual puts more and more energy into storing data and other "*Mental Images*" that mirror *Beta-Existence*, their considerations and willingness become increasingly rigid and fixed—essentially forming "energy ridges" and "mental machinery" to manage and control experience with a physical body-form (*Genetic Vehicle*). This is also one aspect of how an *exterior* Alpha-Spirit became entrapped *interior* to the Human Condition of the Physical Universe.

Some schools of philosophy and spirituality have sought a resolution to this entrapment by treating the entire subject of the Physical Universe—and its facets of *space-time energy-matter*—as "unreal" or a "delusion." Such modes contradict earlier agreements and postulates the Alpha-Spirit is already "carrying" concerning the Human Condition, so the individual gets "hung up" or "stuck" in a "Mystery" concerning their certainty on Reality. These other methods have been attempted by our organization and were found unworkable and unproductive to reaching the ultimate goal of returning to the Spirit its own (true and original) Actualized Awareness and ability of operating as Self, independent and *exterior* to *Beta-Existence*.

In spite of the numerous times an Alpha-Spirit has connected with a *Lifeform* in a *Beta-Existence*, we continue to consistently apply spiritual energy to create our "Personal Universe" in *Alpha-Existence*. Self-Determined knowledge of this gradually fades to black as an individual enshrouds considerations of Self and Reality with further "agreements" concerning the nature of the Physical Universe in exclusion. For this reason, most other "sciences" and "applied philosophies" have entrapped considerations and attention *interior* to *Beta-Existence*—providing no regard for the Spirit, its true nature or abilities.

> The Alpha Spirit *is* at *Cause* in *creating* Universes; Self *is* at *Cause* in *determining* its own true spiritual existence; and the mechanics of *Beta-Existence* are wholly separate, but mirrored in an individual's considerations of a Personal Universe.

The nature and existence of this Physical Universe is simply the result of common denominator agreements made by countless Alpha Spirits **participating** in this *reality* as a Point-of-View (POV) remote from, and simultaneous with, their own true continuing position as a *Spiritual Being* inhabiting a Personal Universe within Alpha-Existence (with is marked at "7.0" on our Standard Model). It is at this "point" that the Alpha-Spirit may turn "180 degrees" to **confront** the *Infinity of Nothingness*, but the fact that we are here now suggests that we became far more interested in the survival of potential *Somethingness.*

Our Standard Model, our Systemology and allegories from "Arcane Tablets" suggest that as Alpha-Spirits became increasingly unwilling to confront communications of a "game" within a particular Universe, their considerations for existence as Self "fell down" or "degraded" to "lower" condensations and goals than former Universes. Descriptions of the Pathway back "up" and *out* are relayed to "esoteric initiates" using symbolism of ascending "Gates." An individual goes "out of" *Communication* with "higher" spiritual levels on their descent *interior* to the present Human Condition. The "Wizard Grades" of our Systemology *systematically* pursue a repair of this.

"Imagination" is the most appropriate semantics we can apply to the Alpha-Spirit's *Creative Abilities* as experienced in the Human Condition. Although an Alpha-Spirit may direct imagery (energetically down the ZU-line) to the "Mind-System" for *Beta-Existence:*

> Imagination is a *creation* originating directly from the "Spirit"—not a *product* of the "Mind."

However, as a *Being* descends in their considerations, *Point-of-View* (POV) and lower "seats" of *Beingness*—particularly below "4.0" on the Standard Model—cumulative programming and implanting of the "surrounding" Mind-System *caves in* on the individual. This promotes automated reactive tendencies, preset patterns of thought and stimulus-response behavior (as treated in our Systemology materials concerning "**Beta-Defragmentation**").

Δ Δ Δ Δ Δ Δ

Each and every one of us has the ability to *incite* or *dissolve* "creation" with our *Attention*—our focused application of *Self-Directed Awareness*. We tend to do this several times a day: forming an **intention** in the "Mind," *creating* an entire "*Mental Image*" within our "Personal Universe" of Reality and then often *erasing* it in fear and/or doubt. Within higher realizations of an Alpha Spirit's "Home Universe" and other shared "Creative Universes" within Alpha-Existence, the same faculty described as "imagination" in *Beta* is actually pure "*Creation*"—perhaps the highest ability and directive purpose *of* the Alpha-Spirit.

Of course, an individual is no *more* "free" to *Self-Determine* the nature of their own "*Creations*" or "*Creative Ability*" than they are in confronting and handling other elements of the "*Reactive Control Center*" and Mind-System, *if* their considerations are still fixed **locally** and exclusively to the Point-of-View (POV) of the *Human Condition*—particularly the specific *Genetic Vehicle* to which it is operating. Such considerations inherent to the *Human Condition*, such as "I" or "Self" being "held in," "snapped in" or "keyed-in" *to* the "body" are implanted "pass-not" barriers to achieving higher states suggested by "Wizard Levels" of **Metahuman** Systemology.

A stable Beta-Defragmentation requires an individual to *know* to the fullest extent of their *Beingness* that they are *not* the "physical body" (*genetic vehicle*)—to the same extent that they had once fixed or trapped their *knowing* in a consideration that they *were* identified as some other "body" or such. An individual *must* knowingly maintain *Actualized Awareness* "outside of" the *Beta* range and limitations of the *Human Condition* in order to move forward and "upward."

Previous attempts at reaching the same goals as our Systemology often failed due to overemphasis on handling "energy" directly. It is now concluded that an individual's inability to directly handle "energy" is supported by the amount of "relays" and "screens" and "filters" and "catalysts" fixed in place to prevent them from doing so—

barriers to direct communication and knowingness. If an individual *were* practiced in handling energy directly, there would be no dependency on using sensory-organs and perceptions of a *genetic vehicle*. One could still do so by choice; there would be no compulsive necessity behind it.

Wizard Level-0 redirects emphasis on precise control, and responsibility for, "Mental Images" and "Masses"—*forms, objects, manifestations* and "*terminals*"—that an individual maintains an energetic circuit-**flow** with. When an individual properly *Self-Directs* handling of their *realizations* of consideration connected to *imagery* and *symbols* representing the "terminals" themselves, the energy-flows simply followed in suit; the circuitry connected to them "defragmented" as if the operator handled the energy.

Highest potential creativity of an Alpha-Spirit and its upper-level *Point-of-View* (POV) is brought down to lower points of *Beta-Awareness* and fixed within parameters of *that* existence, becoming obsessively attached to a *genetic vehicle* (or "physical body") POV for its sense of *Beingness*. Through a long sequence of programmed imprinting on implants reinforced with excessive emotional encoding:

> an individual comes to believe certain factors
> are true of *Self* and their Personal Home Universe,
> when they actually only pertain to considerations
> of the *genetic vehicle* and the *Physical Universe*.

Fragmentation of Beta-thought reduces an Alpha-Spirit's true spiritual individuality as it begins to "identify" itself with other "things." When it too solidly identifies with agreements of low-level *Awareness*, it becomes a locatable "effect" of *Beta-Existence*, succumbing to "mundane forces" of the "Physical Universe." Having forgotten its own creative ability, it is convinced on dependency of a *Beta-Existence* to provide all force, energy, space, matter and so forth—providing the individual with an entirely *other-determined* "reality" in which to exist. This fact is the real delusion of the Physical Universe; not the solidity of its material substance. It continues to persist in existence, as a sort of "prison for Alpha-Spirits," because no one takes responsibility for its original creation and every Observer consistently alters what it *is* (or pretends that what *is*, *is-not*) and makes it more solid.

Inability to control or manage *Self-Determined* flows of energy (communication, reactivity, mental images, &tc.) is remedied by practice of consciously, intentionally and knowingly *Self-Directing* these flows in the same way that their handling has come to be "automated" as "push-button responses" managed by the *Beta*-environment or Physical Universe. The key component to this type of practice or "**creativeness processing**" is *Imagination*—literally, personal control of "Mental Imagery" and recording of experience.

> Mechanisms of the Mind-System store data for "Mental Imagery" which entangles it with the same energy and *Awareness* that is *imprinted* during an experience or **Imprinting Incident**. Not only does this reduce an individual's *Actualized Awareness*, but also leads to **relinquishing** responsibility for creating and handling *Mental Images* over to the automated mental machinery. This same *imprinted* data creates energetic **turbulence** later when reactively incited as an individual's "Reality." This happens if the external environment is similar to an **Activating Event** that stimulates circuitry for a programmed response with a certain *facet*.

Imprints are essentially "stamped" holographic-type imagery—a snap-shot of energetic *facets* associated with an experience. When an individual is not maintaining high levels of *Actualized Awareness*, energetic-flows activate emotional encoding or programming (stored on and as implants). When insufficient "*Presence*" and *Self-Determinism* is applied to its handling, automated response-mechanisms are "**unconsciously**" generated in place of it; they generate a "Mental Image"—and an Alpha-Spirit "*looks*" at *that* in place of the actual energy.

When *Self* is not knowingly at *Cause* in the experience of *Life*, no responsibility is taken for creation of that experience—or one's own Personal Universe. The individual, as an *effect*, tends to put up more "resistance" to the Physical Universe being as *Cause*—therefore making considerations and agreements to *Beta-existence* more solid and apparently less controllable (one thinks) by *Self*.

In Route-3, "energy-flows" are treated as "circuits" on "channels of communication" with "**terminal** nodes." Flows on these circuits are fixed by our "resistance" *against* some rejection, barrier or communication break with Universes and Spheres of Existence all the way down to present-time *Beta*-experience. Over the course of our very long spiritual existence, this has created more solid barriers and added greater solidity to our fixed considerations of what something *is*. This happens "on automatic," using automated response-mechanisms we have created to handle the "circuitry" for us.

> When we analyze the nature of emotionally encoded *Imprinting*, we often find "snap-shots" of what we are resisting against.

In a resonating "Image" remaining from a physical accident, it is a "snap-shot" of what we are attempting to *stop*, and thereby *control*. Failing this, the "Image" remains—it becomes a barrier-wall or backdrop on our Reality (for that "channel"). It contains only stopped motion or no motion and becomes timeless. Of course, because we don't want to *see* or *communicate* with what comes next, we tend to "flip" the "Image" around, now seeing the "backside," which is a kind of "blackness" representing "Mystery."

But *facets* of the *Imprint* (and its mechanisms) all still exist "running in the background," yet now even less under control of *Self*, which no longer *sees* it for what it *is*. This energetic solidity and fragmentation hinders a *Self-Honest* state of true Spiritual Freedom and *Creative Ability*. A remedy for this is found with one of the primary theories behind the application of "systematic processing":—

> to get an individual to consciously, willingly and
> knowingly practice actions that are otherwise
> taking place unknowingly on automatic
> or using response-mechanisms and other filters.

Such mechanisms and filters were once our own creations, but *control* of them became more automatic the longer they were used and the greater they were relied upon as "sensors" for information and experience. Keep in mind, that this same quality of energetic communication is taking place all up and down the Standard Model (ZU-line), including throughout the Mind-System.

in "systematic processing" we practice fluidity of energy-communication (as an alternation) along each channel (to a "terminal") to free up the unlimited considerations an Alpha-Spirit naturally would maintain at its highest basic state. Systematically practice knowingly "duplicating" or "copying" *Mental Images* that are otherwise considered an imposition or barrier. When a *Seeker* recognizes that they "own" it, then the responsibility and command-power of creating all *Mental Imagery* experienced, increases.

△ △ △ △ △ △

Wizard Level-0 material emphasizes techniques that promote responsibility and certainty to control *Mental Imagery*—the ability to *know YOU* are creating the *Imagery*; that you can *choose* to make it more 'solid' and 'real' or simply 'dissolve' it; and realizations that no thing is permanent or can affect the Spirit permanently, except as a consideration that it can.

Grade-III and Grade-IV systematic processing for Beta-Defragmentation treats the *past* in *this* lifetime—"scanning" this lifetime or "resurfacing" a specific event, or an event that is linked to communications from an earlier event by its *facets*. Such methods are not only effective for *this* lifetime, but to have greater applications, the *Seeker* would require an increased Reality on *former* lifetimes—and quite often, the "screens" and "filters" maintained during experience of *this* lifetime (and former ones) act as "blinders" to higher spiritual realizations.

"Route-1" assists an individual in reclaiming energies "entwined" or "entangled" with emotional intensity held from former experiences. It was intended to *assist* an individual in reaching enough *Actualized Awareness* to apply other forms of systematic processing. "Route-2" addresses personal significances, reasoning and *facets* of "associated knowledge" tied to an event (*any* event) or consideration. "Route-3" follows similarly, though it went beyond events, treating communication lines with "terminals" as energetic channels, and *three* specific circuits of *facet imprinting*:

Circuit-1: what *Self* has done (outflows);
Circuit-2: what *Self* has received (inflows); and
Circuit-3: what *Self* has observed of others (crossflows).

All former "Routes" primarily treat the incidents from *this* lifetime—and their "Recall." There is no question that they are effective methods for goals in place at each step of the way. If these other "Routes" should have demonstrated anything to you as a *Systemologist*, it is that you are *here* in the present where "past events" are *not*.

Wherever an "energy-flow" has been fixed in place, or control of a "channel" has been abandoned, or considerations concerning a given "terminal" have been **calcified** or fragmented into debris: an individual can be said to be "out of communication" with that aspect or part of existence. And since all parts work *systematically*, there is an ensuing *systematic* break-down of the remaining systems— at least as it concerns *Self-Determinism*, control and command, of and by *Self*—as Alpha-Spirit. To be effective at all:

the "Routes" of "systematic processing" rely on
a Spirit's ability to *control* and *dissolve* its own *creations*,
even if not instructed specifically as such in directions.

Route-3 includes a further "A.T." application: "Circuit-0," which is what *Self* has created (or is creating) for *Self*— "What *Self* has done to *Self*." This method emphasizes personal responsibility for creating all *Mental Images* and "identity associations" of what things *are*.

Any point where the Alpha-Spirit is using a Mind-System to experience *Beta-Existence* from a POV *interior* to the *Human Condition*, a significant amount of its own spiritual energy is taken up in the "unknown" validation and solidification of various *"wall-like screens"* and *"filter-mechanisms"* inhibiting free circulation of energetic-flow between an Alpha-Spirit's true Beingness and any of its potential creations or POVs.

Fragmentation of any kind "blocks" clear communication maintained between *Self* and anything which it is still creating or in "possession" of. We may carry strong energetic "ties" with terminals in our past that hold a significant amount of our attention fixed—and even other times when attention was too dispersed to be properly focused at all. Routes 1, 2 and 3 allow a Seeker to resume communication with what they *"screened"* or *"filtered"* in the past, thereby reclaiming control and command of those channels.

"Route-1" Resurfacing/Cathartic Proc. (*Tablets of Destiny*)
"Route-2" Analytical/Recall Processing (*Crystal Clear*)
"Route-3" Communication Proc. (*Metahuman Destinations*)
"Route-0" Creativeness Processing (*Imaginomicon*)

The most basic "keyword" used as a "***Processing Command Line***" (**PCL**) of "Route-0" is: "IMAGINE." Route-0 methods may be applied directly to the same types of "terminals" and "events" targeted by other "Routes," but only if applying "IMAGINE" properly to the *Processing Command Line* (PCL) and properly processed. For example, one can easily replace "RECALL" with "IMAGINE" for PCLs suggested in previous texts. *"Imagining"* and/or *"Creating"* also provides a wider range of application as *Systematic Processing*. This includes techniques that increase an ability to *"confront"* what they were previously unable to *"recall"* (or have *"screened"*/*"filtered"*) and points that prove too turbulent for a *Seeker* to approach directly by other "Routes."

ROUTE-0
CREATIVE ABILITY PROC. INSTRUCTIONS
REVISED FROM LIBER-3D

Most any "terminal" or "incident" one might treat by another method of systematic processing could be treated with *Creativeness Processing* (Route-0) *if* the "terminal" or "subject" is within the reach (Reality) of the Seeker. If not, then the same methodology is employed on a gradient scale—getting an individual to simply *Imagine* some small part of the whole, each time gradually increasing the amount of scope (or magnitude) that they *are* willing and able to "*confront.*"

△ △ △ △ △ △

Effectiveness of "Route-0" is dependent on an individual *creating* and *imagining* independent of memory, Betathought or "associative reason." When using "*creativeness processing,*" *i*n no way should an *Imaginary Scene* or *Mental Image* be a duplicate or "*facsimile*" of something that has actually happened (knowingly) unless the technique specifically calls for it. The basic purpose is to resume control of the very mechanisms and functions already causing "associations of identity" to be automatically fixed in "*facsimile imprints*" and ("reaction-response") experiences.

The term "*Mental Image*" is not restricted to only "visual pictures" or "scenery" viewed from the Mind—or within one's Personal Universe. As a Seeker learns in former Mardukite Systemology studies, the *facets* of an *Imprint* include all sensory perceptions along with other associative information. In addition to scenes depicting places and things, "*Crystal Clear*" suggests several other significant *facets* including: brightness/dimness, time of day, time of year, sounds, noises, vocal tones, spoken language, hardness/softness to touch, weights, physical efforts, tastes, smells, temperature, humidity, motion/movement, body actions, body position... the potential list is nearly endless.

True *Imagination* originates from a "higher" point on the Standard Model than Beta-Thought. The source is outside of, or *exterior to*, *Beta-Existence* and the *Human Condition* POV, similar to *"Alpha-Thought."* Alpha-Thought is referred to as "postulates" in past literature: a decision for something *to be* or *not to be*—a much higher level faculty of the Alpha-Spirit than "considerations" or associations taking place as "thinking." In fact, these higher faculties were once used to *create circuitry* of the Mind-System (now relied on for "thinking") as the willingness and ability of the Spirit began to slump into states of *Beta-Awareness*. Therefore, rehabilitation of *Creative Ability* allows an Alpha-Spirit the understanding and certainty to regain freedoms it holds in its truest basic state.

Benefit gained from *Creativeness Processing* is not as a result of a *Seeker* "facing up to" the Reality of *this* Physical Universe. Ability to *confront* this *Beta-Existence* is increased by practicing with their own Personal Universe—which is a truer spiritual existence they closed off responsibly communicating with, by unknowingly superimposing experience and POV of *Beta-Existence* using the *Human Condition*.

"Route-0" is intended to steer away from *real* "scenes" from *this* lifetime. *This* Physical Universe is not the only *Beta-Existence* an individual has occupied—nor is *this* lifetime the only incarnation-cycle that has been experienced in *this* Physical Universe. Unfortunately, the more an individual's POV is entrapped in *Beta-Existence*, the more their considerations fall "in line" or "in step" *with* the Physical Universe; and both become more solid.

When occupying low-levels of *Beta-Awareness* for too long, an individual often "mechanizes" their considerations—rather than willingly controlling "postulates" and knowingly directing "actions" to *create* effects. An individual may also come to believe that Physical Universe is all there is—that it is the source of all the materials and energies within it; that they must use efforts of *Beta-Existence* in order to *Be* or *Have* anything in a Spiritual Universe. Yet, we discover that Alpha-Existence—and one's own Personal

Universe—does not actually require any physical effort in order to *Create*. It only requires "postulates" or "considerations" that things *are*, in order *to be*.

Defragmenting (and controlling) "stores" of *Mental Imagery* seems particularly important for our *Spiritual Actualization*. An Alpha-Spirit "records" personal experience as *Mental Imagery* on a *"Spiritual Timeline"* and this is carried between lifetimes.

An individual is often occupying a POV surrounded by *"screens"* and *"Imprints"* based on fixed locations in "space-time"; which they refer to as "experience." But these experiences tend to "change" the perception of what and who the Alpha-Spirit *thinks* they are; which is a big step down from *knowing*.

Communication of energy is retained as a continuous flow (or "wave") on a particular "channel" up to *now* in present time. An individual isn't really *stuck* anywhere themselves, so much as they have *stuck* "pictures." But the individual is no longer carrying *Actualized Awareness* on that "channel" in the *now*, which is why it is not "actual" *Awareness*, but instead, a "Reality" agreement that has kept a "presence" of *Awareness* fixed on some point in the "past."

Δ Δ Δ Δ Δ Δ

In the beginning, the Alpha-Spirit used its *Creative Ability* for "fun" - for "art" - and its own personal amusement. Getting "lost" and identified with POV of its own *Creations* not-knowing the true nature of *Self* as I-AM, came later.

Meanwhile, here in *beta-existence*, we can employ *Imagination* in systematic processing as a means of handling "assignment of consideration" along a circuit or channel without restricting use only to *"activating events"* which have actually occurred *and* are within the scope of reality for a *Seeker* to effectively confront or recall (reach).

Concepts such as "pain," "loss"—even witnessing violence or death—are compulsively created *imprints* which often seem *more real* to an individual than the true present environment. Of course, these events *did* happen, but a *Seeker* keeps the energy and attention entangled and suspended with *Awareness* around each. This is what holds *Self* back from breaking the gravity of *beta-existence*. Even when unknowingly and compulsively maintaining creation of mental machinery (and its products), the Alpha-Spirit is still *fragmenting* the wholeness of its *Awareness*—hence decline of *Actualized Awareness* "present" at a given moment.

Systematic processing goals are achieved only when a *Seeker* directs actual attention to the exercises, which is referred to as "presence"—or *Awareness* given to the present environment, particularly the session. Processing is directed toward *Self* and not one of the phases or circuits or *imprints* created by *Self*. Instructions are referred to as "commands" because they introduce Alpha-Thought considerations for a *Seeker* to "run" on their own.

When an individual stops *looking*—for whatever reason— they use mental machinery to do the "*looking*" for them.

Therefore, most "objective universe" techniques for increasing attention-on-the-present are concerned *literally* with "*looking*" "*contacting*" and "*communicating*" with the present environment. This demonstrates enough certainty in the "safety" of the environment for *Self* to actually apply its *Awareness*. Proper handling of various "Points-of-Views" (POV) is an integral part of "Route-0" because:—

while this "crystal lens" remains fragmented, so too is the view taken regarding *Imagination* and *Creative Ability*.

At the beginning of a session, a *Seeker* is directed to "look around" at their environment and notice things, one to the next. The environment may even appear to get "brighter" as this happens.

So much of what an individual really believes they are perceiving is actually fragmented by circuits and filters before the information is even communicated to *Self*.

This is better demonstrated, for example, when an individual enters a new environment: more attention is placed on what is around them. It does not take long for "familiarity" to set in. Then "scenery perception" (the setting) is mostly created on automatic—not even really "looked at" anymore. The average individual is not educated to remain at "cause" over their own selective directed attention. There are exercises that direct a *Seeker* to look at precise points, one to the next, as opposed to simply glancing around lightly or casually observing.

"Wizard Level-0" techniques are intended to increase an individual's certainty on operating as the Alpha-Spirit. This includes using *"Zu-Vision"* independent of a *genetic vehicle* or *beta-existence*. The most direct technique (or PCL) —*"Be outside that body"*—is not necessarily the most practical if other strongly held reality agreements and fragmented considerations still impinge on an individual.

> *Systemologist Seekers* practices exercises to increase the reach on *knowing* their own spiritual existence, rather than agreeing to carry a vague idea about it.

We have accepted suggestions as "reality" lending toward our own Self-invalidation. It allowed implantation of considerations rigidly fixed to a POV, such as the standard-issue *Human Condition*. Fear of invalidation can prompt an individual to decrease their willingness and certainty on ability. Regardless of where an invalidating cue or suggestion originates from, only our own acceptance and incorporation of it as a reality agreement allows its effect. The circuits introduced for Route-3 may be applied to handle "Invalidation" with systematic processing.

Δ Δ Δ Δ Δ Δ

There are many instances when the POV of an Alpha-Spirit can be pulled-in or snapped-in on the fields and mechanisms inherently part of a "body." This may take place during intense emotional stress or **trauma** when the perspective of *Self* is fixedly tied in with (and distracted by) sensations and *pings* of a "body." This strengthens the circuitry for an 'Identity', propagating an idea that *Self* is located in a "body." This happens much more often when an individual is already suspended *interior* to a Mind-System, already surrounded by the associative thought and emotional encoding circuits of the *vehicle.*

> The Alpha-Spirit is capable of commanding a *genetic vehicle* and its functions (mechanisms and energetic fields) while retaining its original POV *exterior* and independent of the *vehicle* they are operating and Universe they operate in.

Entrapment in a Mind-Body Identity is possible and later cemented by "*Implants.*" There are many implant platforms on which specific circuits operate. At this present level of work, our concern is with a general realization that they exist and that their installation has a tremendous impact on the POV and considerations remaining with an individual to knowingly handle. Rather than prompting by a PCL directly, the *implants* on which *programming* and *encoding* occurs, are increasingly more accessible (and less sensitive) after a complete and thorough application of all Beta-Defragmentation materials comprising *Grade-III* and *Grade-IV*. *Implants* are treated in upper-level work when they "surface" and/or when a *Seeker* is in a position of *Awareness* (and with techniques) to confront them directly.

> Many who already have a sense of their entry into this Universe and *Human Condition* will often liken it to *falling into* or being *sucked into*, &tc. But in all cases where we have considered the action taking place to "*Implant*" an individual with the *Human Condition* in *this* Universe, the common theme suggests that one is *outside* and then one is suddenly *inside*—and during the disorientation between, *something* happens.

Depending on whether an individual is working with *this* lifetime or has begun *Backtrack* work on the *Spiritual Timeline*, the same methodology is employed to start opening up these channels for exploration. Processing includes considerations (and sensations) attached to "going in" or "getting in" something or somewhere.

Significant "energetic charge" is entangled with "Entry into Universes" or "Implanting." This also means "Wizard Level-0" *can* potentially trigger realizations of how a *Seeker* arrived "here." It is often reacted to without understanding and without realizing the nature of this phenomenon ahead of time. Fragmented automatic-response circuits connected to these events add some difficulty in maintaining high enough Awareness to fully achieve goals set forth for Beta-Defragmentation.

By processing the concepts of moving *inside* and *outside*, a *Seeker* is less likely to handle it with automatic circuitry.

Route-3 and *Route-0* is applied to defragment considerations for accessing "Zu-Vision," operating "*exterior*" to the physical body, or even the handling of space and creation of a "Personal Universe." If a POV (*attention, awareness, &tc.*) can be "snapped in" on the Mind-Body system outside *Self-Determination*, an individual's *Identity* is still very much entangled and associated with those mechanisms.

- Incidents when you wanted to get inside but can't
- Incidents when you were kicked out from where you wanted to be
- Being forced inside
- Incidents of being trapped inside
- Pulled in
- Pushed in
- The feeling or sense that you must get in
- The feeling or sense that you can't get in...

Such types of incidents potentially carry a heavily imprinted charge. This greatly reduces *Self-Awareness* and *Self-Determination* and therefore, *presence*, when left uncontrolled. You can use the above concepts for PCLs to treat circuits with *Recall* or you can *Imagine* incidents and see what *Mental Imagery* seems most correct. In either case, experiencing some release assists handling basics of upper-level work.

Another heavily-charged spiritual incident may also be "restimulated" and "detrimental" to effective progress at

Wizard Level-0 is Collapse-of-Space and Collapse-of-Universes. This is something that all individuals have experienced intensely at some point on the *Spiritual Timeline* at least once (with their Home Universe).

Our exercises depict the basic structure of a *space* or *Universe* as a "cube"—defined by eight "corners" or "points" that **anchor** the boundaries of the dimension. Just as there are experiences of one's own POV "snapping in" or "caving in" on a new plane of *space* or *mass*, so too are there times when the *space* and *energy-matter*—and the very corners of a Universe itself—"collapse in" on the individual. Heavy fragmentation charges on this experience can affect a *Seeker's* willingness to be responsible for the *"Creation-of-Space"* as found in *Wizard Level-0* exercises.

The **"hot buttons"** treated in systematic processing for "Collapse-of-Universes" are quite similar to the "going in" and "interior/exterior" buttons given previously. In this instance, rather than a POV being "snapped in" to some *space* or *energy-matter*, the reverse is treated:

- Incidents of *space* collapsing in on the POV
- The world closing in; the world folding up
- Energy imploding; energy collapsing in on the POV
- Corner-points collapsing; corner-points snapping in on the POV
- Sudden "uncreation" or folding up of all form
- The environment caving in on the POV
- Pulled backward from
- Falling away from
- Sense of everything suddenly becoming unreal...

As with the case of "POV snap-ins," these "creation cave-ins" may be encouraged or prompted by external sources and other-determined events—however, much like "invalidation" and other *facets* of personal (degradation that we *choose* to "accept" or *agree* to as "reality"), experience of any POV is still *Self-Determined* on some level; including "Entry into-" and "Collapse of-" Universes.

Δ Δ Δ Δ Δ Δ

"Creativeness Processing"—Route-0 and "Wizard Grades"—
provides *Seekers* sufficient practice of their own *Creative
Ability* in order to demonstrate that:

> *Self* can create whatever, whenever, and everything
> that is experienced and recorded is copied by *Self* as
> a personal creation. We are, in essence, creating a
> facsimile-copy of the Physical Universe around us
> and treating the *Mental Imagery* of that copy within
> our Personal Universe. All perceptions are commu-
> nicated indirectly through circuitry and relays and
> screens.

The Universe that many individuals occupy when they
close their eyes and *Imagine*, is very often still a duplicated
facsimile of *beta-existence*. This means all their considerations for creation and ability and reality agreements for a
Personal Universe are tied exclusively to *beta-existence* as
well. Systematic application of *"Creativeness Processing"*
and *Imagination* assist in defragmenting these considerations and returning additional certainty to *Self* about its
own true nature as a *Free Spirit*.

Seekers should begin with previous Routes and methods of
Beta-Defragmentation (procedures in *Crystal Clear* and *Metahuman Destinations*). This reduces heaviest charges of
imprinting or reactive *"pictures"* prior to increasing perception of *Mental Imagery*. Otherwise reactive *imprints* are
perceived more vividly and have more "bite."

It may be the case that spiritual rehabilitation of *Creative
Ability* is the master key to stable *Beta-Defragmentation*. All
other systematic processing essentially makes *this* more
possible. For processing, early steps regarding "Presence"
in environment and "Control" of the body are necessary
for increasing *Awareness* enough to actually make *"creativeness processing"* effective for our purposes.

If a *Seeker* (as an *Awareness* point) is not truly "present,"
than all exercises, procedures and fancy PCLs will only be

performed using some automatic response circuit. The individual, as *Self*, may still not be executing the commands at all. "Route-0" techniques focus a *Seeker* on a subjective universe to work from, giving a *Pilot* only certainty on action that is actually observable. If an individual is having difficulties with exercises and processes that *can* be observed and communicated easily, a *Pilot* should be careful **investing** too much time toward applying "upper-routes."

Δ Δ Δ Δ Δ Δ

Increasing a *Seeker's* tolerance of POV and *Creative Ability* involves confronting *space* and "points" in *space*. Traditionally, an individual is more comfortable with *mass*, calcified *energy-matter*. Many "*Wizard Level-0*" exercises and techniques deal with "points" and "spots," which have, in themselves, no *mass* or color or shape or feel. Of course, these "points" can be collapsed within a Universe and condensed into greater solidity—but that is not the level of solidity we are dealing with in higher existences.

"Route-0" emphasizes what *Self* is doing in regards to its own Personal Universe. Our past work has treated other circuits of energy-flow and stored imprints regarding what has happened to *Self*, what *Self* has done to others, and what *Self* has observed others doing to others. All of this is stored within the Mind-System. Even when it does not have strong emotional encoding, if *Self* assigns significance and association to it, this information contributes to what an individual carries for their considerations as Alpha-Thought. But this is entirely subject to an individual's own participation, command postulates and creation—even when information and cues are strongly suggested by external forces.

To knowingly *Be* an *Awareness* at various "spots" and "points" in existence (and be able to scan the "*Spiritual Timeline*"), a *Seeker* must increase their tolerance to *look*. This means actually applying attention to a "locational point" in *space-time*. The Alpha-Spirit has the ability to direct its POV to any location that it is willing to "see." We now practice this differently than previous arcane mystic schools have taught.

> Rather than considering a "spirit in flight," a *Seeker* should strengthen realizations that the true **static** I-AM-*Self* POV is actually a non-local point "moving the scenery"—or rather *creates it*—around them.

Another element of "*creativeness processing*" became more critical the longer our experiments were treating "points" and "spots" with no *mass*. An individual is likely to not feel very well during the session when constantly confronting or standing before *space* (which prompts toward *Nothingness*). An individual finds *energy-matter* more interesting and enticing as their *Awareness* decreases because it gives them something to "know about." When sole consideration is a "Personal Universe" and everything is known, because everything is *Self-directed*, there is no such "game" conditions involved.

Although "games" and "energy" are what got an Alpha-Spirit into trouble early on the "*Spiritual Timeline*":

> it is difficult to increase *Actualized Awareness*
> back to its original state without also consistently
> giving the Alpha-Spirit something
> to *do* with a *purpose*—or something to *play with*.

This is no different than an individual that has come to depend on their stores of *Mental Images*, each assigned meaning from former events that still carry *facets* of significance into the present. This alters how an individual experiences existence. An individual would feel quite lost, disoriented and unhappy if we were to simply take away all *imprints* at once. It became clear to us that for a *Seeker* to "let go" willingly, they would have to be able to knowingly *create* something in its place.

> An individual has grown accustomed to being an
> "energy unit" rather than an "Awareness Unit."

Systematic processing *reduces* emotional intensity, ana-lyzes imprints to the point of *dissolution*, and *defragments* circuits of "pictures" and "programs." A *Seeker* can feel as though they are *losing*, not just the things themselves, but their sense of a "game."

> If this is not handled systematically, a *Pilot* may find that as one "automatic circuit" is reduced, another one "turns on" with full intensity. This can happen if *implanted compulsions* remain where an individual "has to have" something.

Covert goals of *Imagination* and *Creativeness* processes are to assist *Seekers* in being free of implanted compulsions to "*have*" things. Processing "mass" is one basic step to this; or to have a *Seeker* really "*look*" at things around them in the "session room" to orient their presence.

Δ Δ Δ Δ Δ Δ

Refinement of "*Creativeness Processing*" occurred at the Sys-temology Society as an upper-level alternative to Route-2.

> Applications of "Route-0" emphasize what *Self* is *do-ing*, but specifically what it can *create*—or *is* creat-ing. The more a *Seeker* practices handling their *Cre-ative Ability*, the greater the realizations concerning just how significantly *Self* plays a role in compuls-ively and unknowingly creating with various types of energetic-machinery all along. This is incredibly difficult for some individuals to accept properly; but it is among the minimum realizations required for achieving Beta-Defragmentation and beyond.

Working with energy directly is quite obscure to commu-nicate for Beta-Defragmentation techniques. Therefore, we treat *Mental Images* for the energy that they contain; partially like a magician uses a *symbol* in substitution for the *actual*. But it is not the same. Rather than symbols, our *encoded imprints* actually do contain a reserve of entangled energy of personal *Awareness* on a particular channel. Handling circuitry on that channel affects the *imprint*.

Δ Δ Δ Δ Δ Δ

Our *Mental Images* are very personal to us and they carry a lot of personal energy within them. Each time they are restimulated from various *facets* and generated with automatic-mechanisms, the entire fragmented *Human Condition* is given more solidity. This is because an individual is also responsible for continuous creation of the machinery at work. In short: "*Creativeness Processing*" may allow a *Seeker* to regain control over their creation of *Mental Imagery* along a certain channel or representing a specific terminal that is not otherwise resolved easily using other "Routes."

There is a consideration of something specific in "Games Universes" and below that does not exist in an individual's own "Home Universe." This is:

> "Scarcity-and-Abundance"—This exists as a consideration only if there is a dependency on "energy" to communicate actions and intention, rather than direct "Alpha-Thought."

This reality agreement is installed as part of an *implant platform*. It solidifies certain limitations and conditions placed on lower "Shared Universes"—providing a certain order-and-sequence to "forms" moved by "energy" (and creation of both). Everything gets knocked down a notch with each Universe condensation. Everything that was, becomes a "way to" something else. And this continues on.

> The perception of "scarcity" is what causes an individual to cling that much tighter to what they perceive they "have." The more "pictures" they copy, the less an individual begins to *create* on their own. Failing to knowingly create, they hold onto compulsively created *imprint* as something rare.

Most encoded information tends to be a hindrance to experiencing and *Self-directing* that experience. It's easy to see how a very long existence across the "*Spiritual Timeline*" could have a tendency to cumulatively degrade abilities and fragment *Awareness* of an otherwise Unlimited *Spiritual Being*.

Collecting experience hinders *Awareness* for new experience. The only reason we keep it to "learn from" is because we put ourselves into a position of "not-knowing" in the first place —it was something to do; we've done it; now its one more consideration restricting what we will do next.

It is quite difficult for someone still working through heavy beta-defragmentation steps to come to a solid actual realization that: *they are creating this experience*. That is a lot for someone to take responsibility for all at once, espe-cially if pushed before they are ready to handle it. The idea will certainly be rejected if it comes from another source. Therefore, the bulk of "Beta-Defragmentation" hangs on the amount of time it takes for an individual to come to this realization, for themselves, with complete certainty.

Δ Δ Δ Δ Δ Δ

"*Creativeness Processing*" negates automation and as-sociated imprinting along a certain channel by re-placing it with a new creation of the same type, de-gree and frequency, and in the same time and space.

Δ Δ Δ Δ Δ Δ

Ideally, "*Creativeness Processing*" (for defragmentation pro-cessing) requires some type of **assessment** on a *Seeker* concerning the terminals and forms that carry an energet-ic charge. There are ways of even using various "galvanic skin response" biofeedback devices in conjunction with "word-association" ("Route-3G") as even suggested by Carl Jung.[‡] An individual could list out all various items, as best they could, paying close attention to those that they are unwilling to create or be responsible for; also those that they have an emotional response-reaction to.

Some *Pilots* introduced a PCL that query a *Seeker* al-ternately: "What are you willing to create?"/"What are you not willing to create?" Others have used the keyword "confront" in place of "create." This prim-

---

‡   See also "*The Way of the Wizard*" (*Liber-3E*) by Joshua Free.

arily works best for more advanced *Seekers* experienced with *Piloted Procedure*. A less direct PCL would
replace "are you" with "would you be."

Concerning applications to earlier materials: "Route-1"
treats the heaviest incidents that act as the thickest
blinders to maintaining present *Awareness*; "Route-2" employs *"recall"* PCLs, which can be converted to *"imagine"*;
all of the "hot-button" terminals and circuits treated with
"Route-3" can also be converted. Make certain that imagined incidents and events are uniquely and knowingly
created, not something that the *Seeker* has a sense is a facsimile-copy from actual experience. Reactive images are
those that "come to mind" as soon as a terminal, subject
or object is named (or contacted).

In order to take what is *Imagined* and use it for *"Creativeness Processing,"* the *Seeker* must have a sense that they are
actually *creating* it; not a reactive-response. It must not be
generated for them by some other mechanism that they,
long ago, set up to deliver "pictures" on a "screen."

> A *Pilot* can suggest any particular terminal (object,
> mass, &tc.) for the *Seeker* to *"Imagine."* This is fol-
> lowed up with a PCL to "make it more solid."
> Essentially take what one has imagined to *be* and, by
> consideration, grant it *more beingness*. Until this is
> effectively done by postulate command, a *Seeker* can
> start with making many copies and pushing them
> together to make a solid or turning up a "dial" to
> make it "brighter." At first, in lack of certainty on
> direct postulates or Alpha-Thought, a *Seeker* may be
> likely to rely on *imagining* a means of accomplishing
> the action in a way that is "in agreement" with ex-
> perience of the Physical Universe.

Because an individual is constantly creating *energy-masses*
that snap-in or pull-in on their POV, whether that is the
genetic vehicle "body" or some other consideration of
"Self," it is necessary to facilitate this on one's own determinism. However, a PCL directing this:

should *never* be a "pull" action (from inside),
but rather a "push" or "shove" (from outside).

The individual has enough "caving-in" on them when they are fixed to a *genetic vehicle* POV. Therefore, we employ methods to establish a "secondary POV" that allows them to "push" or "shove" their *Creations* into the *genetic vehicle* from a point *exterior* to it. This is also excellent *pre-A.T.* practice for "*Zu-Vision.*" The *Pilot* should direct an end-cycle to each *Creation*, alternating: "push into that body" and then "throw away." If necessary, the *Seeker* can "squish it into a ball" before the end-cycle action.

Realization goals for *Wizard Level-0* include: handling automatic and compulsive creation of *Mental Images*; freeing associative restrictions on *Creative Ability* and *Imagination*; detaching *fixed POV* from the *genetic vehicle*; assuming responsibility for *Creation-of-Space* and handling *points* in *space*; and ability to maintain a stable Alpha-Spirit POV to freely experience a *Personal Universe* that is independent from, outside of and exterior to the *Physical Universe*.

ROUTE-3E
INTEGRITY PROCESSING INSTRUCTIONS
REVISED FROM LIBER-3E

In most instances, increased Awareness means an increased ability to "foresee" future results and act toward them. This includes maintaining a wide-angle view of the entire Standard Model at all times. Individuals that can only "think" or "operate" regarding the first few spheres have a tendency to be shortsighted. This is worse when an individual is not even Actualized (defragmented) regarding the *First Sphere* as Self. Such individuals are "Potential Dangers" to **optimum** survival of both the Systemologist and the community at large. The only resolution we have discovered is our systematic processing; making it the most important activity you can *do* for someone.

A standard-issue (fragmented) Human being does not know to "process out" their perceived "problems" and thereby applies shortsighted actions to resolve them. Such efforts are referred to as "*Harmful Acts*" in Systemology, or more accurately "**counter-survival**" actions.

> *harmful-act* : a counter-survival mode of behavior or action (esp. that causes harm to one or more *Spheres of Existence*)—or—an overtly aggressive (hostile and/or destructive) action against an individual or any other *Sphere of Existence*; in *Utilitarian Systemology*—a shortsighted (serves fewest *Spheres of Existence*) **intentional** overtly harmful action to resolve a perceived problem; a revision of the rule for standard *Utilitarianism* for Systemology to distinguish actions which provide the least benefit to the least number of *Spheres of Existence*, or else the greatest harm to the greatest number of *Spheres of Existence*; in *moral* philosophy—an action which can be experienced by few and/or which one would not be willing to experience for themselves (*theft, slander, rape, &tc*); an **iniquity** or iniquitous act.

Fragmentation and energetically **charged** masses (sometimes called "ridges") are connected to *Harmful and Hostile Acts*. This includes what we have done to others, others have done to us, and what we witness others having done to each other. These are all "systematic processing" points (and **Hot Buttons**). These are critical for achieving "Wizard Level-1" and working through *Mardukite Grade-V*, where *iniquities* must be "incinerated" in order to rise above. Therefore, the **Ethics** (*Route-3E*) portion of the *Pathway* is not an afterthought, filler or some arbitrary supplement— it is a detrimental factor for Ascension through the upper "Wizard Grades."

> The individual, as "I-AM"/*Self* or Alpha Spirit, beneath fragmentation, is basically "*good.*"

This truth about the "Spirit" (of *Lifeforms*) is what allows Systemology techniques (systematic processing technology) to yield positive effects in *defragmenting* veils of erroneous consideration clouding or distorting clear vision of what is "right" and/or (for) the "highest good." All individuals act in Beta-Existence to "SURVIVE" and thus, in their own fragmented POV (which they refer to as their "own right" or "opinion"), believe themselves acting "justly" for what is "best." None truly believe that they are acting upon "evil" or "false" fixated purposes for the sake of "evil" alone; not even the "villains."

An individual's "*Spiritual Timeline*" is explored in greater detail as they progress through the Wizard Grades. At this juncture, we can determine that the *Alpha Spirit* begins its existence with a very high *Ethics*, superior to even what is demonstrable within the Standard Model of Beta-Existence. Proper *Ethics* is actually an upper-level dynamic system, equivalent to a "*Ninth Sphere*"—or more accurately, *First Arc of Infinity*, carrying a "harmonic" with Alpha-Existence **relative** to the *First Sphere* in Beta-Existence.

The Alpha-Spirit seeks to operate and act in the most optimum manner, which is most evident with their original "Home Universe." Eventually, cohabitation considerations within "Shared Universes" and "Games Universes" (which are, themselves, superimposed over one's own personal "Home Universe") results in more and more behavior that is less and less optimum—and from which a being may lose its ability to *Hold-Back* the *Harmful Acts.*

> **hold-back** : withheld communications (esp. actions) such as "*Hold-Outs*"; an intentional (or automatic) withdrawal (as opposed to reach); Self-restraint (which may eventually be enforced or automated) to not practice *Harmful-Acts*; not reaching, acting or expressing, when one should be; an ability that is now restrained (on automatic) due to inability to withhold it on Self-determinism alone.

Loss of high-level *Ethics* forms a perceived need for *moral codes* and *penalties* as a guide. This also leads to *Hold-Outs.*

> **hold-outs** : withheld communications; energetic withdrawal and communication breaks with a "*terminal*" and its *Sphere of Existence* as a result of a "*Harmful-Act*"; unspoken or undiscovered (hidden, covert) actions that an individual withholds communications of, fearing punishment or endangerment of *Self-preservation* (*First Sphere*); the act of hiding (or keeping hidden) the truth of a "*Harmful-Act.*"

We selected the term "*Hold-Outs*" for our Utilitarian Systemology semantics, based on its application in professional photography—where numerous snapshots/pictures are *withheld* from final selections openly communicated to present an event, &tc. Oftentimes, an individual carries around many *Hold-Outs*—hidden, but occupying their attention. They are fed energy as compulsive creations. The individual participates in Reality with a constant anxious worry (problem) that someone else will "find out." Therefore, they are forced to *Hold-Back* their reach and communications (**energetic-exchange**) *outside* of *Self-Honesty:*

> these *Harmful-Act–Hold-Out* sequences are what keeps a Spiritual Being entrapped within a Prison Universe.

The Wizard's *Way Out* of Beta-Existence requires *clearing* the **slate** of what is emotionally and energetically carried as "mass"/"matter" by the Spirit: to be certain that the "heart" is "light enough" to be weighed against a feather.[‡] Many religions have established their own methodologies for confessional procedures. None seem to be effective for *systematically rehabilitating* the Power and Beingness of the Spirit. Former attempts simply enforced "guilt" and other enforced programming, fixing attentions on a *moral code* rather than a higher *Ethic*.

Ethics is the lowest *Arc of Infinity* for Alpha-Existence. Imposition of a *moral code* (and *penalties* when an individual *fails*) resulted in construction of "Penalty Universes" or "Prison Universes." The *Beta-Existence* (Physical Universe) we consider present, is actually a "Penalty Universe" created by those (once) occupying a previous manifested universe, referred to (in our Systemology) as the "Magic Kingdom." Even the "Magic Universe"—similar to *this* one, except that the "electron is free" (and able to be utilized without "wires")—was itself first constructed as a "confined existence" *beneath* an even wider **encompassing** shared "Games Universe." Hence, *Ethics* is no small matter once we consider how large a part it plays in why an individual consistently finds themselves "located" in (and "fixed" to) a *Beta-Existence* "space-time" as they do.

The I-AM-*Self* once experienced an essentially unrestrained existence as a *Free Spirit*, due to the naturally high *Ethic* "in" place. During accumulation of experience across a *Spiritual Timeline*, this deteriorated into rigid *moral codes* that promote imposing (or enforcing) restraints (*Hold-Backs*) on Self and others. **Validation** of "guilt" leads to further "*Hold-Outs*" due to regret—*Hold-Backs* and *Hold-Outs* being "no-action" *imprints*, or else of "regret" when one did not *Hold-Back* an action and now *Holds-Out* admission and responsibility for it. Just as *facets* of other types of *Imprinting* and *Programming* can affect the freedom of an

---

‡   Alluding to "afterlife judgment" in ancient Egyptian mysticism. See also "*The Vampyre's Handbook*" by Joshua Free.

individual Alpha-Spirit, so too will these energetically charged masses tied to *Harmful-Act/Hold-Outs/Hold-Backs.* These specifically affect ability to reach optimum states of *Self-Honesty* with our "Wizard Level" work.

Once a *moral code* is in place (or *Ethics* are implanted), a series of "hidden" restraints are agreed to and become Reality—even when an individual operates in opposition to this programming. In fact, when a *Seeker* negates *morality*, they are at once in **conflict** with their own true values (and nature) as Alpha-Spirit. In addition to *Hold-Outs* and struggles over *Hold-Backs* (personal restraint), an individual will also employ a sequence-"**pattern**" or programmed-circuit of "justification" to explain motivation for their *Harmful-Acts.* In many instances, this **displaces** personal responsibility onto some "other" *terminal*—which further **inhibits** one's own *Self-Determined* restraint. This creates mechanisms that automatically *Hold-Back* ability.

Once the **threshold**-cover was lifted on Wizard-Level "Alpha/Ascension-Tech" (*Actualization Techniques/*"A.T."), it became quite clear that *Ethics* is the fundamental "keystone" for accessing (and surviving) the "Fifth Gate" and its *immolation of iniquity.*

Δ Δ Δ Δ Δ Δ

Where a "*Hold-Out*" involves the Seeker's own undisclosed actions (which should still be addressed in **Ethics Processing**), a "*Missed Hold-Out*" involves someone else's actions. It is possible that the "*Hold-Out*" was not even treated as such by the Seeker—may not even be thought about ever—until the energetic charge on the incident is nearly found out and then missed. This directly restimulates any charge on the energetic-mass. Since the Seeker is erroneously left with an *uncertainty* to "wonder" about (thereby reducing Awareness and presence), the whole sequence-chain is a source of present-time fragmentation.

For this specific application, the nature (or contents) of the "*Hold-Out*" itself is quite secondary in significance (by comparison) to the primary fact that: "*something* was almost found out"—contributing to the fragmented state of a *Seeker's* present condition. Unlike systematic methods for processing-out *Imprinting Incidents*, the exact moment of uncertainty (or Mystery) should be "spotted" on the *Backtrack* (and realized/discharged "*As-It-Is*"). Otherwise, a *Seeker* risks accumulating additional "*Hold-Backs*" due to a perceived confusion and/or **degree** of (un)willingness to act or reach.

All "circuits" are applied to *Ethics Processing*. Failure to do so proved to be a shortcoming in the original version of Route-1. "Processing-out" each circuit or POV on an incident (or event type), even if one or more has to be *imagined*, provides opportunities for optimum energetic release on that channel. This means for any *Harmful-Act* you have committed and then *Held-Back* ("**circuit-1**"), you would also *run* the concept of having someone else commit it against you ("**circuit-2**"), and of course, another/others to another/others ("**circuit-3**"). This will remove enough residual energy from a channel to prevent incidents from restimulating "*automated motivation*" or considerations for future actions and responses.

> **hostile-motivation** : an *imprint* of a counter-survival action ("*Harmful-Act*" or "*Hostile-Act*") committed by another against Self, stored as data to justify future actions (retaliation, &tc.); any *Sphere of Existence* (though usually an individual) receiving the effect of a "*Harmful-Act*"; an *imprint* used to rationalize "motivation" or "justification" for committing a "*Harmful-Act*"; in systematic *games theory*—the modus operandi concerning "payback," "revenge" and "tit-for-tat."

The "Mind-System" records and stores all parts (*facets* and *POVs*) of similar incidents on an associated-knowledge chain. As a result, there are some instances when fragmentation remaining from incidents of "being the effect" (something happening *to you*) will not "process out" (or reduce in charge) until similar incidents of "being the cause" (doing something *to others*) are fully confronted. If not resolved systematically, these "action-motivation sequence-chains" can actually remain suspended (actively awaiting restimulation) across many lifetimes/incarnations.

Along the course of an Alpha-Spirit's long existence on a *Spiritual Timeline*, many patterns of harmful behavior are recorded and stored. Therefore, it is also necessary to **flatten** "Circuit-3" turbulence in *Ethics Processing*, which is frequently overlooked. Witnessing the actions of other "beings" (even when imaginary or fictional) has a tendency to restimulate energetic charge and/or solidify fragmentation of the first two *circuits*.

Δ Δ Δ Δ Δ Δ Δ

A *Class-3E Pilot* must operate at high-Awareness with ability to *confront*—face-to-face handling and proper management—of "discreditable" and "hostile" *Hold-Outs* by certain individuals using the "*phase*" of a malevolent personality-package. An Alpha-Spirit does not directly set out to occupy a POV from an "evil" *phase-personality*.

Many systematic *Grade-IV* PCLs introduced for "Route-3" and "Route-3C" within SOP-2C also apply to "Route-3E" for *Ethics Processing*. During *Piloted systematic processing*, if a *Seeker* is painfully struggling to achieve *Grade-IV* realizations, has not effectively achieved any, or is not progressing forward on the *Pathway*, it is only due to one or more of the following:—

— the *Seeker* is feeling hungry, thirsty, tired or restimulated by the environment;
— the *Seeker* is maintaining a misunderstood word/concept;
— the *Seeker* is not applying presence to the session, due to attention fixed on an outside problem;
— the *Seeker* is not trusting of Systemology methods, or has been mishandled by a Pilot;* or
— the *Seeker* is suspended in place, maintaining *Hold-Outs* and *Hold-Backs*, or with attentions directed at *Harmful-Acts* and even *Hostile-Motivators*.

∞   This includes actual or imagined events.

It is detrimental to successful application of our methods that these conditions be determined or resolved. This list should be briefly checked-out before starting *any* systematic processing session, *Piloted* or not.

Whether or not a *Pilot* (or *Seeker*) utilizes mechanical **biofeedback** tools (described later) to assist, the ability to provide high-power processing in Systemology requires high-level intuition and proper application of this applied philosophy. The keyword here is *"applied"*—that means you're supposed to *do* something with it. When it comes to *Wizard-Grades*—when it comes to *Actualized Alpha Ascension*—you won't be able to just *think* your way up and out. Handling the *"Way Out"* requires a high-tone ability to *Confront*; as does the gradient of *Gatework* we are presently treating.

In some situations, an early emphasis on *Ethics Processing* is necessary just to get an individual *moving* at all on the *Pathway*. It is not for us to judge a *Seeker's* misdeeds. Our only interests concern improvement of their own ability and spiritual freedom. Progress on the *Pathway* is the importance—and some *Seekers* find the weights they have burdened themselves with in this material existence, prior to pursing this *Pathway*, are already too much for them to *Confront* and resolve at their present *Awareness*-level.

For this reason, Route-3E (and *Liber-3E*) is introduced for Grade-IV rather than Grade-V. It may be introduced immediately as an integral of Route-3 (described in *Metahuman Destinations*). Therein, we process *Three Circuits* regarding channels of *Communication, Interest* and *Agreement* (in that sequence). The emphasis of those series regarded *Recall* and *Analysis* of "demands" (enforced, coerced, &tc.) and "rejection" (withdrawal, inhibition, &tc.) on those lines. This is quite similar to our present focus on what someone *"has done"* and what they have *"held back."* When an individual *rejects* some thing, they are *Holding-Back* on those lines, and essentially withdrawing responsibility.

To our existing array of PCLs, we have but to add "*Hold-Outs*" to each of the series. For example: where we have *Communication Demanded* of others, of us, and cross-flow; then *Communication Rejected* by others, by us, and cross-flow; we then add *Communication Held-Out* on others, on us, and cross-flow. A Grade-III or early Grade-IV *Seeker* may need to have explained that a "*Hold-Out*" is an intentional inhibition, withdrawal or refusal to reach, communicate or connect. PCLs are not effective if a *Seeker* is uncertain of a word's meaning, or if the meaning they associate is misapplied.

> Initially, we are not as concerned with targeting justifications (or excuses) in basic "Route-3/3E" as much as we are interested in distinguishing imprinted considerations (and *facets*) of a particular space-time event as separate from present-time and present-environments. Personal computations and justifications are often revealed when properly processing (more accessible) considerations.

ROUTE-3E
ETHICS PROCESSING CHECK-OUT
STANDARD SPHERES ASSESSMENT
"SP-R3E" EXCERPT FROM LIBER-3E

The following PCL-skeleton (SP-R-3E) is a systematic formula for applying *Ethics Processing* to all key areas and any
applicable terminals representing *Spheres of Existence*. It
may be used as a general assessment, as a check-out, or
specifically targeting charged "turbulent terminals." We
are concerned most here with *Confronting* all actions, *Hold-
Outs* and *Hold-Backs* that are accessible.

The systematic logic we have applied here is:
"Defragmentation via Direct Confront As-It-*Is*."

It may be that lighter more reachable answers must be
pulled off the channels before deeper heavier incidents
(and imprinting) can be contacted and released (knowingly and willingly).

The method applied here introduces "R-3E"—literally the Standard Procedure for (back of and beneath) all *Ethics Processing* as "Route-3E." It differs
from traditional *"Expanded Route-3"* because this is
intended to resurface key points of specific data,
rather than analyzing and distinguishing intertwined or entangled *Communication Circuits*, which
is the systems logic behind "Route-3." This is a
Wizard-Level Procedure, systematically intended
to not exclusively restrict answers to this lifetime
or incarnate-body when run extensively at high-
Awareness levels.

*Basic Terminals (as Sphere-Representations) for Ethics Pro-
cessing*—(1) "YOUR BODY"; (2) "SEX" "CHILDREN" "FAMILY"
"HOME"; (3) "WORK" "COMMUNITY" "A 'TYPE' OF PERSON"; (4)
"SOCIETY" "HUMAN SPECIES"; (5) "ANIMALS" "NATURE"/"EN-
VIRONMENT" "PLANET EARTH"; (6) "A 'TYPE' OF OBJECT OR
MACHINE" "SOLAR PLANETARY SYSTEMS" "GALAXIES" "PHYSI-

CAL UNIVERSE." Treating higher *Spheres* such as (7) "SPIR-
ITS" *&tc.*; (8) "RELIGION" *&tc.* are also important, especially
given the *'religio-mystical'* backgrounds many *Seekers* have
before finding the *Pathway* with our Systemology.

Advanced Wizard-Level Applications—this same formula may
be applied to upper-level work to handle terminals representative of the *"Arcs of Infinity"* (the upper-Alpha
Spheres beyond "8" on the Standard Model of Beta-Existence for the Human Condition) which concern a truer Al-
pha-Directive, primarily with "SURVIVAL" of *Creations* and
Universes, rather than an already "ETERNAL" *Alpha-Spirit*
that is only convinced of its need to survive through a
body after heavy implanting and entrapment in *Beta-Existence* systems.

** When using a **Biofeedback** *Device*, it is important to
check each individual word of a PCL for an existing
charge prior to use in session processing. Every series or
process should begin with communication between *Pilot*
and *Seeker* regarding what process is about to be run and
the words used for it. It is possible that a particular button or concept carries a *charge* on its own; it is also possible to get charge-reads on a misunderstood word. **

[*Ethics Processing* is a *Seeker's* best chance to get everything
out in the open—to confront, handle and discharge
everything accessible *As-it-Is* prior to upper-level *Wizard
Grade* check-outs and further ("*A.T.*") *Actualization-Ascension Tech.*]

— What *Actions* have you done involving __ ?
\ What have you *Held-Back* from doing involving __ ?
— What *Actions* has another done involving __ ?[‡]
\ What has another *Held-Back* from doing
involving __ ?
— What would you permit others to do involving __ ?[∞]

---

‡ Or "*have others*"—based on an agreed upon PCL patter that the
Seeker understands to mean "circuits other than 1."
∞ Alternative patter to "*permit*" (preferred) includes firstly "*allow*"
and secondly (if needed) "*find acceptable for.*"

\ What have you *Held-Back* others from doing involving ___?

— What could you allow others to find out about you involving ___?[Δ]

\ What have you *Held-Out** on about yourself involving ___?

— What could others allow you to safely find out about themselves involving ___?

\ What have others *Held-Out* on about themselves involving ___?

Δ   "*Find out*" implies discovery or a revealing, as opposed to another version of this: "*What would be acceptable for others to know about you?*" A *Professional Pilot* may have to work, or rather "*word*," a PCL around an individual's acceptance level (reach and understanding) as discussed prior to simply running a series of command lines out of the blue. There is an exchange of direct communication during the setup of each process or series. Lack of such communication will limit the success rate of our applied philosophy.

*   This assumes a seeker understands the intended systematic meaning of the phrase "*Hold-Out*," otherwise alternative patter would be "*kept hidden.*"

ROUTE-θE
CONCEPTUAL PROC. INSTRUCTIONS
"SP-CR-3E" EXCERPT FROM LIBER-3E

Conceptual-Certainty Processing is applicably effective for any *Seeker* at any gradient; however, its refinement at the Systemology Society was reserved for experimental developments at Wizard-Levels. It is part of the original *"Route-0"* research series, beginning years prior to the publication of *"Imaginomicon"* (*Liber-3D*). Starting with *Grade-III*—as an early precursor to *Imagination* and *"Creativeness Processing"*—it was discovered that:

> a *"Concept"* of something can be systematically processed
> even if an actual *Recall* is difficult to obtain or
> a specific memory unavailable.

However, in late 2019 (and throughout developments of 2020), newly apparent shortcomings suggested it not be recommended as a direct or primary route to *Beta-Defragmentation*. Where it came to treating terminals, the actual "energetic-mass" (fragmentation) did not always fully resolve because the "Source"/"Cause" was still *not-known* and often remained *non-confronted*. Difficulties found in processing certain *computations* with *Conceptual-Certainty* led us directly to the existence and subject of *Implants*—yet this would require further investigation that surpassed the scope of the *"**Master Grade**"* (*Grade-III*) and *Wizard Level-0* (*Grade-IV*). [In fact, this upper-level experimental research and development cycle is still ongoing at the Systemology Society and Mardukite Academy through 2021.]

"Route-0"—as specifically treated in *"Imaginomicon"*—became our *Grade-IV* solution (or alternative) to *Conceptual-Certainty Processing*. *"Route-0"* is applied to our first official completed version of *Beta-Defragmentation Standard Procedure*.[Σ] However, for systematic practice-drilling personal ability to freely or fluidly manage *Alpha-Thought*

Σ   First issued in the June 2021 premiere edition of *"Imaginomicon."*

(*considerations* and *postulates*) fully on Self-Determination, the formerly given "*Route-0*" methods are either like using dynamite where shovels are needed, or else quite the opposite if a *Seeker* is still in preliminary stages of systematically developing "*Creative Ability*." **Conceptual Processing** also makes some *Ethics* processes accessible/workable earlier on the *Pathway*, rather than only waiting until after a *Seeker* has officially worked with *Imagination* and *Creativeness* at the end of *Grade-IV*.

Wherever a PCL reads, "Get the sense of..." "Get the idea of..." "Think of..." and even the more obviously blatant "Get the concept of...", we are treating considerations of a *concept* (as a thought or consideration, &tc.) and not a "feeling" or "sensation." Much like proper use of "IMAGINE" PCLs, processing *concepts* is useful for defragmenting *Imprints* and automation at a reactive (RCC) level; mainly because understanding and handling *concepts* is not restricted to associative-analytical thought levels. Many "computations" an individual makes about life are based on implanted *concepts* used as a foundation to encode relative *Imprinting* later on. And this is also where a *Seeker* comes around to face the nature of *Alpha-Thought* (*considerations* and *postulates*).

> *Concepts* may be run, but they do not represent "mass"
> —and therefore are not "terminals" themselves.
> But, "*Conceptual-Certainty*" may be run on "terminals."

Conceptual-Certainty was among the first methods used to handle "automaticities" during early days of the Systemology Society. The logic is rooted in very ancient spiritual practices pertaining to consciously "making" the body/mind *do* what it is doing on an automatic circuit, and thereby taking control. When a concept is run long enough (or high-power enough) for *certainty*, then total command is resumed by *Self* determining a change to the nature, motion or speed of the tendency, &tc. For example, if you are sitting down while reading this now:

—*Get the concept of you making that body sit in a chair.*
Or, alternatively:
—*Think of you making that body sit in the chair.*
Compare to an objective application:
—*You make that body sit in the chair.*
Or, a command postulate:
—*Sit in the chair.*

"Route-OE" is not exclusively intended to handle physical behaviors. However, Mind-System response-patterns often promote obvious or observable reactions, **compulsions** and behaviors. The behavior exercised as physical effort in *beta-existence* begins as a thought—even if a programmed one; and if so, it most likely has emotional encoding or some other facet of sensation associated with it that might "***ping***" the *Seeker*. It is important to continue through the process completely, even if a given concept, subject or consideration is causing physical discomfort. Safeguards and system-protections exist embedded into the basic foundation of fragmented Implant-programming patterns. These may then be encoded by some related event to have a "physical response" where a *Seeker* withdraws their reach on handling them due to an automatic "*ping*" or re-occurring chronic ailment that flares up each time.

Using these methods, a *Seeker* reclaims "energy-bits" of their past attentions that have been suspended on the *Backtrack* in connection to a particular area, subject or terminal. Typically, these units of our attention—or **AttEnergy**—were either *rigidly fixed* or *widely dispersed* by some "other-determined prompting" (communication and social activity with others).

Whatever impinging or obsessive thought an individual has, they would systematically process (or "run") the concept of having that thought (as *Self-Determined*). If the obsessive thought is, for example, a worry over buying a house; the *Seeker* runs the concept of worrying over buying a new house. Eventually, the "worry" can be turned off or changed into a "healthy interest" or even "enthusiasm" (on the *Beta-Awareness Scale*). Preferably, a *Seeker* runs the process until not only is there no automatic obsession to worry about buying houses, but no intrusive compulsion to think about buying houses at all. Afterward, the individual is free to more clearly think about, or not think about, buying houses as they choose—and without attached misemotional facets of anxious worry.

There is also the other side to consider. We have mentioned the obsessive circuit, but—what about a desired or intended thought or idea that is not surfacing? Rather than being compulsively fixed, there are matters that an individual finds difficulty "thinking on" by choice. If a *Seeker* finds that they are unable to "think" on a certain line or channel, run a process on the concept of being *denied* access to that line or *Held-Back* from reaching a certain *Sphere* (of existence or actions)—since that is what is automatically taking place.

> *Hold-Outs* and *Hold-Backs*, by semantic definition, "hold" **Attenergy** to an incident on the *BackTrack*.

Even if the exact mechanism qualifying this condition has not yet been "spotted" in space-time on an individual's *Spiritual Timeline*, just work with what is readily apparent at this stage of the *Pathway*—and do your best. As standardization of our *Beta-Defragmentation* procedure is reaching completion, we still seek to handle management of any accessible response-tendencies inhibiting a *Seeker's* total freedom and ability to knowingly "reach" and "withdraw" their attention, energy and personal power on their own determinism.

Key Concepts (Hot-Buttons) for Route-OE Ethics Processing—"INVALIDATING" "BEING CRITICAL" "WORRYING" "ATTACKING" "HOLDING BACK" "FAILING TO **HELP**" "LOSING CONTROL" *and* "MISCOMMUNICATING."

** When using a *Biofeedback Device*, it is important to check each individual word of a PCL for existing charge prior to use in session processing. Every series or process should begin with a communication between *Pilot* and *Seeker* regarding what process is about to be run and the words used for it. It is possible that one of these buttons or concepts carries a *charge* on its own; it is also possible to get charge-reads on a misunderstood word. **

** *A point-of-fact for training* :: This PCL makes an excellent example of demonstrating the systematic relationship between the *Circuits* (in most of our "Route-3" processing methods) and the *Spheres*. **

[Run the entire process inserting the same *"Key-Concept"* in the blanks. Flatten any significant turbulence on a *circuit* before leaving off of it for another. Record notes regarding any contacted or surfacing thoughts, memories, realizations or additional *Harmful-Acts*, *Hold-Backs*, *Hold-Outs* and other charges discovered on channels to terminals, communication-circuits, **phases**/identities, *Spheres*, and so on. *Ethics Processing* is a *Seeker's* best chance to get everything out in the open—to confront, handle and discharge everything accessible *As-it-Is*, prior to upper-level *Wizard Grade* checkouts and further ("*A.T.*") *Actualization-Ascension Tech*.]

Circuit-1 — Get the concept* of ___ *something.*‡
     \ Get the concept of not ___ *something.*
     \ Get the concept of *something* being ___ .

Circuit-2 — Get the concept of another ___ *something.*
     \ Get the concept of another not ___ *something.*
     \ Get the concept of *something* being ___ to another.

Circuit-3 — Get the concept of others ___ *something.*
     \ Get the concept of others not ___ *something.*
     \ Get the concept of *something* being ___ to others.

---

*   If needed, the alternative standard patter is "Get the idea of..."
‡   The PCL can be left general ("*something*") unless there is a particular terminal (person, animal, place, thing) that is assessed as heavily "charged"—preferably "reading"/"indicating" as such on a mechanical *'Biofeedback'* device.

C-0/A.T. — Get the concept of ___ yourself about
something.
\ Get the concept of not ___ yourself about
something.
\ Get the concept of *something* being ___
to yourself.

After running *Expanded Route-0E Conceptual Processing*
(above) to a completion, the next step is to run the same
"Key Concepts" with *Basic-Conceptual Route-0E* (below). Emphasis here returns specifically back to *Self*—what has *out-
flowed* "from" and *in-flowed* "to" the *First Sphere of Existence*,
representing the perceived position and POV of *Self* experiencing *Beta-Existence*.

Circuit-1 — Get the concept of ___ .
\ Get the concept of not ___ .
Circuit-2 — Get the concept of another ___ you.
\ Get the concept of another not ___ you.
Circuit-3 — Get the concept of others ___ *something.*
\ Get the concept of others not ___ *something.*
C-0/A.T. — Get the concept of *you* ___ yourself.
\ Get the concept of *you* not ___ yourself.

ROUTE-3EX
SEARCH & DISCOVERY ON THE CIRCUITS
"EXPANDED-3E" EXCERPT FROM LIBER-3E

We each maintain some level of reality agreement with whatever we identify with, or are in communication with. In any situation where there is actual contact or flow, both sides must 'duplicate' the full cycle of communication to share *Reality*. A person acknowledges, recognizes or identifies a certain individual as the *Source* of the communication just as much as they must '*duplicate*' the content communicated by willingly being a receipt point. The entire '*Cycle-of-Action*' must be projected as *Reality* and '*duplicated*' by each each party "**A-*for*-A**" in order to have actual communication. And all of these *Mental Images* (and subsequent encoding from the content) are stored along each appropriate channel and contribute what we "take away from it" or register as "experience."

> Our "experience" is not a source of "fragmentation" until we find ourselves not-confronting it "As-It-*Is*." That means not only the "acceptance" of what is done but also the "willingness" to be at either *Point-of-View*.

Ethics Processing is introduced on the *Pathway-to-Self-Honesty* to systematically resolve this issue. There are some individuals that do not seem to earn any stable gains from the *Pathway* until this area is resolved. It is not so much a matter of the actions themselves, but the significances assigned to them and other considerations attached. Most encounters are not permanently fragmentary, but that which is not-confronted directly will hang up on the *Spiritual Timeline* as a confusion—a fragmentation of the certainty, muddying clear vision and experience of *Reality*.

> During a "*Harmful-Act*" there is a '*duplication*' of all **viewpoints** by all persons, easily allowing a "*Phase-shift*" with the others.

There is a tendency for an individual to **dramatize** what has happened to them—or solicit assistance and support from others—with the old "look what they've done to me" while occupying a *Victim-phase*. This is derived from a basic survival tactic that projects "I am already wounded; please do not attack." The tendency is validated and strengthened by memories and imprints of when others might have "taken care of the individual"—such as with a childhood illness or injury. This tends to apply mostly to encounters with other friends and loved ones, where one might earn "**sympathy**" as the sole means of remaining in communication.

There are environments throughout the *World-at-Large* where this computation of victimization is a highly counter-survival mistake to employ. In such instances, the individual likely takes on a (more aggressive) *Malefactor-phase*, based on a completely separate computation that "*that one* is the winning position to be in," or the mode one must operate with in order to achieve a surviving position. So we have the issue of fragmented personality-packages that "turn Evil" solely because of being on the receipt (*enforced effect*) end of too many non-confronted "Evil" acts.

The original "*Route-1*" technique overlooked important aspects of fragmentation, such as what the individual, themselves, has done as an "*out-flow*." The total sum of these aspects contributes to "acceptance levels" or *Hold-Outs* on free-flow communication and *Hold-Backs* that Self-impose a restriction or unwillingness to act, or else *reach*.

| What is non-confronted becomes a "hidden influence." |

The *malefactor* committing a "*Harmful-Act*" carries just as much, if not more, fragmentation even at *Cause* as their "victim" does at *Effect*. Keep in mind that the experience of both POV is recorded by both. This means that when an individual is unwilling to confront their own created effects or completely unwilling to experience the "other side" of the situation, the event and all of its facets will be registered and carried as a fragmentary energetic-mass suspending *Awareness* and attention on the *Spiritual Timeline.* It is simply waiting to be "pulled in" and manifested against themselves as a "*Hostile-motivator.*" Subscribing to the balance of all action in this Physical Universe, the *malefactor* has an incident happen to them "after the fact" that would seem to justify or motivate the former action— but it is happening afterward. This phenomenon is misunderstood as *karma.*

Before treating more significant Ethical concerns, "empathy" may be **repetitively** practiced (or "drilled") with a partner free of the inhibition that may be applied to casual contact in public or with strangers.

—Entire instruction behind the exercise is simply: to attempt a '*duplication*' of sensations from another POV.

—If you are even just speaking with someone, *Imagine* the impression you are projecting (how you appear and sound) from their POV.

—If there is physical contact, *Imagine* the feeling or sensation of touch received by the other POV.

When we refer to "*Harmful-Acts,*" we are not exclusively treating physical violence. All manners of projected unkindness apply to *Ethics Processing,* particularly where the effect is a reduction (any perceived "*Loss*") in an individual's *Beingness* and/or *Awareness*-level. "*Pain*" and "*Unconsciousness*" are simply two common examples of more violent acts. We are reaching for genuine ability to face-up to the *BackTrack* as we increase progress on the *Pathway.* To ensure "wins" for a *Seeker,* the "lighter" incidents should be treated masterfully prior to tackling "bigger" *Ethical* hang-ups in one's past.

Empathy may be applied to "supercharge" effectiveness of '*Forgiveness*'—as given in the Ethics/Integrity series.

In fact, an ability to actually confront environmental facets and personal experiences from all POV of an incident "As-It-*Is,*" is a high-power key to discharging accumulated turbulent energetic-masses that restrain (or *Hold-Back*) true freedom of the Alpha-Spirit.[†]

Δ Δ Δ Δ Δ Δ

Standard and Conceptual methods of *Ethics Processing* usually reveal quite a bit of material to resolve. It may be, however, that at a certain stage of release (or even at the very start) some significant attention must be given directly to a "search and discovery" effort. Although no specific instructions are given to restrict its application to *this* lifetime, there are also no specific instructions given in *Wizard Level-0* (*Grade-IV*) for targeting a *Seeker's* "*past lives*" directly.[∞] [This is an experimental formula directly distinguishing communication-circuit energy-flows as treated throughout *Ethics Processing*.]

NOTE: Energetic discharge and sense of release only takes place if what is discovered is fully confronted "As-It-Is" using Route-3E methods. "Discovery" and "Discharge" processes may be more effective when conducted by *Professional Pilots* and when using a mechanical biofeedback device (Route-3G) to assist.

"Search and Discovery on Circuits" is worded very directly for use by experienced Systemologists. It is originally intended as a *Pilot's* "tool" for accessing layers of significance surrounding *Ethical* fragmentation. Each circuit is treated separately. The four PCL are run alternately in se-

---

[†] When processing an incident (or running "*Forgiveness*"), also *Imagine* the experience from the opposing POV. The Mind-System tends to classify and group imprinting incidents on a "chain." If a your sense of an incident is becoming stronger (more solid) in its restimulated charge (rather than releasing), spot a similar non-confronted incident "parked" earlier on the *BackTrack*.

[∞] An exception being the note regarding incidents that do not readily discharge because they are linked to a larger, stronger, *older* "chain" requiring a *Seeker* to "scan for" and "spot" a similar type of incident earlier in "time." This sometimes inspires *Seekers* with a "*sense*" of something that is only logically connected via a former incarnation.

quence repeatedly (1-2-3-4; 1-2-3-4) for a single circuit until a *Seeker* has no more readily available answers, they are
interested in the discovery process and optimistic or relieved by the results. [If a *Seeker* reaches this point on one
PCL of a circuit before the rest, that one part may be omitted from repeated runs.] This process may be run *Solo* as a
personal data-inquiry toward *Self*, but its function is
primarily to "root out" information—a list of which should
be recorded for later use.

Circ-1 — What have you made another *Out-Flow*?
What have you made another *Hold-Out*?
What have you made another *In-Flow*?
What have you made another *Hold-Back*?

Circ-2 — What has another made you *Out-Flow*?
What has another made you *Hold-Out*?
What has another made you *In-Flow*?
What has another made you *Hold-Back*?

Circ-3 — What has another made others *Out-Flow*?
What has another made others *Hold-Out*?
What has another made others *In-Flow*?
What has another made others *Hold-Back*?

Circ-0 — What have you made yourself *Out-Flow*?
What have you made yourself *Hold-Out*?
What have you made yourself *In-Flow*?
What have you made yourself *Hold-Back*?

ROUTE-3G
GSR-METER PROCESSING INSTRUCTIONS
REVISED FROM LIBER-3E

"*Psycho-Galvinometers*" (*GSR-Meters*; *Galvanic Skin Response*) measure electrical resistance of the skin surface. Experimental use of *GSR* for "transpersonal psychology" is as old as "psychology" and "psychoanalysis" itself. It has been little more than 150 years—since the field of Psychology separated itself from general Philosophy. That the surface of skin is electrically active—and that detectable resistance changes occur based on emotional stimulation—dates back to the mid-to-late 1800's. Early "word association" investigations by Carl Jung compared measurable "critical arousal" (**electro-dermal activity**) to "emotional charge" held by an individual regarding key words and concepts.

By the 1930's, the field of criminology applied *GSR*-equipment as a key component of the "polygraph," which also measures heart-rate, temperature, blood pressure and breathing. For both legal and practical reasons, a *full* "polygraph" is not employed within our Systemology—the additional measurements being quite unnecessary. However, it is no surprise that *biofeedback* devices and instruments used to gauge our *Ethics Processing* for *Personal Integrity* are also associated with what is commonly referred to as a "lie detector." But again, we are dealing with something called "*Self-Honesty*"—so...

GSR-Meters (*EDA-Meters*) detect *emotional fluctuation*, measures *energetic fragmentation* and monitors changes in *Awareness* whenever a *Seeker* contacts "charged" terminals, *imprints* or *implants* on a particular channel. A *Systemologist* (*Pilot* or *Seeker*) does not require an extensive background-education in electricity/electronics in order to understand and operate a *GSR-Meter*.

Electrical "current" is electrical energy "flow"—meaning a *flow* (motion or action) of *electrons*, usually through a conductive wire; much like a flow of water moves through pipe or a hose. A "closed-loop" where electrons circulate is called a "circuit." We quite often treat personal energy "flows" and "circuits" in our Systemology. However, when referring to "electrical resistance" of a circuit, we quite literally mean: an "energetic-mass" (material) with an ability to "restrict" (slow down) electron flow. Larger or greater resistance in a circuit indicates greater or denser "mass" *resisting* free-flow of electrons in that circuit. And unless an individual intends on constructing their own Meter, this is really the extent of traditional electrical knowledge that a *Seeker* or *Pilot* needs.

The basic electrical circuit used to measure an un-known (or variable) value of electrical resistance is called the *"Wheatstone bridge"*—named not for its original inventor (*Samuel Hunter Christie* in 1833), but for *Sir Charles Wheatstone*, an English scientist that improved and popularized its application and notoriety in 1843.

When a *Seeker* holds *electrodes*[Σ] (*"sensors"*) of an *Electro-Psychometer* in their hands, they are part of a closed-circuit. A small unnoticeable amount of electrical current (usually no more than 2 volts) is passed through the body, which now acts as one "leg" of "resistance" in the circuit. To determine the unknown value of resistance from the body, a *"potentiometer"* (*"variable resistor"* and "range adjuster") is attached to the other "leg" and controlled externally by a rotating "knob" or "arm." This "balancing arm" (or

---

[Σ] Although semantically and scientifically accurate, a few experimental participants at the Systemology Society found terms like "electrode" and "probe" to personally carry reactive association with something *invasive*. If not applying physics vocabulary, as above, to introduce a proper electrical-education (*"how they work"*), a preferred day-to-day name (and for sessions) is *"sensors."* Another acceptable term is *"cans"*—which is part of the original terminology found in this practice. It simply references the fact that metal soup-cans were actually the first standard *"electrodes"* applied—attaching to the meter wire-leads with alligator-clips. Even after specially manufactured "electrodes" were designed, the term *"cans"* has remained in use among practitioners all the way up to the present.

"baseline control") is manually rotated to a position where the "display-dial needle" is visibly at the "set" point, indicating a "balance point" is reached for the circuit. While the "needle" is at the "set" point, the circuit is balanced: the "balancing arm" (or "baseline control") position on one "leg" or "side" of the "circuit bridge" is indicative of the electrical resistance value present across the surface of the skin on the other "leg" or "side" of the circuit.

> This fundamental action compares to applying weights (with known values) on one side of a "balancing scale" in order to determine an unknown, but equivalent, weight (value) on the other side.

Bringing attention out from the inner workings and mechanisms, it is more critical that all operators (*Pilots, Co-Pilots* and *Solo-Seekers*) are familiar with external controls and dials of whatever model/type is chosen for use. Basic functions and controls of an *Electro-Psychometer* have remained standard for at least half-a-century. Whether using older styles, where every detail is represented by an analog knob, or newer models* that employ digital technology—and even computers or phones, the operation is the same.

Rather than indicate a display of the actual "electrical resistance"—measured in "*Ohms*"—by the biofeedback Meter, early models by Mathison and Hubbard used a scale of basic numbers "1" through "6" (sometimes even up to "7"). The balance-set position is indicative of some things, but it is really needle motion and pattern characteristics that become the critical "reads" during systematic processing.

At *basic*—meaning emotionally and reactively defragmented; unaffected by any turbulence from the Spiritual Self—the meter-reads on bodies were consistently 5,000 *Ohms* (*5000Ω* or *5kΩ*) for females and *12,500Ω* (*12.5kΩ*) for males.

---

* In addition to models based on *Mathison* or *Hubbard* patents, there are also biofeedback devices appropriate for Systemology referred to as an: "Ability Meter" (UK), "Clearing Meter", "Clarity Meter" (US), "C-Meter" (AUS), "Delta-1 Meter" (GER), "Phoenix Meter" (US), "OM-Meter" (RUS), and "Theta Meter" to name a few.

These figures are actually simplified on a "standard" Balance-Arm as "2" and "3" respectively. These set values are also useful to know for device calibration before each use. In a *Traumatic Incident Reduction* (*TIR*) manual, "Beyond Psuchology" by Frank A. Gerbode, it also states that:—"...in most people, under ordinary circumstances, the resistance will be found in the range of 5,000–15,000 *Ohms*."

Some *GSR-Meter* models do display actual electrical resistance in *Ohms*—otherwise the "standard" applied to most modern "New Thought" practices is:

Balancing Arm	Electrical Resistance
1	400 Ω
2	5000 Ω
3	12,500 Ω
4	25,800 Ω
5	56,500 Ω
6	190,400 Ω

An *Ohm*-meter, such as you would find in a hardware store, does not work well for detecting *fragmentation*. Usually the display-dial will cover such a large range that you are not going to see precise movements, if at all. High quality *GSR-Meters* allow an individual to display a smaller portion or range—and generally have controls that increase or decrease amplification (sensitivity).

Δ Δ Δ Δ Δ Δ

The intended purpose of *Systematic Processing*—as described in *Grade-III*—is to bring undesirable, implanted and artificial *programs*, *imprints* and *postulates* into clear view for a *Seeker* to analytically inspect. Suppressed *fragmentation*, *imprints* and *programming* are uncovered in layers—as some is taken off, more becomes accessible that previously might not even register on a Meter. This is elevation of *Actualized Awareness* in action and objectively on display.

"When restimulated mental content is confronted, repression dissolves into Awareness. When not confronted, detachment may suffice, but if further involvement is enforced, then anxiety results."

—Peter Shepherd, GSR Meter Course
Tools for Transformation, 1994-2001

An individual that avoids "handling their stuff" runs the risk of having the *charge* restimulated by their environment in everyday life. Energy-flows encounter resistance from *mass*, just like damming up a stream of water. Hence, in most cases, the higher the resistance, the greater the *mass* encountered. Here we mean quite specifically and literally "*mental mass*" (or "*fields*") surrounding certain 'ideas' and 'concepts'—or as Carl Jung was researching, associated with certain 'words' and 'memories'.

As *energetically-entangled mental masses* are brought up to the surface for a *Seeker* to confront, the resistance increases—or "*rises*." When the *mass* is actually confronted As-It-Is and disintegrated with the *Seeker's attention* ("*attenergy*")—*Actualized Awareness* —then the Meter reads a resistance reduction, or "*fall*."

Biofeedback devices are not a substitute for understanding Systemology. A *Seeker* would already have to be familiar with vocabulary and concepts applied to a *process* or *PCL*. For example, a misunderstood word given in a *process* can cause false readings. Therefore, it is also important to check each of the actual words used in a *PCL* prior to applying them in order to be certain they do not already have a "charge" on them. This goes back to the original Jungian application of *GSR* for "word association."

A Meter is particularly useful when *Piloting* a *Seeker*. Although they do not indicate exactly *what* the *Seeker* is thinking about or confronting, they will indicate shifts in attention and *how* the *Seeker* is handling it. They do not necessarily "read" the *Mind*—but they do register how the *Mind-System* is affecting the body as it operates. By observing the *Seeker* and Meter, a *Pilot* can determine when a "*hot-button*" is 'pressed' or *reached* during processing—or when the *Seeker* is *withdrawing* (backing off) from the same.

There are indications for when the *Seeker* is experiencing restimulation of an *Imprint*—and when there is no longer a "charge" of entangled energy remaining on a particular circuit or channel. The Meters are intended only as *tools* to assist *systematic processing*. A *Pilot* is processing the *Seeker*; not the biofeedback device itself. It is also not a substitute for observing the reactions and behaviors of a *Seeker*.

Δ Δ Δ Δ Δ Δ

In spite of the fact that excessively sweaty, cold or dry hands can affect the baseline read from the electrodes (and should be remedied before a systematic session begins), use of a GSR-Meter as we describe and apply it does not have anything to do with perspiration—which is what many skeptics and critics suggest. The human body does not sweat and "un-sweat" rapidly enough to provide the kind of instant reactive reads and changes we look for an observe during systematic use. By reactive read, we mean literally within an instant or second of a Pilot completing a statement, word or PCL. More than three seconds and you are dealing with latent thought.

> "Detection and recording of galvanic skin response is often combined with detection and recording of other autonomic-[ANS (Autonomic Nervous System)]-dependent psychophysiological variables such as heart rate, respiratory rate and blood pressure. The device that detects and records these (additional) variables is called a *polygraph*—meaning *'many measures'*. Changes in emotion associated with intentional falsification of answers to carefully selected and worded questions involuntarily and subconsciously alters autonomic output in such a way as to cause recognizable changes in recorded physiological variables."
>
> —Pflanzer & McMullen,
> *Galvanic Skin Response & The Polygraph*
> *Lesson 9, Biopac Systems Inc., 2000*

As high-level *fragmentation* is already a state of energetic suspension and confusion (yielding lower states of *Beta-Awareness*), when we increase involvement, reach or arousal (by triggering heavier traumatic experiences), it produces stress, tension, anxiety and discomfort. In what might be considered "excitement" under other circumstances, we are pushing limits of tolerance while *systematic processing*. When an individual is in a relaxed state, the detachment or withdrawal from worldly matters is invited and generally pleasant. But when the same reaction is applied in *systematic processing*, the *Seeker* is "dodging" or moving away from what should be confronted, which produces tension and stress. This is why, in session, we are most interested in points when a *GSR-Meter* indicates a sudden reduction of resistance—or "fall"—because it denotes something that the *Seeker* is able to handle, reach for and is ready to confront; it denotes an increase in *Awareness* applied and a willingness to take responsibility. An increase or "rise" would indicate the opposite of this.

In order to have "falls" during a session there must be points when the Meter reads a rise, or that the Balance Point is a higher resistance. But, we generally only *process* an individual item or terminal, *imprinting incident* or event that *reads*. A particular area or focus is indicated for *processing*, then the needle (display) will indicate a reduction of resistance when the *Seeker* is no longer resisting the handling of it. A *Pilot* makes certain a question or item is *"reading"* before it is *systematically processed* to an **end point**. *Processing* a "charged" terminal or incident continues so long as there is still a "read" (change) taking place. Of course, if there was no indicator or "read" to begin with, there would be no way to gauge this; there would be no way to determine when a *Seeker* had flattened that *wave-action*—or what is considered an energetic *"ridge."*

A "ridge" is perhaps one of the most *solid-state* **waveform** patterns encountered when an individual is working with energies. It is essentially an energetic-mass formed from two energy-wave flows, typically in opposition to one an other. In some ways, all of "matter" could be considered a highly condensed and compacted energetic "ridge"—and in all likelihood, that is how it came to be so in *beta-existence*. But rather than dissolving solid matter, we are concerned with **flattening** the "solidity" of the **collapsed wavefunctions** which have formed and collected as "energetic-masses" around the individual.

Δ Δ Δ Δ Δ Δ

To learn the basic "yes"/"no" *Meter*-reads and reactions by working with a list of questions (or generating them at the time) for which there is no mystery about the answers. For example: Are you sitting down? Are we presently inside/ outside? Do you drive a car/have a license to drive a car? But nothing that digs to deep under the surface. To get an even further handle on what is taking place when using a *Meter* in session and for Ethics (or Integrity Checkups), you can instruct the *Seeker* to intentionally "lie" about an answer to a question that is otherwise obvious. If they are sitting down—if they are indoors—have them answer that they aren't to each and see what and how things *read*.

> "When material [a mass or '*ridge*'] is restimulated by events or in session—if the material is too hard to experience or confront, it is repressed and there will not be an instantaneous response on the meter. The *ridge* will remain in restimulation but out of consciousness, until attention is directed to the item and it is confronted. This is a flight away from the material. If the client is able to view the material, some of the suppressed emotional charge is released, causing a *fall* in resistance. This happens instantly. However, mental defenses may kick-in and cause a backing off or resistance to the material, because its content may be hard to face. This stops the release of charge and the resistance may *rise*—still accessible but the client is fighting against it. A *rise*, then, relates to material that is being confronted, but is also fought against. If viewed directly, the contents may overwhelm the

client, and the client moves away from it in fear, which causes high emotional arousal and *fall* in resistance, followed by a blocking-off of the material and subsequent *rise* in resistance and suppression of the experience."

—Peter Shepherd, <u>GSR Meter Course</u>
Tools for Transformation, 1994-2001

When working with a *GSR-Meter* for *systematic processing*, the most common term is "read"—such as when you hear someone say, "That *reads.*" More often than not it is indicating a decrease in resistance or *"fall."* There are also rare instances where the *Meter*, or more accurately, the observed *needle*, doesn't read anything at all for anything no matter what you do. The term "stuck" is often applied and all this means is that the *Seeker* is not offering their presence to the session. There is a break in communication or reality for whatever reason. It is important to know whether or not a reaction is going to read, otherwise it gives an illusion that there is no "charge" on something that otherwise will be blown over—or *flown* over—when it should have been handled. Operating a session in this way, when the *Seeker* is not providing presence, will actually reduce a *Seeker's* participation even further because the session, methods and *Pilot* (ability) loses credibility—even at "subconscious" levels; even when the *Seeker* is the one causing, allowing or validating the break in reality or attention themselves.

So long as the sensitivity is kept constant—checked at the beginning with "squeeze and release" tests—the *reads* on a *Meter* are able to be compared to other *reads.* For the *"falls"* you would be looking for the "largest" read or *"largest fall"* in relation to other reads. This is important when you are seeking to scout out a particular answer among variables. If you were to ask a *Seeker* which of their former jobs contributed the most fragmentation, there may be some "charge" on more than one answer; therefore you are looking for the biggest reaction or *read* when each is given. More details on specific "reads" are given in *Liber-3E.*

ROUTE-3Y
JUSTIFICATION & RESPONSIBILITY PROC.
REVISED FROM LIBER-3E

Although programmed purposes and implanted goals are treated more directly at higher level Wizard Grades, it is easy to see that this subject reoccurs sporadically within our *Systemology* Routes and Grades all along the way. Even in *"Crystal Clear (Handbook for Seekers)"* we began to ask a *Seeker* if the goal and motivation for their behavior is actually their own—*Self-determined*—or does it come from another—*Other-determined*—source.

Accumulated involvement in dangerous situations, states of confusion, unjust destruction and being at the effect end of faulty—or blatantly false—information, all lend to fragmented purposes that may very well be painted to appear "for our own good." Instead they are actually non-survival (or counter-survival) oriented, leading us away from routes to achieve "greater heights"—higher more ideal states of *Beingness*—including "Universes" preceding this one.

For a *Seeker* that is 'approaching' the Wizard Grades, there are many amazing and fantastical vistas yet to be explored within our work. But it is entirely critical for any lasting success in the higher ranks and levels of if of our *Systemology*. By reclaiming a true Ethic—by resolving the matters of *Hostile-Acts* and *Hold-Backs* that are determinable from *this* lifetime—the way forward is cleared much faster.

The *Pilot* must address any and all *"Problems"* that a *Seeker* has their 'present attention' (*Pressence*) on—focus on the *"elephant in the room"* (*actual* or *imagined/realized*) before addressing other considerations. Systemology of "Problems" is taken up in Grade-IV, but the truth is that the lower on the *Beta-Awareness Scale* an individual is, the more of their attention and sense of *Beingness* is wrapped up or entangled with problems—the more problems they perceive they have which are not solved. In fact, the lower a person is in *Awareness*, the more insistent they are that the problems have to be solved "right now." [If the GSR's *Balance Point* is high at the start of session, *do not* conduct '*standard processing*'; find out what the *Seeker's* attention is on and/or what "*Loss*" they are 'sad'/'upset' about. No other '*systematic*' gains will occur while a *Seeker* is in this position.] In order to dissolve significance of emotional **entanglement**, a *Seeker* should be prompted to identify as many aspects of the event, time and place *As-It-Is.*

In the instance of Goals and Purposes, problems are often hidden or buried from view—they are not "confronted" and when using GSR in processing, they cause the needles to "*rise*" significantly. Basically, the individual is increasing their resistance against whatever it is they don't want to face. We might say it indicates being overwhelmed. This is where we find the "breaks" in *communication* and/or *reality*. This is why our *Ascension* is handled on a gradient scale—an individual must have *reality* on it—*realizations*—before they can find themselves confronting the *actuality.*

The effects on a *Seeker* may be reduced if the "imprinting incident" (*&tc.*) is resurfaced—but it must be at the point of origination, the very first moment or instance of the event. Otherwise the results will not be permanent. It is not unlike a chain, which is found in *systematic processing* to only reduce if the earlier incident or earlier beginning is found. Otherwise the imprinting and/or associative Mental Imagery can potentially become stronger. This is why after being processed a couple of times, the *Pilot* asks the *Seeker* if the intensity or imagery is getting stronger or thinner. If it does intensify, then you're not working with the "whole thing." Just as if the *fall* on the GSR continues, there *Seeker* still has more *Hold-Backs* -or- the incident is rooted in a "past life" and the *Seeker* has no reality on it.

A *Fragmented Purpose* is rigidly fixed in place in such a way that the *Seeker* didn't likely agree to it or may not even be 'aware' of it—thus it is not *Self-determined* and is certainly not resolved (or dissolved) "*As-It-Is*" in basic processing or managed in regular every-day life. Such a purpose may or may not be overtly displayed with *Hostile* or *destructive* intentions, but they are certainly present—even if, again, beneath the surface and outside the normal reach of a *Seeker*. When 'processing-out' a *Fragmented Purpose*, the *Seeker* must confront the nature of the actual intention they have and not simply a statement of action or what someone else intended. When it comes to *Ethics Processing* and personal integrity strengthening, we are concerned primarily with the "intention" that the *Seeker* had—and without attempts to justify it. When asked what they've done, too often a *Seeker* will set up their *Awareness* on the "defensive side" and immediately begin to give obvious facts, excuses and justification. These are not the type of answers we want to see accepted in Route-3E series, *&tc.*

Fragmented Purposes reduce an individual's **apparent** integrity. They are not necessarily always "on" or dramatizing the programming—it may be triggered or stimulated into action by any number of things. However, when they are in this *"mode,"* they often are perceived by others to be at least a little bit "crazy" if not fully "insane" depending on the intensity of the programmed purpose. The *Pilot* is looking to find the underlying *Fragmented Purpose* that systematically leads to a behavioral-chain or pattern of *Hostile-Acts. Fragmented Purposes/Goals* are typically installed as between-lives implants and thus handled as *"BackTrack."*

As long as the *Pilot* handles *processing* fully and systematically, which may include necessary application of *"The Systemology of Justification and Responsibility,"* it is possible to free up the *Seeker* enough to pursue the higher-level Wizard Grades. However, if the *Pilot* does not maintain proper control and steering of the session, allowing the *Seeker* to run all around the actual procedure, then it's a waste of time. It wasn't until intensive work on *Grade-V* began at the *Systemology Society* in 2021, that we realized the Route-3E series on "Ethics Processing" (in *Liber-3E*) was critically necessary to ensure stable Beta-Defragmentation.[*]

---

[*] All fundamentals should be run as a repetitive PCL until the *Seeker* appears to run out of answers. Any further answers hidden may be

Another critical step to handling and elevating *Personal Integrity* is *"justification defragmentation."* If the matter is not obvious—assuming the *Seeker* has not focused on their own *justifications*, they can be obtained by asking for them. Whenever a *Hostile-Act* or *Hold-Out* is discovered, the *Pilot* simply asks if the *Seeker* has justified that behavior in any way. If using GSR, the matter should be asked about until there is no charge regarding the act. Although standard *Pilot* training in "3E" (3G) distinguishes a "read" on a *GSR-Meter* to mean "yes," it can also mean that there is still a charge on a line. So if after there are no immediate reads on a **interrogative** question, and you ask "Do you agree that this PCL is clear/defragmented?" and you get a read, then there is still a charge on the line.[‡]

You do a *Seeker* a great disservice by allowing vague answers and generalities to "fly" during *Personal Integrity Defragmentation*. A *Pilot* is encouraged to have gotten their own *Hold-Outs* defraged (as part of their *"Class-3E"* certification) so that they are not likely to sidestep the same areas in others. Although we are concerned with actions, the 'things' a *Seeker* has "heard" (from others) or "thought" (but not acted on) can also create "mental mass" and thus should be flattened with two-way communication, but not emphasized or targeted directly. Spending an entire session on such will not advance the *Seeker*; yet, parts of these actually relate to a *Seeker's* "justifications" and so they are (to that degree) important. However, *Hold-Outs* on actual *Hostile-Actions* are immensely more important. Also pinpoint the time-place of events to be certain a *Seeker* desensitizes charge As-It-Is. If *GSR-Meter* reads aren't quieting down, ask for a similar occurrence that took place earlier in the past. You want to target the *first* time the *Seeker* ac

---

detected by GSR—asking the *Seeker* what '*that*' is that came to mind each time there is a read (however slight or tiny).

‡ According to an anonymous professional therapeutic processor that this article is written in collaboration with, the *Pilot* should never say "that *still* reads" and should say instead that "there *is another* read here" or "I'm getting *another* read here." Otherwise you risk invalidating the *Seeker.*

ted in such a way—which is the basic *imprinting incident* on which all other mass/fragmentation is built upon.

When using the *GSR-Meter*, a *Pilot* learns to recognize the significance of an immediate reaction of the needle or '*instant read*'. Even when the *Seeker* does not have an immediate answer, because they are now searching their databases for it, the immediate response of a needle should be used as the indicator. Assuming the *Seeker* does take a moment to '*think*' about it, it is likely that when they hit upon it, the *Pilot* will see the same quality of needle reaction on the *Meter*. With these kinds of processes, it is *then* that a *Pilot* should indicate a '*read*' to the *Seeker*, by saying "*there*" or "*that*" or "*what is* that(?)" (of which a *Seeker* would know from previous experience or education that they are being asked *What-Is-It* they are looking at; and the *Pilot* is to acknowledge the *As-It-Is* answer received).

As expressed throughout Grade-III and IV work, "*Willingness to be Responsible*" has nothing to do with blame and guilt; it has everything to do with *True Power*—the ability to be *at cause* over things. "Justification" is a common occurrence when handling "Route-3E" because when an individual acts in a manner that is later considered "wrong," there is a natural encoded tendency to "lessen the importance/significance" or else "justify" the actions. This not only strengthens the imprinting of the "*Harmful-Act*" but also requires that the individual maintain certain false beliefs in order to support these "justifications." Maintaining any falsehoods is a conflict with *Self-Honesty* and perpetuates distortions in '*thinking*' and the way in which one views and interacts with the '*world*'. It is high-time that you are able to confront (*face up to*) actions without feelings of regret, blame or urge to justify them; without which it is impossible to shed skin of the Human Condition and rise above the gravity of this *beta-Existence*.

ROUTE-30*
DEFRAGMENTATION INTENSIVE PROC.
GRAND TOUR & IMPLANT CHECKOUT

This processing-skeleton is culminated from all basic Beta-Defragmentation techniques for Wizard-Level applications at Grade-V and above. It represents the minimum of what is applied to Class-4 *Piloting* of *Implants* and the *Backtrack*. This "Grand Tour" essentially employs all basic Routes. It consists of the most basic PCLs from each category. Additional systematic processing techniques are only utilized if the direct route does not seem to be achieving the results.

There are many applications for this "Intensive"—which is why it is included in *"Systemology-180."* It should be understood that its original purpose applies to *Implanting* on the *Backtrack*; removing "charge" from 'goals' and 'roles' that are apparently programmed—*implanted* artificially; then dramatized and built upon during one's lifetime. But this skeleton may be modified to fit more appropriate wording for processing some other type of "terminal" &tc.

"Route-2" assists in increasing willingness to confront, but it also tends to take heat off the turbulence when a *Seeker* recalls positive aspects of the processing subject. By using multiple circuits, a *Seeker* is also able to analyze the goal or terminal from the outside, so to speak. PCLs are run alternately in series repetitively. They original targeted a type of 'phase' or 'personality role' (to dramatize a goal).

RECALL being ___.

RECALL another person being ___.

RECALL others being ___.

As demonstrated in Grade-III, component factors of attention are tied to communication, reality agreement and the degree of "likingness" (liking, attraction) shared between an individual and a terminal or environmental aspect.

---

* Released at the Spring 2023 *"BackTrack"* lectures by Joshua Free.

This application of "Route-2" assists in accessing memory. The basic *facets* of each instance should also be *spotted*. If no event easily *resurfaces*, an "IMAGINE" PCL can be used.

> RECALL a time you were in good communication with a(n) ___.
>
> RECALL a time a(n) ___ was in good communication with you.
>
> RECALL a time another was in good communication with a(n) ___.
>
> RECALL a time a(n) ___ was in good communication with another.
>
> RECALL a time others were in good communication with a(n) ___.
>
> RECALL a time when a(n) ___ was in good communication with others.
>
> RECALL a time you agreed with a(n) ___.
>
> RECALL a time a(n) ___ agreed with you.
>
> RECALL a time another agreed with a(n) ___.
>
> RECALL a time a(n) ___ agreed with another.
>
> RECALL a time others agreed with a(n) ___.
>
> RECALL a time when a(n) ___ agreed with others.
>
> RECALL a time you felt you liked a(n) ___.
>
> RECALL a time a(n) ___ liked you.
>
> RECALL a time another felt they liked a(n) ___.
>
> RECALL a time a(n) ___ liked another.
>
> RECALL a time others felt they liked a(n) ___.
>
> RECALL a time when a(n) ___ liked others.

Communication is indicative of a free flow of energy that can be exchanged. Breaks in communication lead to the development of *barriers*, automatically generated masses. Use "IMAGINE" techniques to conceive of a continuous out-flow of communication (speech) between terminals. With the running of each PCL, IMAGINE the largest out-pouring of speech possible. A PCL is run excessively until it begins to slow; then switch to the next one.

IMAGINE saying specific things to a(n) ___.
IMAGINE a(n) ___ saying specific things to you.
IMAGINE another saying specific things to a(n) ___.
IMAGINE a(n) ___ saying specific things to another.
IMAGINE others saying specific things to a(n) ___.
IMAGINE a(n) ___ saying specific things to others.

Part of an individual's break in communication, and other turbulence on a particular line, results from accumulated failures to help and assist others. Fragmentation results if the *Seeker* does not also balance the "failures" they hold on to with the memory of times when they are successful. On the *Backtrack*, a particular 'goal' and 'role' decays into the next one (usually an opposing one) after so much "failure" using a particular *personality-phase* has been calculated. If these cannot be *spotted* with 'RECALL', then use 'IMAGINE', as with the remainder of this Grand Tour.

RECALL a time you helped a(n) ___.
RECALL a time a(n) ___ helped you.
RECALL a time another helped a(n) ___.
RECALL a time a(n) ___ helped another.
RECALL a time others helped a(n) ___.
RECALL a time a(n) ___ helped others.

Another "hot-button" coinciding with *Help* is a failure to *Protect*. Such imprints are generally more intense and may even include violence. A *Seeker* runs into their stream of "losses" (including "love")—as well as matters of trust and betrayal. "Route-2" will not reduce emotional entanglement associated with "loss" and so the *Seeker* should focus on the other end of the **spectrum**.

RECALL a time you protected a(n) ___.
RECALL a time a(n) ___ protected you.
RECALL a time another protected a(n) ___.
RECALL a time a(n) ___ protected another.
RECALL a time others protected a(n) ___.

RECALL a time a(n) ___ protected others.

One of the issues with using a '*personality-phase*' or an implanted 'goal/role' to solve "problems" is that once this is done, an individual is likely to *calcify* that method of behavior (or thought or effort) and use it as an absolute for the handling of all difficulties. This leads to further problems, often of a greater magnitude. An individual is operating in such a way as to solve the problems that oppose the 'goals' they are fixed to.

When applied to unravel the *Backtrack,* a *Solo Pilot* will *spot* a particular problem (with the first PCL) and then as many solutions accessibly *spotted* afterward. Then another problem is selected as a target. As one *spots* earlier and earlier 'goal-problems' on the *Backtrack*, one realizes that "solutions" eventually lead to another "goal" on a 'chain' that was first implanted far back on the *Spiritual Timeline.*

   a) -What problem might a(n) ___ have with another
      (or others)?
      -What solutions might a(n) ___ have to that problem?
   b) -What problem might another (or others) have with
      a(n) ___?
      -What solutions might they have to that problem?
   c) -What problem might a(n) ___ observe between
      others?
      -What solutions might a(n) ___ have to their problem?
   d) -What problem might a(n) ___ create for themselves?
      -What solutions might a(n) ___ have to that problem?

"Route-3E" reveals that an individual does things and then hides them and withdraws reach and communication. It doesn't really matter what the original intention was; in the end, they begin to hold-back their action as Cause. It is important to rehabilitate realizations of being Cause and not just focus on more negative 'Harmful-Acts'—although these do need to be handled. We are concerned with all *out-flow*; both those acts which have actually been performed and those which have been *Held-back.*

a) What might a(n) ___ do to another?
   \ What might a(n) ___ hide from another?
b) What might another do to a(n) ___?
   \ What might another hide from a(n) ___ ?
c) What might a(n) ___ do to others?
   \ What might a(n) ___ hide from others?
d) What might a(n) ___ do to themselves?
   \ What might a(n) ___ hide from themselves?
e) What might you do to a(n) ___?
   \ What might you hide from a(n) ___?

Another *hot-button* for *processing* is "*change.*" A *Seeker* that is resistant to change is also unwilling to improve. A compulsive insistence on change is no healthier. The '*Identity-Phases*' attached to "goal/roles" and problem-solving tend to be resistant to change (which is treated in Grade-IV).

a) What might a(n) ___ want to change in another?
   \ What might a(n) ___ prevent changing in another?
b) What might another want to change in a(n) ___?
   \ What might another prevent changing a(n) ___ ?
c) What might a(n) ___ want to change in others?
   \ What might a(n) ___ prevent changing in others?
d) What might a(n) ___ want to change in themselves?
   \ What might a(n) ___ prevent changing in
   themselves?
e) What might you want to change in a(n) ___?
   \ What might you prevent changing in a(n) ___?

Flows on a circuit are comprised of considerations toward communication, agreement and liking—all of which contribute to how an individual *understands* such-and-such. An upset occurs when these considerations are compulsively desired, forced, held-back and/or rejected. The most common PCLs for these combinations of *buttons* and *considerations* are listed here for *Backtrack* processing.

What communication might a(n) ___ inhibit in another?
What communication might another inhibit in a(n) ___?

What communication might a(n) ___ inhibit in others?

What communication might a(n) ___ hold-back from saying?

What communication might you inhibit a(n) ___ from saying?

What communication might a(n) ___ force on another?

What communication might another force on a(n) ___?

What communication might a(n) ___ force on others?

What communication might a(n) ___ force on themselves?

What communication might you force on a(n) ___?

What communication might a(n) ___ desire from another?

What communication might another desire from a(n) ___?

What communication might a(n) ___ desire from others?

What communication might a(n) ___ make themselves desire?

What communication might you desire from a(n) ___?

What agreement might a(n) ___ reject from another?

What agreement might another reject from a(n) ___?

What agreement might a(n) ___ reject from others?

What agreement might a(n) ___ make themselves reject?

What agreement might you reject from a(n) ___?

What agreement might a(n) ___ force on another?

What agreement might another force on a(n) ___?

What agreement might a(n) ___ force on others?

What agreement might a(n) ___ force on themselves?

What agreement might you force on a(n) ___?

What agreement might a(n) ___ desire from another?

What agreement might another desire from a(n) ___?

What agreement might a(n) ___ desire from others?

What agreement might a(n) ___ make themselves desire?

What agreement might you desire from a(n) ___?

What might a(n) ___ inhibit another from liking?
What might another inhibit a(n) ___ from liking?
What might a(n) ___ inhibit others from liking?
What might a(n) ___ hold-back themselves from liking?
What might you inhibit a(n) ___ from liking?
What might a(n) ___ force another to like?
What might another force a(n) ___ to like?
What might a(n) ___ force others to like?
What might a(n) ___ force themselves to like?
What might you force a(n) ___ to like?
What might a(n) ___ desire another to like?
What might another desire a(n) ___ to like?
What might a(n) ___ desire others to like?
What might a(n) ___ make themselves desire to like?
What might you desire a(n) ___ to like?

By following game-conditions "TO SURVIVE" in *Beta-Existence*, an individual allows themselves to commit "Hostile-Acts"—which are then buried under layers of justification. Once an action is *spotted* (in the first PCL), many answers can be given in response to justification. When the first pair are *flattened*, move to the second. When there are no more answers for the pair, run it again for new responses.

a) What would a(n) ___ do to ensure their own survival?
   \ What justifications would they have for that?
b) What would a(n) ___ stop others from doing to
   ensure their own survival?
   \ What justifications would they have for that?

A *Seeker's* primary justification computation or justification imprint is generally attached to the implanted "goal/role." In a nutshell the processing determines what an individual uses (as a consideration) to justify themselves as right and make others wrong—as stated in the PCLs.

How might a(n) ___ make themselves right?
How might a(n) ___ make others wrong?

In order to check-out that there is no significant charge on a channel remaining after the Grand Tour, the following is a "Route-0" communication process that may even allow a *Seeker* to experience "Zu-Vision" as an *End-Point.* This is not the absolute purpose of the defragmentation, but may ensue as a result. If this Grand Tour has not fully defragmented the channel (or implant or goal, &tc.), at least the bulk of the turbulence and fragmentation will have been lifted off of the line, allowing for enough *Actualized Awareness* to approach other systematic processing techniques. An experienced *Pilot* knows the ultimate realization of this technique already,[‡] but it should still be answered within the rules of handling systematic processing sessions.

From where could you communicate to a(n) ___?

From where could a(n) ___ communicate to you?

From where could a(n) ___ communicate to others?

From where could a(n) ___ communicate to themselves?

[‡] The supreme realization is that anything can communicate with anything from anywhere. But individual locations should be *spotted* to assist in "grounding" a *Seeker* at the end of the Intensive.

SYSTEMATIC PROCESSING TECHNIQUES

GRADE-III
CRYSTAL CLEAR PROC. TECHNIQUES
EXTRACTED FROM LIBER-2B

<u>AN INTRODUCTION TO BASIC ANALYTICAL RECALL</u>

Practice with the following *processing commands*:

—RECALL a scene that was very colorful. *What was it? Where was it? What did you hear?*

—RECALL a scene that was very peaceful. *Where was it? How did it smell? What did you hear?*

—RECALL a sound that was very loud. *Where was it? What was loud? What else did you see?*

—RECALL a sound that was very soothing. *Where was it? Who was there? What else did you hear?*

—RECALL a sound that was not understood. *Where was it? What/Who made the sound? What emotion did you feel?*

—RECALL an object that felt sharp. *Where was it? Who else was there? How bright was the space?*

—RECALL an object that felt soft. *Where was it? What did you hear? What emotion did you feel?*

—RECALL a taste that was sweet. *What was it? Where were you? What did you hear? Who else was there?*

—RECALL a smell that was strong. *What was it? Where were you? What actions were happening?*

—RECALL an object moving away from you. *What was it? Where were you? What did you hear? What else did you see? Who else was there? What did you smell?*

—RECALL an object moving toward you. *What was it? Where were you? What did you hear? What else did you see? Who else was there? What did you smell?*

—RECALL the time you first heard of Systemology. *Where were you? What did you hear? Who else was there? What emotion did you feel?*

—RECALL the time you started performing this "*Analytical Recall*" session. *What position was your body in then? What position is your body in now?*

HANDLING SPIRITUALITY WITH ANALYTICAL RECALL

—RECALL a time you were in a church. *Where is it? What do you see? What do you hear? What do you smell? What time of day is it?*

—RECALL an earlier time you were in a church. *Where is it? What do you see? What do you hear? What do you smell? What time of day is it?*

—RECALL a time you were made to go to a church. *Who is enforcing you to go? What are they saying? What else do you sense? What emotion do you feel?*

—RECALL a time you were made to feel guilty. *Where is it? Who else is there? What do you hear? How bright is the space? How large is the space?*

—RECALL the moment you decided to go some place on your own. *What position is your body in? What actions or motions are happening? What emotion do you feel making the decision?*

—RECALL the place you decided to go to. *Where is it? What do you see? What do you hear? Who else is there? What do you smell? How bright is the space?*

—RECALL a place you enjoy visiting. *Where is it? What do you see? What do you hear? Who else is there? What do you smell? How bright is the space? How large is the space?*

LIGHT PROCESSING OF LOSS WITH ANALYTICAL RECALL

—RECALL a moment when you discarded something you later needed. *What is it? Where are you? What do you hear? Who else is there? What emotion do you feel after discarding it?*

—RECALL the moment you realized you needed what was discarded. *Where are you? What do you hear? Smells? What else do you see? Who else is there? What emotion do you feel?*

—RECALL a moment when you were forced to have something. *What is it? Where are you? Who is making you have it? What are they saying? How large is the space? How bright is the space? What emotion do you feel?*

—RECALL a moment you discarded something you were forced to have. *What is it? Where are you? Who made you have it? What time of day is it? What emotion do you feel after discarding it?*

—RECALL a moment when you discarded something you didn't want. *What is it? Where are you? What do you hear? Who else is there? Smells? What emotion do you feel after discarding it?*

—RECALL a time you enjoyed throwing away something old or broken. *Where are you? Who else is there? What do you hear? What time of day is it? What emotion do you feel?*

PROCESSING ATTENTION PATTERNS WITH ROUTE-2

—RECALL a moment when someone *did* something that confused you. *Who is it? Where are you? What do you hear? What do they say? What position is your body in?*

—RECALL a moment when someone *said* something that confused you. *Who is it? Where are you? What do you hear? What do they say? What time of day is it?*

—RECALL a moment when you were really focused on something. *What is it? Where were you? What actions are happening around you? Is anyone else there? What position is your body in?*

—RECALL a moment when you focused your attention and were suddenly distracted. *Where are you? What were you focused on? What broke your attention or confused you? What do you hear? What else do you see? Who else is there? What do you smell?*

—RECALL a moment when something suddenly fixed your attention. *Where are you? What focused or fixed your attention? What actions are happening around you? Is any-*

one else there? What do you hear? What else do you see?
What do you smell?

—REPEAT the *last two* "command lines" several times, alternating between, then end the session.

<u>HANDLING ATTENTION WITH OBJECTIVE PROCESSING</u>

Resolution for *attention (presence)* is processed very simply with "spot-identify" alternations of *Awareness*. The effectiveness is so sharp that this may be used at the beginning *and* end of a session if desired, or also at any point during *Self-Processing* where you feel you may be digging into something (or some aspect) deeper than you are ready to handle. It is not enough to just glance—really focus attention on the object, notice its points of solidity and identify it at analytical levels. Then touch it and analyze any additional *facets*.

—LOOK around you and SPOT an *object* in space.
IDENTIFY its *solidity* and CONTACT its *substance*.

(*Do this several times with various objects, walls and corners, until completely "in phase" and interested or extroverted about your Path; alternatively practice with eyes closed and only imagine you are moving to touch objects in the room.*)

<u>DEFRAGMENTATION USING ANALYTICAL PROCESSES</u>

Significant *Actualized Awareness* must be present to process information, perception and **experiential** memory *analytically*. Everything short of this is hardly "**valid** memory" because it is stored as "erroneous programming" and "conditioning." Much of this has been enforced by efforts literally *against* our WILL. *Literally.* This is what we are *Processing-out*—"resolving"—to regain an actualized state, the original, basic power and ability of WILL. You may practice on this now.

—RECALL an incident when you were invalidated by someone.

—RECALL an incident when you invalidated someone else.

—RECALL an incident when someone invalidated someone else.

—RECALL a moment when you were suddenly interrupted by someone.

—RECALL a moment when you interrupted someone else.

—RECALL a moment when someone interrupted someone else.

—RECALL the last time you were told to know something important.

—RECALL the last time you told something important to someone else.

—RECALL the earliest time you were told a secret.

—RECALL the earliest time you told a secret to someone else.

—RECALL an incident when a belief was enforced on you.

—RECALL an incident when you enforced a belief on someone else (or others).

—RECALL an incident when someone enforced a belief on someone else (or others).

—RECALL the earliest time you told a secret to someone else.

—RECALL a time that someone lied about you.

—RECALL a time that you lied about someone else.

—RECALL the last time when someone lied to you about someone else.

—RECALL the last time when you watched someone lie to others.

—RECALL a time that you lied about someone else.

—RECALL a moment when you were picked or chosen.

—RECALL an event you won at or a time when you were best at something.

—RECALL the last time when you discovered something to be untrue.

—RECALL the last time when you discovered something to be true.

—RECALL the last time when you were stopped from finishing something.

—RECALL an instance when you stopped someone from finishing something.

—RECALL a moment when someone stopped someone else from finishing something.

—RECALL a time that you successfully completed a task.

—RECALL a time when you were satisfied with results.

—RECALL a time when you were right after all.

CONSIDERATION PROCESSES: THOUGHT, WILL & EFFORT

Personal management—and *Processing* used to rehabilitate it—are possible only because of an amazing faculty of *Self*: we call "**consideration**." We may apply *right effort* to yield results of optimum efficiency of results—and then there is everything else that falls short of (or even exceeds) this. *Consideration* is the faculty enabling a proper gauge of *effort* toward "manifestation of things" or "actualization of beingness."

Our ability to properly analyze, evaluate, realize, actualize—and get "*effective*" results—is a matter of "*right consideration.*"

—RECALL an instance when you heard someone say the word: *Effort.*

—RECALL a moment when you used the word: *Effort.*

—RECALL a time when you applied *Effort* to accomplish something, and you were successful.

—RECALL a time when you applied *Effort* to accomplish something, and you were unsuccessful.

—RECALL an instance when someone said to you: *Give it more Effort.*

—RECALL an instance when you said to someone: *Give it more Effort.*

—RECALL an instance when someone said to someone else to: *Give it more Effort.*

—RECALL an instance when someone said to you: *You're trying too hard.*

—RECALL an instance when you said to someone: *You're trying too hard.*

—RECALL an instance when someone said to someone else: *You're trying too hard.*

—RECALL an event when you witnessed someone applying *Effort* to accomplish something, and they were successful.

—RECALL an event when you witnessed someone applying *Effort* to accomplish something, and they were unsuccessful.

—RECALL a time when you applied *Effort* and someone applied *Effort* against you.

—RECALL a time when you applied *Effort* against the *Effort* of someone else, and you were effective.

—RECALL a time when you applied *Effort* against the *Effort* of someone else, and you were ineffective.

—RECALL a moment when you witnessed someone applying *Effort* against the *Effort* of someone else, and they were effective.

—RECALL a moment when you witnessed someone applying *Effort* against the *Effort* of someone else, and they were ineffective.

—RECALL an event that you made an *Effort* to attend and were successful.

—RECALL a place that you made an *Effort* to visit and were successful.

—RECALL a time when you successfully moved an object.

—RECALL an instance when you found an object too heavy to move.

—RECALL a time you picked up an object that was lighter than you expected.

—RECALL an instance when you unstuck a door or drawer.

—RECALL a moment when you felt truly successful.

—RECALL a time when you guessed the right answer.

DEFRAGMENTATION USING SUBJECTIVE PROCESSING

Self-directed personal management of high-frequency actualization includes ability to properly manage what is referred to as "*stress.*" Humans are not socially instructed with coping skills. They are told to "suck it up" and "hold it in" until weight of the load becomes to much. This is a poor way to operate *beta-existence*. Whenever a shift-change occurs for a state or condition, the *motion* creates a situation of "stress."

> Directed *Awareness*—or any focused concentration of *Awareness*—whether it is subjectively ("internally") *or* objectively ("externally") oriented... it is COMMUNICATION of CONTROL.

Therefore every *Self-directed Alpha Thought* or "*Processing Command Line*" (PCL) is communication of "control"—so:

> *Who is in control of your life?*
> *Who are you accepting commands from?*
> *Who is directing your attention?*
> *Who is demanding that you "listen" to them?*
> *Who is demanding that you "pay attention"?*

Anyone making demands of us does so an intent to "control." *Self-Realization* requires looking outwardly at personal interaction with others treated as *beta-influences:*

> Sources of *imprint* restimulation;
>
> *Enforcers* of Reality agreements;
>
> *Programmer-authorities* of information-data; and
>
> Those who actively use *effort* against us.

Consider those who outflow their energies at you against your will; or those that reject your own advances and communication. We are not interested in placing "blame" with these exercises. With our *Systemology*, we primarily are interested in identifying systematic relationships contributing to *our decisions* and Reality agreements. "Blame" only leads to a reduction of personal responsibility as "cause."

—IDENTIFY persons which you *presently* consider strong *beta-influences* in your environment (home, school, family, work, &tc.) or directly concerning your beliefs and past programming in this present lifetime.

—*List them below.*

1.) _____ ‡ ___
2.) _____ ‡ ___
3.) _____ ‡ ___
4.) _____ ‡ ___
5.) _____ ‡ ___
6.) _____ ‡ ___
7.) _____ ‡ ___
8.) _____ ‡ ___

—EVALUATE your past/present experiences with these persons enough to estimate a basic ZU association for each. Use *Systemology* education and personal experience with the *Emotimeter* and *Awareness Scale* as your basis.

—*List these "numeric values" for each name, on the corresponding space marked* with a "‡" (a symbol often used in *Systemology* to indicate the "ZU-line" itself or "Self-directed Will-Intention on the ZU-line"). *How much and in what ways do you think these persons affect (or have affected) your beta-personality?*

—RECALL the most commonly used verbal statements spoken by each person in your list or their most commonly demonstrated emotional state. —IDENTIFY any key words or phrases that you might resurface when considering these individuals and their influence on you. EVALUATE this data: assign it a value from the ZU-line (which may or may not be the same from the previous list).

—*Record this information below for each.*

1.) _____ ‡ ___
2.) _____ ‡ ___
3.) _____ ‡ ___
4.) _____ ‡ ___
5.) _____ ‡ ___
6.) _____ ‡ ___
7.) _____ ‡ ___
8.) _____ ‡ ___

Putting aside your present *Awareness* of these influences for a moment, take some time now to consider your own *beta-personality* and evaluate the answers you gave on the "BAT" test.‡ Obviously the test is generalized enough to gauge a numeric evaluation against objective standards. When you answered the questions, you were merely asked about the intensity of specific *Self-determined* values expressed in your lifetime—or ranking priorities: personal significance of each aspect (category) of *Life Management.* *Your* scores are based on *your* own decisions and choices. Granted, many times *Self-direction* is fragmented by low-levels of *Awareness.* But a *Seeker* while on the *Pathway* that even these conditions were agreements made by *Self. After* receiving some type of fragmentation. We later go on reinforcing fragmentation with additional agreements and reasoning based upon the same.

---

‡ The "BAT" or *Beta-Awareness Test* is given in "*Liber-2B*", "*The Systemology Handbook*", and "*The Way Into The Future*" volume.

Take a thorough review of *Self* and the previously evaluated statements evaluated of the "BAT" in relation to any personal realizations established (or changed) at this point in your present cycle (run-through) of *Grade-III* work. Run the following *Analytical Processes* and take notice if any particular *facets* connected with each evaluation are: emotional reactions; relevant keywords describing mental states; Self-affirmations (or "*Self-talk*"); or finally, associations often vocalized to others, since those are personal statements (agreements/postulates) about ourselves.

—ANALYZE the present condition of your physical body. *How do you feel about its condition? What words would you use to describe its condition? What influences your beliefs about it? What influences your intentions in using it? In what ways might it be improved? How might you do that? In what ways have you attempted to improve conditions and were not successful. In what ways have you attempted to improve conditions are were successful? What information of it have you observed from others? What words, phrases or expressions do they use? What information of it have others attempted to enforce on you? What words, phrases or expressions do they use? What parts of it are you most certain of? What are your favorite parts?* *

—ANALYZE the condition of your physical possessions.

—ANALYZE the emotion that you feel most often.

—ANALYZE whether your typical thought-patterns primarily concern the past, present or future.

—ANALYZE how certain you are in your ability to maintain your existence in this lifetime.

—ANALYZE the responsibilities that you have accepted.

—ANALYZE any responsibilities you are shying away from.

—ANALYZE what additional responsibilities you could accept.

---

* *Seekers* should consider similar types of questions regarding each line of analysis. Make note of the best or most accurate words and phrases used to describe each part. Record this information in a *log*.

—ANALYZE your certainty in communicating/expressing to others about things you know.

—ANALYZE your degree of trust/certainty about your environment.

—ANALYZE the amount of gossip, hear-say, and falsehoods that regularly appear in your communications/expressions to others.

—ANALYZE your accuracy retaining or passing along information.

—ANALYZE aspects you are presently blaming yourself for.

—ANALYZE aspects you are presently blaming others for.

—ANALYZE what/who in your environment assists you.

—ANALYZE what/who in your environment threatens you.

—ANALYZE what/who in your environment forces you.

—ANALYZE goals and ideals that motivate your actions.

—ANALYZE your feelings/attitudes regarding others you meet.

—ANALYZE your feelings/attitudes about all Humans.

—ANALYZE your attitudes about all animals and plants.

—ANALYZE your feelings/attitudes about planet Earth.

—ANALYZE your attitudes about the Physical Universe.

—ANALYZE your attitudes about the Spiritual Universe.

—ANALYZE your attitudes about Supreme Infinity.

Compare data you collected in this *Self-Analysis* to previous *evaluations* involving those considered "influences" in your *Self-direction*. We carry many goals and ideals that have been "implanted" from other sources. These aspects also contribute to our *beta-personality*; which by definition, operates in some degree of *fragmentation* if retaining significant amounts of erroneous programming. Basic operation of the Human Condition—and communication with others that also operate a *beta-personality* as Human—is *always* a potential "source" of *fragmentation*.

DEFRAGMENTATION USING OBJECTIVE PROCESSING

Emotional energy is closely tied to efforts and actions in *beta-existence*. In *Processing*, we are concerned with the degree of personal "control" to manage physical activity. It is important to understand and *defragment* the RCC at this step on the *Pathway*. Information coming in (input or *inflow*) from the environment (or consequences of action) necessarily passes through the *emotional range* of our Mind-Body connection before again reaching *analytical Awareness*. Close examination of all esoteric texts and practices regarding spirituality or mysticism reveals unilaterally: "Self-Control of Emotion" is perhaps one of the most fundamental steps on *any* version of the *Pathway*.

—IDENTIFY an *object* in your environment that is neutral (harmless) and of which you are primarily indifferent to. [Start with something you have no preexisting emotion attachment to, a neutral item such as a rock or paperweight. Teachers operating within the **"Ancient Mystery School"** often used something like a candle or a pebble.]

—LOOK at the *object* with your full attention and *Awareness* and ANALYZE the extent of your indifference and neutrality regarding its condition "*to be.*"

—IMAGINE that the *object* is suddenly the most awesome, useful, positive, valuable "thing" presently assisting your existence. Spend several minutes *realizing* this until your emotional frequency raises up to the highest "elated" degrees of joy and enthusiasm that you can possibly actualize. ANALYZE any additional *facets* directly experienced as a result. [This is *your present* (4.0) on the *Emotimeter*.]

—IMAGINE that the *object* is now suddenly an even more amazing, beautiful, breathtaking, intricate and perfect demonstration of manifestation. Spend several minutes *realizing* this until your elated state has increased into appreciating the *object* as the most **archetypal** piece of art, music and verse all combined in one. ANALYZE any additional *facets* directly experienced as a result.

—IMAGINE that the *object* is suddenly the most trivial, useless, negative, distracting "thing" presently attacking your existence. Spend several minutes *realizing* this until your emotional frequency lowers down back into the range of *Emotion*. The more intensely this *Awareness* is applied, the lower the *degree* that is actualized, including a pass-by of the former feelings of indifference, into feelings of anger, rage, perhaps also even fear if a true *realization* is reached that this *object* is suddenly pure **anathema** to your existence, to which point we will eventually be able to be so low that we are complacently "at one" with the *object*, and are subdued by its control. ANALYZE any additional *facets* directly experienced as a result. [This potentially demonstrates your present "full curve" or "*Pitfall*" potential from (2.5) down to (0.1) on the *Emotimeter*.]

PRACTICE shifting your *attitudes* and *emotions* between states as well, making sure before the end of the session to leave yourself in a high-frequency state—though generally indifferent, again, to the *object* itself. The *object* is a focal tool only. YOU can be in control of these states of *Awareness* at will—at any and all times. (And *that* is the goal.) Make certain to end the session at high-frequency *Awareness* after practicing emotional fluctuation.

Practiced self-controlled ability to shift *emotions* (and other *states*) at *Will* by *Intention* is innate and yet not realized equally by all. For some *Seekers*, it requires practice. Logic behind the systematic design of these *Processes* is not always clear at the start, or even always readily apparent at this *Grade*. Bottom line: they yield progressive effective results toward our ultimate goal, and it is for that reason alone that they *are* suggested.

The previous exercise may be applied several times *on the same object* and it may be applied to a different *object* during the same session. You may even use *two objects* at the same time, choosing one to be "positive" and one as "negative" and then alternating focused attention as rapidly (but fully) as you can. To extend this practice further, one would select *two of the exact same object* and apply this alternation, but with arbitrary selectivity of one from the other, named uniquely from *Self*, or as *"Paperweight-A"* and *"Paperweight-B."* These *Objective Processes* draw a *Seeker's* attention toward *Self-Control* of *Emotional* energy.

PROCESSING SELF-DIRECTION OF WILL AND INTENTION

The basic functions of the "Mind-System" all relate to one or another steps regarding:

- Critically Analyzing a Problem or Condition
- Applying and Communicating Energy/Data
- Evaluating Results of Applied Personal Efforts

[*Subjective-Processing (example)*]

—RECALL a moment when you *decided* to *push* against something.

—RECALL the *effort* you applied to actually *push* the object.

—RECALL an instance when you were *pushed* by someone else.

—RECALL the *effort* you applied to actually withstand the push.

[*Objective-Processing (example)*]

—LOOK around and select an object you could move.

—IDENTIFY the object and then *you* touch it.

—DECIDE to apply the *Will-Intention* to move the object.

—APPLY the *Self-Command* that: "You move the object."

—DECIDE to apply the *Effort* to move the object and then *you* move the object.

An individual uses knowledge of previous *efforts* that *Self* has applied in order to gauge future *efforts*. *Fragmentation* is also imprinted from *efforts* that others apply toward us— meaning counter-efforts used against us. Solving problems is a matter of *certainty* combined with *correct* information.

Whenever energy/communication is *fragmented, held-back* or *enforced*, the amount of *certainty* and *information* is diminished along with *Awareness*. Examine a few examples affecting you now in your actual life by listing the first problems entering your thoughts or that have been bothering you, which have not yet been dealt with (or not yet been solved):

A. _____

B. _____

C. _____

D. _____

It is very likely that these lingering problems remain unresolved as a result of *fragmented, withheld* or *missing information*. If you find this is the case, write down the information that would resolve the equation/problem:

A. _____

B. _____

C. _____

D. _____

With these considerations in mind, decide whether or not new information is still necessary to solve the problem. If it is, write down how you might go about determining this information. If new information is not necessary, decide whether or not the problem can be resolved with *Analytical Processing*. If you have already determined the course of actions required to solve the problem, than write down the *Will-Intention* required.

A. _____

B. _____

C. _____

D. _____

Many "problems" a *Seeker* faces in this lifetime are part of basic *Game-conditions* inherent whenever *Self* interacts with the Universe. If a Primary Decision (*Alpha Thought*) is actualized that a "problem is a non-problem," then realization will follow. If, however, an agreement is already made that it *is* a "problem," then a *Seeker* will need to *"Process-out"* or dissolve the original agreement/belief through to its entirety. One cannot label and reinforce something as a "problem" *and then* decide that "oh, well, I guess I won't deal with it" and expect that it won't be problematic later.

Individuals superfluously accumulate an entire museum library full of *beta-problems* with fixed concrete solutions. An individual *uses* this accumulation as a quality of their *beta-personality*. This, too, should be *"Processed-out."* The alternative is holding onto old erroneous "problem-solutions" that later affect solving of problems in the *future*.

Consider any problems faced in the *past* with environmental situations, other individuals and physical masses— problems that you very seriously considered "problems" and which remain unsolved. As previously instructed, list the first such unresolved problems that come into mind:

A. _____

B. _____

C. _____

D. _____

Similar to the treatment of present concerns, write down any *fragmented*, *withheld* or *missing information* that you could have used to resolve this past equation/problem if you had known it at the time.

A. _____

B. _____

C. _____

D. _____

With these considerations kept in mind, decide whether or not this new information has since surfaced to resolve past concern. If it has, write down how you determined this information. If necessary information was never disclosed, decide to resolve past concerns with *Analytical Processing*. If necessary, *process-out* any lingering fragmentation. An unresolved problem is simply an unanswered equation.

ANALYTICAL PROCESSING OF GOALS AND PURPOSES

Failed and unrealized goals are a source of *fragmentation*. This includes goals and purposes that we decide to take on from others. We also have certain *expectations* concerning results of our *Efforts*. When these are misaligned or met with *counter-efforts*, the outcomes change how we accept new inflowing information. This contributes to a "personality" of likes, dislikes, inclinations and tendencies, &tc. Very few of these, if *processed*, will be found as *actual* aims and goals of the "I" or *Alpha Spirit*.

Make a list of all basic "goals" and elaborate "ambitions" which you have *realized* for your life, and perhaps that you are still working to *actualize* in the present (and future).

1. _____
2. _____
3. _____
4. _____
5. _____
6. _____
7. _____
8. _____

Consider all the different people you have encountered in this lifetime—those which you considered "close" to you physically and shared an emotional "liking." Consider those you have shared this "closeness" with—and which have since departed from you, either as a result of death or some permanent disconnection. List these names, each on a numbered line.

1. _____
_____
2. _____
_____
3. _____
_____
4. _____
_____

5. _____
   _____

6. _____
   _____

7. _____
   _____

8. _____
   _____

Consider any unfinished plans, goals, fears and dreams—
realized but not bought to *full actualization (manifestation)*—
for each one and list them below the name. These are the
failures to actualize that you perceived for those closest.

> If you find any of these *failures to actualize* are simil-
> ar to your own present goals or future purposes,
> circle the entire name section and make a note of
> the relationship on your own personal goals list.

If RECALL of any of these individuals (or their relationship
to you) causes emotional reactions or deep distress, then
process-out the entire relationship with this individual to
the fullest *analytical* extent. Do this until you are comfortable recalling memory of them without a stress response.

[*Identity-Phase Processing (example)*]

—RECALL the first memory of when you met ___ .

—RECALL the first instance you made the decision to
   like ___ .

—RECALL any moment you made the decision to
   like ___ .

—RECALL the first instance you made the decision to *be*
   like ___ .

—RECALL any moment you made the decision to *be*
   like ___ .

—RECALL the first instance you *realized* that you *were*
   like ___ .

—RECALL any moment you *realized* that you *were*
   like ___ .

—RECALL the first instance you made the decision to *be sympathetic* toward ___ .

—RECALL any moment you made the decision to *be sympathetic* toward ___ .

—RECALL the first instance you *felt anger* toward ___ .

—RECALL any moment you *felt anger* toward ___ .

—RECALL the first instance you *regretted* something you did to ___ .

—RECALL any moment you *regretted* something you did to ___ .

—RECALL the first instance when you tried to *help* or *assist* ___ .

—RECALL any moment when you tried to *help* or *assist* ___ .

—RECALL the first instance when you successfully *helped* or *assisted* ___ .

—RECALL any moment when you successfully *helped* or *assisted* ___ .

—RECALL an enjoyable event or memory you shared with ___ .

—REPEAT the above processing cycle again. (*Repeat it several times—as needed.*)

—RECALL the instance you started this processing session.

—RECALL the instance you completed the last cycle of processing.

—RECALL the most recent time you enjoyed what you were doing.

PROCESSING BEING AT CAUSE FOR EMOTIONAL EFFECTS

When an individual makes someone else a *cause* through "blame" and "misappropriated responsibility" they lend their own power of *Self-direction*. The more we make others responsible for what happens to us, the less that we are able to manage what is actually within our responsibility. Likewise: the more we consciously accept inappropriate blame and guilt, the greater our emotional *imprinting*. After elevating *Awareness*, a *Seeker* operating at high-frequency can sustain their personal **vibrations** when engaging in communication (even about blame). A fully actualized WILL can confront lower *beta* energies without succumbing to them.

Without *Self-Honesty*, when an individual takes on *beta-experience* of an "ill effect," there is a tendency to quickly assign "blame" and "responsibility" to an external source. It is "natural " for *beta-systems* of *Awareness* to want to *distance Self* as far as possible from "ill effects"—but it is not *Self-Honest*, nor does it promote actualizing *Self*.

—RECALL a moment when you heard someone say the phrase: *You're bringing me down.*

—RECALL a moment when you said the phrase: *You're bringing me down.*

—RECALL a time you saw someone entering a room.

—RECALL an instance you *felt* someone enter a room.

—RECALL a time you saw someone exiting a room.

—RECALL an instance when you *felt* someone leave a room.

—RECALL a time when you *made* someone cry.

—RECALL a time when you were *made* to cry by someone else.

—RECALL an event when you watched someone *make* someone else cry.

—RECALL a moment when you tried to *make* someone feel better and were rejected.

—RECALL a moment when someone tried to *make* you feel better and you rejected them.

—RECALL an event when you watched someone try to *make* someone else feel better and they were rejected.

—RECALL a moment when you tried to *make* someone feel better and succeeded.

—RECALL a moment when someone tried to make you feel better and they succeeded.

—RECALL an event when you watched someone *make* someone else feel better and they succeeded.

—IMAGINE your physical body is enshrouded in a sphere of light.

SELF-DIRECTING WILL WITH OBJECTIVE PROCESSING

If a state or condition is *Self-directed*, created by *Self* and "owned" with responsibility, there is little danger of lasting *fragmentation*. When a *Seeker* is fully *Aware* that *imprints* and *beliefs* are their own creations to form and transform—even recall back energy during *dissolution*—than any constructive use of WILL is limited only to one's own imagination and creative expression—which are *Alpha* qualities.

Seekers may practice energetic work using esoteric methods. An initiate was told to take an "ordinary" object, such as a rock, or small piece of metal—some kind of trinket—and "charge" it with an "intention." The basic principle is always the same: *Self-direction* of *Intention* via *Will*. All that's required, is to bring up, conjure, recall or imagine a certain aspect to the fullest extent of *"Alpha Thought"* that you are able—directing a complete and detailed impression and then releasing it toward the object with the fullest extent of *Will-Intention*. This may be practiced on any neutral object.

(PART A)

—IMAGINE your physical body is enshrouded in a *sphere of light*.

—LOOK around and IDENTIFY a small neutral object you could hold.

—DECIDE that *you will* go and pick up the object; and then *you* do it.

—IMAGINE the object is a **sentient** being that is capable of emotion.

—CREATE the emotional feeling of *happiness/joy* and hold it in Mind.

—WILL the emotional feeling of *happiness/joy* into Being.

—INTEND the object to fully experience *happiness/joy*; and then Will it.

—REPEAT the intention and direction of Will several times until *you* are *certain* that the object is experiencing and expressing *happiness/joy*.

—REPEAT the above four steps using the emotional feeling of *sadness/grief*.

—REPEAT the primary steps using the emotional feeling of *ferocity/anger*.

—REPEAT the primary steps completely, alternating emotional feelings fully, making certain that your own emotional state remains independent of emotional fluctuation. Practice repeatedly. (*End session on a neutral emotion, just as at the start.*)

(PART B)*

—INTEND the object to be *fiercely angry*.

—RESURFACE an emotional feeling of *fear* of the object. ANALYZE any *facets* you associate with this feeling.

—IMAGINE the object is genuinely *afraid* of you.

—RESURFACE an emotional feeling of *anger* toward the object. ANALYZE any *facets* you associate with this feeling.

—INTEND the object to be experiencing *grief-stricken sadness*.

—RESURFACE an emotional feeling of *sympathy* for the object. ANALYZE any *facets* you associate with this feeling.

—IMAGINE the object to be *sympathetic* toward you.

—RESURFACE an emotional feeling of *relief* and *interest*. ANALYZE any *facets* you associate with this feeling.

—INTEND the object to be experiencing *happiness* and *joy*.

—RESURFACE an emotional feeling of *happiness* and *joy*.

---

*   Part-B may be practiced as an extension of the previous Part-A session. If practiced as a separate session, use the first four steps from Part-A to properly establish the *Process*.

ANALYZE any *facets* you associate with this feeling.

—REPEAT the above steps (of PART B) completely several times until you start to feel that you have greater personal management (*Self-control*) of directed emotional energy and the response-reactions tied to emotional energy from external sources.

Goals for this *Processing* are achieved when the *Seeker* has reached a point of personal certainty (knowing) that a Willed *Intention* is carried to action. *Objective processing* always involves increasing the *Seeker's* certainty regarding personal abilities to manage *Self-direction*.

PART C is a basic demonstration of the **axiom** that: "All Intentional Acts are Magical Acts" (as stated by our esoteric predecessors). This process is similar to *earlier* parts, except the goal is to *realize* a direct communication line of *Will-Intention* between the *Seeker* and the *object*. This includes communication of *Will-Intention* as "control" (using *command lines*) and an "acknowledgment," regarding the *object* as endowed with sentient faculties you can contact and *with* motor functions. (The *object* is treated as a living being.) The *Seeker* makes a *Self-directed* command of *Will-Intention* to the *object* to the fullest extent imaginable; then they actually perform the physical action to achieve the desired *effect* and genuinely "thanks" the *object* as to acknowledge the *result*.

<u>A GRADE-III APPROACH TO "A.T." WIZARD LEVELS</u>

"**Collapsing a wave**" is *Awareness* taking a wave of potential states and fixing it as a "peak" or "ridge" of specific arrangement for interaction. we take all that *could be* and make a decision as to what *is*; we make a definitive decision to agree on what something is *to be* in exclusion to that it is *not to be*. It has now become an *effect*. It is solid as we peer down from *Self*. If we now "***flatten***" this obstruction—running it to *process-it-out*—than we can return the "wave" to its original state of potentiality.

We can control WILL and the *effort* produced from emotional energy on command. When you close your eyes,
what do you see? Is it energy patterns? Geometric shapes?
Images from your lifetime or memory? Is it pure blackness? If it is mostly darkness, are there any variations?
Practice taking a "snap-shot" image of whatever you are
seeing in your "**Mind's Eye**"—copying everything you are
able to perceive. WILL a copy of the image to form next to
the original. Do this several times. Stack the copies on top
of each other. What does this do to the sensation and presence of this image? Does the image become more solid and
dense or more transparent and thin?

—IMAGINE your physical body is enshrouded in a
sphere of light.

—LOOK around the room and IDENTIFY an *object* that
you like.

—FOCUS your *attention* solely on the *object* and nothing
else; no other external activity in the environment and
no internal activity in the Mind.

—SIT comfortably and just look for a while, doing your
best to just *be* with the *object* and commit it fully to
your *Awareness* without analyzing any reactions or associations.

—CLOSE your eyes and IMAGINE a copy or facsimile of
the *object* firmly in your Mind's Eye.*

—IMAGINE the facsimile *object* as closely to the original
object as possible.

—WILL the brightness of the *object* to increase; then
WILL the brightness to decrease; then increase again.

—WILL the color of the *object* to change; make it blue;
then turn it red; then change it to green; then return it
to its original color.

—OPEN your eyes and FOCUS your *attention* back solely
on the original *object*.

---

* When realized at *Alpha Awareness* levels, these types of processes
(indicating the "Mind" or "Mind's-Eye") may be conducted from
"Spirit Vision" ("Zu-Vision") as an advanced application.

—WILL the brightness of the *object* to increase; then WILL the brightness to decrease; then increase again.

—WILL the color of the *object* to change; make it blue; then turn it red; then change it to green; then return it to its original color.

—CLOSE your eyes and make facsimile copies of anything that enters your Mind—each time an image or thought enters your mind, IDENTIFY the *image*, then copy it and duplicate it next to the original. DUPLICATE the image again. DUPLICATE the image again. Keep doing this several times until all *Awareness* of the image dissolves.

—OPEN your eyes and FOCUS your *attention* back solely on the original *object*.

—IDENTIFY the *object*, then make a mental facsimile-copy of it in your Mind and duplicate it a few feet in front of you.

—DUPLICATE the image again, placing it behind you.

—DUPLICATE the image again, placing it on your right side.

—DUPLICATE the image again, placing it on your left side.

—DUPLICATE the image again, placing it below your feet.

—DUPLICATE the image again, placing it above your head.

—DISSOLVE the imagery and IMAGINE your physical body is enshrouded in a *sphere of light* before ending the session.

PROCESSING SYMPATHY AND LOW-ENERGY ENCOUNTERS

While there is absolutely nothing wrong with assisting others, there *is* something wrong with succumbing to the same states we were "hoping" to assist. High-energy individuals are able to assist and direct energy toward others without falling prey to such energy circuits—and without further propagating circuits of *fragmented* energy.

—IMAGINE your physical body is enshrouded in a *sphere of light*.

—REVIEW moments during your lifetime when you affirmed *illness* or *personal inability* as an *excuse* to avoid going somewhere you didn't want to *go*.

—ANALYZE your intentions motivating each of these instances. *Where didn't you want to go? Why didn't you want to go? What facets are encoded in this imprint?*

—REVIEW moments during your lifetime when you affirmed *illness* or *personal inability* as an *excuse* to avoid completing a task you didn't want to *do*.

—ANALYZE your intentions motivating each of these instances. *What didn't you want to do? Why didn't you want to do it? What facets are encoded in this imprint?*

—REVIEW moments during your lifetime when you affirmed *illness* or *personal inability* as an *excuse* to avoid participating in a role you didn't want to *be*.

—ANALYZE your intentions motivating each of these instances. *What didn't you want to be? Why didn't you want to be it? What facets are encoded in this imprint?*

—REVIEW moments during your lifetime when you affirmed *illness* or *personal inability* as an *excuse* to avoid accepting something you didn't want to *have*.

—ANALYZE your intentions motivating each of these instances. *What didn't you want to have? Why didn't you want to have it? What facets are encoded in this imprint?*

—REVIEW moments during your lifetime when you exhibited *illness* or *personal inability* as an *effort* to gain *sympathy* or *assistance* from others.

—ANALYZE your intentions motivating each of these instances. *Who did you solicit sympathy from? What was the motivating failure? What efforts did that person provide —and what did they do?*

—RESURFACE any *sensations* or *facets* associated with each of these event-instances. ANALYZE any emotion expressed by others—and your own emotional response to their *efforts*. ANALYZE any statements verbalized by others—*and* your own thoughts associated with their *intentions*.

—REVIEW moments during your lifetime when you expressed *sympathy* or *sympathetic effort* in a response to *assist* another being's *Beingness*. [This includes any living organism, physical object or creation.]

—ANALYZE your intentions motivating each of these instances. *What failures motivated a response? Who/What did you provide sympathy to? What efforts did you express—and what did they result as?*

—RESURFACE any *sensations* or *facets* associated with each of these event-instances. ANALYZE any emotion you expressed in your effort—*and* the other's emotional response. ANALYZE any thoughts associated with your *intentions—and* any verbal statements expressed by others in response to your efforts.

—IMAGINE the scene of an *injured child.* —REVIEW your level of *sympathy* and sympathetic effort or emotional response. —ANALYZE how you could *help* this situation.

—IMAGINE the scene of an *injured parent.* —REVIEW your level of *sympathy* and sympathetic effort or emotional response toward. —ANALYZE what you could do to *help* this situation.

—IMAGINE the scene of an *injured beloved pet.* —REVIEW your level of *sympathy* and sympathetic effort or emotional response toward. —ANALYZE what you could do to *help* this situation.

—IMAGINE the scene of a *burning forest.* —REVIEW your level of *sympathy* and sympathetic effort or emotional response toward. —ANALYZE what you could do to *help* this situation.

—IMAGINE the scene of an *injured stranger.* —REVIEW your level of *sympathy* and sympathetic effort or emotional response toward. —ANALYZE what you could do to *help* this situation.

—RECALL a time you successfully assisted another being and felt relief and satisfaction of *directing* the *cause* of *effects*. RECALL many pleasant times. End the session.

GRADE-IV
METAHUMAN DESTINATIONS TECHNIQUES
EXTRACTED FROM LIBER-3C

PROCESSING PROBLEMS AS A GOALS-BASED PROTEST

We approach the subject of "Human Problems" as an extension of *"Communication Processing."* "Protest"—as a communication barrier—contributes to fragmentation when it operates as a "compulsive" mechanism. Early implants were installed prior to *Self* taking on a stringent Human Condition POV; they stem from deeply seeded imprinting that falls within the domain of "past lives."

If we consider the POV from *Self*, the systematic processing to reduce charge on imprinted channels that are presently engaged in "protest" and/or "rejection" (especially as an automatic tendency), would run repeatedly as follows until a Seeker resumes control over the "communication barrier."

1: What is it that you are protesting?

2: How have you communicated that protest?

3: Who should be acknowledging your communication?

A.T.: (*Visualize the terminal accepting the communication.*)

A Seeker begins with most recent and easily accessible examples, then processes them out. It may very well be the case that an earlier similar "protest" or "rejection" appears from an earlier incident or event. This begins a personal journey of exploration into various degrees of higher and higher barriers that have been generated and agreed to over time. It did not happen all at once.

Whatever state a *Seeker* is in today, they did not arrive there overnight. And systematic imprinting and programming is laid in or keyed in differently for each individual. Encoding is embedded to a line of implanted systems programming that is generally found similar across the board of all individuals; although an individual may be found to dramatize different phases of various "goals" and "roles."

After the *Seeker* has worked effectively through the most accessible events regarding "protest" and "rejection" of communications from *other* terminals and source-points, the same systematic techniques can be used to approach circuits on each direction of flow regarding, in this case, terminals representing "protest" and "rejection." For example—

1 : "What is (*terminal*) protesting/rejecting about you?"
2 : "How are they communicating that?"
3 : "Who should acknowledge them?"

This can even be applied to the third sphere of existence regarding mass communications of society as a whole, such as: "What are *others* protesting about *others*?" and so on. The time-tense of the PCL can be changed to "have" instead of "are" in order to better apply to past instances if necessary (only after "present" ones have been reduced).

Self not only goes out of communication with other "living" terminals or entities, but also its own "things" and "creations." This manifests greater pain and illness when identifying too closely with a physical body or genetic organism itself. When an individual experiences "pain" tied to a specific part of the physical body or even a physical locale, the reactive-response tendency is to "avoid" such; which the RCC assumes its doing us a favor by manipulating perceptions of reality to demonstrate the best chances of material survival. It simply registers everything that is connected to imprints of 'pain' or 'loss' as "to be avoided," rejected and protested *automatically*, and therein lies the fragmentation.

A Pilot can apply this basic systematic processing formula to defragment channels at each of sphere of existence. For example: "What have you protested about that physical body?" "What have you protested about your home? Family?" "What have you protested about your career?" "What have you protested about your organization? Church? Neighborhood? City?" "What have you protested about the Human Condition? Life on Earth?" ...and so on.

When tendencies, patterns or compulsions manifest in this lifetime, which appear to be outside of the Seeker's control, our current practice is to begin with *Analytical Recall* ("Route-2") and determine what the mechanism is a response to. It may require some repetitive inquiries before the "Mind" sheds its veil on better answers; and it may very well be that these answers seem utterly ridiculous to the present lifetime or even *this* Physical Universe.

It may be too far of a reach to simply ask a *Seeker* "What are you protesting with that behavior?" or "What were you protesting when you started doing such and such?"— but you may be able to approach the truth with the PCL: "What could you protest by doing *X*?" Get the Seeker to come up with some possible reasons why they would have set up that communication line in the first place. You may not be able to eliminate the original "Alpha" nature of an implant by processing events from *this* lifetime, but you *can* discharge some of the energy that keeps an individual from being able to ever reach back any further.

CONSIDERATIONS OF ACCEPTANCE AND REJECTION

Tendencies toward "acceptance" or "rejection" are tied to closeness and proximity, or else willingness to keep something close; meaning it would be safe to keep close. When we are dealing with tendencies and reactive-response mechanisms, keep in mind that these are all originally built upon a **premise** of logic that was structured for survival. That which was deemed "safe" or would contribute to survival was deemed "acceptable." This is all fine and good until it begins to have its values assigned (or "determined") on an automatic or reactive basis that eliminates *Actualized Awareness* of *Self*. In the past we alternately have asked Seekers "What could you accept about *X*?" and "What could you reject about *X*?" until they realize that whatever they are rejecting, blocking, not wanting or avoiding is all based on past emotional imprinting. In other words, the "threat to survival" is not clear and present, but instead cast up into one's reality as a reactive-response with mental imagery intended to control thought and action in place of a Self-determined Alpha Spirit.

A "Route-3" PCL formula may be used to discharge some fragmentation on these channels. After running the process on general events, the *term* "someone else" could be replaced with another appropriate "terminal" requiring specific attention. These PCLs are alternated within each circuit to prevent from getting "mentally spun" running only negative command lines.

Circuit-1: What wouldn't (someone else) want you to present to them?

What have you presented to (someone else)?

Circuit-2: What wouldn't you want (someone else) to present to you?

What has (someone else) presented to you?

Circuit-3: What wouldn't (someone else) want others to present to them?

What has (someone else) presented to others?

The same methods used to defragment channels of events during *this* lifetime may be further applied to access deeper laden implant data carried between lifetimes. In some experiments involving past lives, or spiritual **continuum** (*Backtrack*), the first two circuits are reversed to see if any further information is gleaned concerning motivators.

ACCESSING HIGHER REALIZATIONS WITH SELF-HONESTY

When we speak of willingness to communicate, reach, accept, help &tc., we are not enforcing any moral ethic on what an individual *should do*. What we discovered is that unwillingness on any lines is a point of other-determined control. We tend to add more solidity to that which we are rejecting and protesting. Ability to freely alter considerations and evaluations allows *Self* to *know* they are doing it.

You don't have to agree with the way things are in the world; and you don't have to like "so-and-so" enough to want to be around them; and you don't have to necessarily become a "teacher" or "law enforcer"; and you don't necessarily have to be a "vegetarian" or sit through long lessons about "math, science and history"... but shouldn't you be freely able to consider any of these things willingly without some automated response-mechanism kicking in and taking command of your attention, focus, energy and behavior? You can practice this fluidity easily enough by **repetitively** using the following formula with whatever you may find that you are protesting with a lot of emotional energy. This can also be practiced as an objective processing exercise on arbitrary (neutral) items.

> —*Contact* the channel of mental energy connected with the "terminal" or "condition" that you are protesting.
> —Get the *Sense* (or POV) that <u>you</u> are "protesting" X.
> —Get the *Sense* (or POV) that <u>you</u> are "admiring" X.
> —Get the *Sense* (or POV) that <u>you</u> are "creating" X.

If this is not effective after several runs through the process, it may be that the content of the channel needs to be handled on a gradient scale; meaning that perhaps too "large" or "general" of a terminal is being processed. Keep in mind that a *Seeker* can only reduce emotional charge on *facets* and *imprints* related to events that they are prepared to "confront" as they actually are, not just as they seem to be from a fragmented state.

When you are blocking, inhibiting, rejecting or protesting a line of communication, *you are doing* something. This is a projection of energy and active use of creative spiritual ability. This is far and beyond simple "dislike" or "disinterest" of some creation. This literally creates a spiritual "beam" of energy; a wave of personal emotional energy that is sent out *in response* to another **waveform** so as to keep it at a distance. This, of course, also creates an additional layer to the individualized concept of "distance" within one's personal universe, and therefore "space."

Anything you want to actively keep out of your "personal space" or "personal universe" is being *protested against.* While this may have first started out Self-determined and freely chosen, the patterned tendencies developed into their automatic mechanisms relying on personal creative power. By taking over **responsibility** for creative ability, to be at every point-of-view, and yet not remain fixed or reactive to any, the freedom to selectively apply these energies—at Will—is rightly returned to *Self.*

CONCEPTUAL PROCESSING OF HUMAN PROBLEMS

In this first set of PCLs we are dealing with "concepts" and the intention or spiritual consideration behind them, which is to say "sense." We are not asking for any specific concrete imagery to come to mind; we are simply asking a *Seeker* to *get a sense of a concept.* In esoteric terms, we are asking to "conjure" or "evoke" to Mind, because in actuality, it is always *Self* that produces the *sense of a concept*—so we want to practice this knowingly.

These PCLs are applied following instructions given for *SOP-2C* and "*Route-3*" and guidelines for "*Route-2.*" A *Seeker* or *Pilot* should work one "circuit" through (alternating positive and negative flows) until it is handled with ease (before working with the next one). Then after working through all the circuits, a return to the first one again is beneficial because it may be treated at a "higher level" of understanding than formerly.

Circuit-1: Contact a sense of solving a problem.

Contact a sense of not solving a problem.

Another example of this PCL could be stated:

Circuit-1: Get the concept of solving a problem.

Get the concept of not solving a problem.

The idea of "contacting a feeling" or "conjuring the idea" is also acceptable for beginners. Whatever PCL pattern is selected, the same should be used throughout each circuit.

Circuit-2: Get a sense of (*terminal*) solving a problem.

Get a sense of (*terminal*) not solving a problem.

Circuit-3:   Get the sense of others solving a problem.

Get the sense of others not solving a problem.

It may be, without supplemental book instruction, that a *Seeker* in session will need to work up to the idea of even treating the subject of problems.

Circuit-1:   What (is a) problem could you confront?

Or using another style of PCL—

Circuit-1:   What problem would be acceptable for you to confront?

Following the *Route-3* formula, this PCL series continues—

Circuit-2:   What problem could (another/ terminal) confront?

Circuit-3:   What problem could others confront?

Even small "problems" are quite challenging for some Seekers to approach, simply because they are still hung up on basic semantics associated (and encoding) to even the very word "problem." For some Seekers, being directed with a PCL that implies confronting the entire problem is too steep of a gradient. A solitary Seeker can easily become hung up on a part of the processing with no other expert advice or support on how to move through it. So as an alternative, the *Seeker* can consider (or be directed by a *Pilot* to consider) some type of problem and then inquire as to "what part of the problem" a *Seeker* could confront. It may be that even small problems must be confronted in pieces until an individual develops the certainty to manage the whole package.

A similar exercise is applied to increase the range of considerations regarding the conception of "problems" and "solutions." After the object has been properly *identified* (as a "terminal") for processing, the following PCL are run similar to the first process in this chapter-lesson.

Circuit-1:   How could (terminal) be a problem to you?

How could (terminal) be a solution to you?

Circuit-2:   How could (terminal) be a problem to (other terminal)?

How could (terminal) be a solution to (other terminal)?

Circuit-3:   How could others be a problem to (terminal)?

How could others be a solution to (terminal)?

Circuit-AT: How could you be a problem to (terminal)?

How could you be a solution to (terminal)?

Some of the answers to these may seem hard to come up with at first, but when considerations expand, even more ridiculous answers can be accepted as an increased realization that it is *Self* determining these evaluations, now and always.

Another "objective processing" technique that may be employed between "subjective processes" could include the same or similar item with the intent that a Seeker invents ways in which the object is the answer or solution. In fact, this technique can be applied to problem terminals just as usefully as it can be applied to creative practice.

Circuit-1:   What problem could you have with someone with which (terminal) is the solution?

Circuit-2:   What problem could someone have with you with which (terminal) is the solution?

Circuit-3:   What problem could others have with someone with which (terminal) is the solution?

Circuit-0:   What problem could you have with yourself with which (terminal) is the solution?

Δ Δ Δ Δ Δ Δ

Our intention is to get a Seeker to increase their willingness and ability to solve problems by understanding that they can just as easily create conditions for the problem as the solution simply by reassigning evaluations. This is an ability true to the actual state of the Alpha Spirit, always.

PROCESSING "CHANGES" AND WILLINGNESS TO CHANGE

Ability to manage "change of energy"—which includes *all motion* of energy—is characterized by a willingness and certainty to channel energies, which is *not* here used in the same sense the mystics may have referred to channeling entities in the past. The "channel" here implies application to "communication" semantics, regarding personal energy and its interaction with "terminals." This means the *Self-directed* intention to "hold energy" and "move energy"; which we can apply demonstrations of as "objective processing" in material existence.

"Change"—and *alteration* in general—is a basic property of systematic control. Other than the initial start and stop of a flow or circulation of energy, about the only other thing energy actually does within and as any system is "change." Even the motion of energy itself is a "change" in state or location, which creates a flow-pattern that we measure in cyclic waves and generally define as "time." The concept of change may also be applied to processing a "terminal."

Circuit-1:	Get the sense of changing something. \ Get the sense of stopping something from changing.
Circuit-1:	Recall a time you changed something. \ Recall a time you stopped something from changing.
Circuit-2:	Recall a time when (*terminal*) changed something. \ Recall a time when (*terminal*) stopped something form changing.
Circuit-1:	What would you be willing to have changed in "another"?[‡]
Circuit-2:	What would you be willing to have another change in you?

[‡]   This terminal is generally treated as "another person," though it could also be treated as any other "lifeform" or even the Spheres of Existence; or else a "turbulent terminal" is processed

Circuit-3:   What would you be willing to have
               another change in others?
A.T. (*Opt.*): What would you be willing to change
               in yourself?

The Mind-System has a unique way of collecting and registering its data; in both instances, acting as a mirror and crystalline lens between the "observer" and the "observed." These mechanisms all act to create, store and display "mental images" which are essentially *facsimiles* or *copies* of what is registered as experience of existence. The motion of energies captured on these images is what gives a sequential record of "time."

An individual goes along thinking and acting as though such and such just *must be* the case so much, even against all odds, that they are unwilling to channel any other energy free-flow. They come up hard against objective the reality of other energies with repeated personal invalidation. The mere unwillingness to *be* in any other POV is going to give them a difficult situation to manage and contribute to an existential demise; because we know that the willingness and ability to manage and adjust to all conditions freely is the key to our continued survival and upward progression.

Circuit-1:   What *could* you change?
               What *would* you leave unchanged?
Circuit-2:   What *could* change you?
               What *would* leave you unchanged?
Circuit-3:   What *could* change others?
               What *would* leave others unchanged?
A.T. (Opt.):   What *could* you change about you?
               What *would* you leave unchanged
               about you?

Objective processing may be applied using the same formula, simply having a Seeker look around the room, locating and identifying what they could change and what they would be willing to have remain unchanged. Essentially, the underlying *realization* behind all of this is to demonstrate a fluid acceptance about the state of conditions taking place in one's environment. Eventually use the term "accept" and "reject" again, since these words similarly qualify but often carry heavier emotional encoding.

Circuit-1:	Get a sense of you changing X.
	Get a sense of not changing X.
Circuit-2:	Get a sense of X. changing you.
	Get a sense of X. not changing you.
Circuit-3:	Get a sense of others changing X.
	Get a sense of others not changing X.
Circuit-1:	What do you want changed about X?
	What do you want to remain about X?
Circuit-2:	What does X. want changed about you?
	What does X. want to remain about you?
Circuit-3:	What does X. want changed about *others*?[‡]
	What does X. want to remain about *others*?

An individual can certainly decide to change something, but on their own determinism and not simply because they are compelled to or even forced to by other-determined factors. Willingness to change is often what empowers one to handle opposition.

Likewise, willingness for things to remain as they are also puts us in a position of acceptance and the ability to knowingly create, copy or duplicate something, again entirely on one's own determinism and without the obsessive need to repeat an action.

These are some of the most critical skills of proper energy handling that seem to have escaped most mystical esoteric schools in the past. . . *They directly lead a Seeker to metahuman destinations. . .*

---

‡ Alternatively, "What do others want changed about *X*?" or else "Others" can be treated as a "Sphere of Existence" terminal. The additional A.T. Circuit-0 would include *X* as *Self (to Self)*.

BETA-DEFRAGMENTATION OF THE "HELP" BUTTON

To engage or receive help from any sphere is to be in communication with it and to be willing to freely give and receive help—which is a high level of communication—on those channels. We could just as plainly state that the resolution of beta-fragmentation regards the handling of communication, problems, protest, change and willingness —and the common point that employs all of these is snow-capped with this concept of "help and assistance."

A sense of "betrayal" is often inherent in failed efforts, failed communications, failed change and ways we have become fragmented on the communication channels regarding help and assistance. "Failed help" does not just mean a failure *to* help, or apply the intention to *help*. What prompts this imprint pattern is when we did make those intended attempts in the past and the efforts failed; or when others genuinely intended to help us but it seemed that it didn't work out. These "experiences" start to get added up and associated with the concept of help, just as much as any other imprinting or programming. The Mind associates our ability to help with our ability to reach.

When processing is expanded to include general "terminals" as opposed to specific events, incidents and persons, we approach a wider range of potential *recall* in our processing. This is what immediately led to our research in exploring "past lives" (*Backtrack*). For example, processing of "parents" or "bosses" as a terminal accesses more of the Mind-system than only treating a specific target from *this* life, such as your specific biological or adoptive parent from *this* life, or an employer from *this* life, &tc.

By tapping into the greater content of a "terminal" with a broad approach, there are reactive-response tendencies and programming that may **resurface** that just don't seem to fit with events and memories of this lifetime. This becomes the entire subject of our forthcoming Grade-V.

PCLs for systematic "help processing" use the same circuit pattern methodology applied to "*Route-3*" and "*Route-2*."

The "Route-3" approach often allows for more creative answers that are not restricted to a specific time something happened. When we use a PCL with "*could*" or "*would,*" we are in no way insisting action—only considerations, and whether or not they are reactive (automated-responses).

Circuit-1:   Who (or what) would you be willing to help?

Who (or what) would be acceptable for you to help? (*Alternative version*)

Circuit-2:   Who (or what) would you be willing to have help you?

Who (or what) would you be willing to accept help from? (*Alternative version*)

Circuit-3:   Who (or what) would you be willing to have others help?

Who (or what) would be acceptable for others to help? (*Alternative version*)

The most basic systematic processing we have on these lines has run in "New Thought" circles for nearly one-hundred years. The most important part of defragmentation is clearing predisposed inclinations and associations that close off our communicative energies along the channels we are connected to. Only once these are all opened up can we hope to be free of the fixed considerations that hold the abilities of the Mind-System to *this* Physical Universe. So, we have the *Pilot* direct a five-way series of PCLs that should get a Seeker over the basic humps of help.

Circuit-1:   How could you help "someone else" (*terminal*)?

Circuit-2:   How could "someone else" (*terminal*) help you?

Circuit-3(a):   How could "someone else" (*terminal*) help others?

Circuit-3(b):   How could "someone else" (*terminal*) help themselves?

Circuit-AT: How could you help yourself?

Instead of processing the general idea of "communicating with" such and such a terminal (or sphere or object or concept), we are using "helping" as an active expression of high-level communication.

Circuit-1:	Get the sense of you helping "someone else" (*terminal*)?
Circuit-2:	Get the sense of "someone else" (*terminal*) helping you?
Circuit-3(a):	Get the sense of "someone else" (*terminal*) helping others?
Circuit-3(b):	Get the sense of "someone else" (*terminal*) helping themselves?
Circuit-AT:	Get the sense of you helping yourself?

It is obvious that the RCC has registered and imprinted many "failures" and "losses" onto our stores of experience and memory—but it has not always been found to be the best route of systematic defragmentation to exclusively process out turbulence with commands that focus on "failure." If you start running the Seeker with PCLs on all the times everything has failed, you're just going to get them spun and shut down to where they don't want to communicate at all. This is a dangerous point to reach since all of our systematic processing is rooted in communication.

There are lower levels of processing one could scrape at here if necessary. All we need to do is go back into our arsenal of PCLs and start plugging in "help." Most of them will work. For example, you could theoretically run something as basic as "What help could you accept?" and "What help can you reject?" up to a point where the Seeker understands that they should not automatically reject any consideration of true help.

If you want to link this work with problems, you might use something like "What problem *could* your help be to another?" or even "What problem *has* your help been to another?" if you are approaching it from the *Analytical Recall* angle. If you do this, make certain to then apply the other circuits from "*Route-3*" for a full *beta-defragmentation* regimen, such as "What problem another's help has been to them" and so forth. Once you understand the patterns inherent in the PCLs of our systematic processing, it becomes easier to apply the right type or level of processing to the individual.

When dealing with the *Backtrack* implants, we cannot completely get around the energy attached to "failed help," but that isn't the wording that we plug into our PCLs. You combine *Recall* with "*Route-3*" and alternate "help" and "no help" on each circuit. You may need to state the PCL as "given help" and "not given help" or "giving no help."

There is also those situations of betrayal by certain social roles that are supposed to help but don't and then we cut off lines of communication and put up blocks because we don't see how we can help them any longer either.

Circuit-1: What help have you given to (another)?
What help have you not given to (another)?

Circuit-2: What help has (another) given to you?
What help has (another) not given to you?

Circuit-3: What help has (another) given others?
What help has (another) not given to others?

Circuit-0: What help have you given yourself?
What help have you not given yourself?

This general formula works pretty well with all terminals and Spheres of Existence. This could be run on any terminal that symbolizes the various Spheres of Existence and influence, primarily: mother, father, or parent, guardian; child, stranger; spouse or lover; teacher; healer or doctor; priestess, priest or even holy man; policeman, states official; and the Green World of the animal kingdom and nature as well. There has been a communication break between the Human Condition and the planet Earth as a living organism and all of its creatures for far far too long. When I am asked about Help? How to help? You processing others. Teaching others to process others. You getting processed. But above all else—HELP ONE ANOTHER!

GRADE-IV
UTILITARIAN PROCESSING TECHNIQUES EXTRACTED FROM LIBER-3E

"FORGIVENESS" ON THE PATHWAY TO SELF-HONESTY

Forgiveness is treated at a high order of meaning, next to "Understanding." It suggests that one *understands* something "*As-it-Is*." In systematic processing, "Forgiveness" is a *concept*, not a *terminal*, because it is not a "mass" (object) or even an "energetic-mass" (implant). It is, however, descriptive of the quality of a channel (to a terminal) or personal significance given to an "energetic-mass" by consideration. Therefore, when applied in processing:—

| The *concept* of "Forgiveness" *may be run on* a terminal. |

What we are dealing with is another avenue for "release" of "emotional encoding" and "freedom from" fragmentation. It is, essentially, letting go of the hold on, or a rigid fixed attachment to, the space-time-event that has already passed and survived. An unprocessed fragmented state tends to stick one's POV in treating experiences of the present time environment as if the previous conditions are still present in it.

| "*Failed Help*" and "*Betrayal*" are the two aspects contributing greatest to the collapse of communication channels with any relevant terminal—and further to entire *Spheres of Existence*. They are detrimental to Ascension. They individuate a person away from higher Spheres and put them in a position to think and act as if they are the only one. |

Whether applying solo-exercises or receiving formal *Piloting*, an individual should get a sense of "relief" by confronting their actions—and should understand that they are *forgiven*. If this acknowledgment is not positively received, or a *Seeker* is still feeling heavy emotion, it is likely that only part of a *Hold-Out* or *Harmful-Act* has been confronted or processed. Acceptance of "Forgiveness" is then an excellent monitoring tool regarding the completeness of Route-3E-type applications.

In order to pursue upper-level Wizard-Grades with full effectiveness, a *Seeker* simply cannot have attentions still rigidly fixated on *guilt, Hold-Outs* or low-level *justification cycles* of any kind. Thus, we impress achievement of *Self-Honesty* more strongly.

The most direct "Route-0" *forgiveness* PCLs include:

A.) IMAGINE you are treating others with *forgiveness*.

B.) IMAGINE others are treating you with *forgiveness*.

C.) IMAGINE others treating others with *forgiveness*.

An advanced (*A.T.*) "Circuit-0" application would include the concept of *Self-Forgiveness*, or else "treating *Self* with *forgiveness*." Ultimately this is what it all leads up to: each individual having to fully let themselves *off the hook* from stored/charged energies of what has happened in the past.

When we consider how long the Alpha Spirit has existed—how many Universes it has occupied, how many roles it has identified with—it is not surprising that each of us has *done* virtually all you can possibly think of *doing*—both good or bad. It is also not very surprising that many of us would rather choose to forget a lot of the misdeeds. Apparently, there are *Hold-Outs* we *Hold-Back* from ourselves. Of course, these accumulate—building up energetic-mass over time—and often conceal or close off channels with various Spheres of Existence and entire Universes. Somehow or another, this is the case for each and every one of us involved with this whole mess of operating (or entrapment to) the Human Condition in the Physical Universe.

> An individual decides "I don't want to know"
> and winds up on the effect end of a Mystery.

Ethics Processing allows a *Seeker* the freedom to consider a wider range of possibilities that are not restricted to *known* (consciously recalled) events from this lifetime. Often times there are some nearly-automatic practically-reactive "ideas" that one has regarding personal events on the *Backtrack*. Without need of validation or concern about whether one's speculations are accurate, *Route-0* may be used to treat real matters that remain just below the surface of *Awareness*. If the imagined event is fictitious, *Creativeness Processing* will add greater fluidity to considerations a *Seeker* maintains on the line, which is still progress. However, if the imagined event does, in fact, include facets of an actual event (even if "out of sight") than the processing can actually assist in resurfacing more of what is hidden— or at least, provide a very real sense of relief and release.

> Circuit-1 — What *Harmful-Act* "might" you have done?
> \ IMAGINE yourself being *forgiven* for it.
>
> Circuit-2 — What *Harmful-Act* "might" others have done to you?
> \ IMAGINE them being *forgiven* for it.
>
> Circuit-3 — What *Harmful-Act* "might" another have done to others?
> \ IMAGINE them being *forgiven* for it.
>
> Circ-0/A.T. — What *Harmful-Act* "might" you have done to yourself?
> \ IMAGINE you *forgiving* your Self for it.

ROUTE-3E ETHICS/INTEGRITY PROCESSING: HOLD-OUTS

To our existing array of PCLs, we have but to add "*Hold-Outs*" to each of the series. For example: where we have *Communication Demanded* of others, of us, and cross-flow; then *Communication Rejected* by others, by us, and cross-flow; we then add *Communication Held-Out* on others, on us, and cross-flow.

A Grade-III or early Grade-IV *Seeker* may need to have explained that a "*Hold-Out*" is an intentional inhibition, withdrawal or refusal to reach, communicate or connect. PCLs are not effective if a *Seeker* is uncertain of a word's meaning, or if the meaning they associate is misapplied.

> Initially, we are not as concerned with targeting justifications (or excuses) in basic "Route-3/3E" as much as we are interested in distinguishing imprinted considerations (and *facets*) of a particular space-time event as separate from present-time

|and present-environments. Personal computations
|and justifications are often revealed when properly
|processing (more accessible) considerations.

Circuit-1 — RECALL a time you *held-out* communication on someone.

Circuit-2 — RECALL a time someone *held-out* communication on you.

Circuit-3 — RECALL a time someone *held-out* communication on another.

Notice that some existing *Grade-IV* PCLs already cover similar ground. *"Inhibited Communication,"* where an individual is demanding someone *not* communicate with someone or some thing, is the same as *"Enforced Hold-Outs."*

Circuit-1 — RECALL a time you *held-out* on liking someone.‡

Circuit-2 — RECALL a time someone *held-out* on liking you.

Circuit-3 — RECALL a time someone *held-out* on liking another (or others).

Circuit-1 — RECALL a time you *held-out* on agreeing with someone.

Circuit-2 — RECALL a time someone *held-out* on agreeing with you.

Circuit-3 — RECALL a time someone *held-out* on agreeing with another (or others).

EXPANDED DEFRAGMENTATION OF THE "HELP" BUTTON

"Route-3C" (*Grade-IV*) closed with considering various persons, places and terminals (even *Spheres of Existence*) with the aspect: "HELP." We considered "willingness to help," "help given" and "help not given," but focused on mostly "positive" expressions. We did not touch upon more serious detrimental imprinting regarding *"Failed Help."* This facet (or aspect) and *"Betrayal"* are the two key *hot-buttons* from *Grade-IV Processing* that **correlate** the most to *Harm-*

---

‡   Or "something"; or a specific charged terminal, if applicable.

ful-Acts and *Hostile-Motivation* in *Ethics*. In turn, these are the avenues leading to close-off reality channels (total "*Hold-Back*") in an existing Universe. These PCL may be used during the earlier series of "Help" if the individual is not gaining new realizations with that aspect; otherwise they are standard practice for a *Route-3E* Ethics-cleanup prior to Grade-V.

Circuit-1 — How has your *help* been a *problem* to another?
\ Tell me about it. (*Two-Way Comm.*)

Circuit-2 — How has another's *help* been a *problem* to you?
\ Tell me about it. (*Two-Way Comm.*)

Circuit-3 — How has another's *help* been a *problem* to others?
\ Tell me about it. (*Two-Way Comm.*)

C-0/A.T. — How as *helping* yourself been a *problem* to you?
\ Tell me about it. (*Two-Way Comm.*)

It is important for a *Seeker* to realize that there are *no real problems* with actual *Help*. A "problem" is two *flows*, postulates, goals, modes, considerations (&tc.) directly in conflict with one another. We are mostly concerned now with flattening any turbulence on the lines of *Help*, correcting and defragmenting a *Seeker's* willingness to reach at terminals that they have had difficulties with. This includes general *facets*, those similar terminals that are tangled up a cross-association with a "past failure."

> By processing general terminals rather than only specific names, the range of consideration for application is increased to include other earlier similar aspects that could be contacted. Early on, this is also one of the keys to tapping into memory of "past-lives" (*Backtrack*)—or other "hidden data" that has not yet resurfaced about *this* lifetime.

The following are processed by running alternate PCLs of each circuit repeatedly to a satisfaction or realization before treating the next circuit.

Circuit-1 — How might you reject another's *help*?
\ How might you fail to *help* another?

Circuit-2 — How might another reject your *help*?
\ How might another fail to *help* you?

Circuit-3 — How might another reject *help* from others?
\ How might you fail to *help* others?

C-0/A.T. — How might you reject *helping* yourself?
\ How might you fail to *help* yourself?

Experiencing *"Failed Help"* and/or perceived *"Betrayal"* promotes (or prompts) *Hold-Outs* and *Hold-Backs*— fragmentation, *"justifications"* (*illogical computations*), *"Self-created disabilities"* and *"motivations"* (*hostility*).

In the systematic process below, make note of all names and terminals that surface. Turbulent terminals should have the original "help" series run on them afterward.

Circuit-1 — Who have you intended to *help*?
\ Who have you intended not to *help*?

Circuit-2 — Who has *helped* you?
\ Who has intended not to *help* you?

Circuit-3 — Who has *helped* others?
\ Who has intended not to *help* others?

C-0/A.T. — How have you *helped* yourself?
\ How have you intended not to *help* yourself?

ROUTE-3E PROCESSING: BASIC CONCEPTUAL PROCEDURE

Key Concepts (Hot-Buttons) for Route-OE Ethics Processing—"IN-VALIDATING" "BEING CRITICAL" "WORRYING" "ATTACKING" "HOLDING BACK" "FAILING TO HELP" "LOSING CONTROL" *and* "MISCOMMUNICATING."

** When using a *Biofeedback Device*, it is important to check each individual word of a PCL for existing charge prior to use in session processing. Every series or process should begin with a communication between *Pilot* and

Seeker regarding what process is about to be run and the words used for it. It is possible that one of these buttons or concepts carries a *charge* on its own; it is also possible to get charge-reads on a misunderstood word. **

[Run the entire process inserting the same "*Key-Concept*" in the blanks. Flatten any significant turbulence on a *circuit* before leaving off of it for another. Record notes regarding any contacted or surfacing thoughts, memories, realizations or additional *Harmful-Acts*, *Hold-Backs*, *Hold-Outs* and other charges discovered on channels to terminals, communication-circuits, **phases**/identities, *Spheres*, and so on. *Ethics Processing* is a *Seeker's* best chance to get everything out in the open—to confront, handle and discharge everything accessible *As-it-Is*, prior to upper-level *Wizard Grade* checkouts and further ("*A.T.*") *Actualization-Ascension Tech*.]

Circuit-1 — Get the concept* of ___ *something*.‡
\ Get the concept of not ___ *something*.
\ Get the concept of *something* being ___ .

Circuit-2 — Get the concept of another ___ *something*.
\ Get the concept of another not ___ *something*.
\ Get the concept of *something* being ___ to another.

Circuit-3 — Get the concept of others ___ *something*.
\ Get the concept of others not ___ *something*.
\ Get the concept of *something* being ___ to others.

C-0/A.T. — Get the concept of ___ yourself about *something*.
\ Get the concept of not ___ yourself about *something*.
\ Get the concept of *something* being ___ to yourself.

---

*   If needed, the alternative standard patter is "Get the idea of..."
‡   The PCL can be left general ("*something*") unless there is a particular terminal (person, animal, place, thing) that is assessed as heavily "charged"—preferably "reading"/"indicating" as such on a mechanical *'Biofeedback'* GSR-metering device.

After running *Expanded Route-0E Conceptual Processing* to a completion, the next step is to run the same *"Key Concepts"* with *Basic-Conceptual Route-0E*. Emphasis here returns specifically back to *Self*—what has *out-flowed* "from" and *in-flowed* "to" the *First Sphere of Existence*, representing the perceived position and POV of *Self* experiencing *Existence*.

Circuit-1   — Get the concept of ___ .
           \ Get the concept of not ___ .

Circuit-2   — Get the concept of another ___ you.
           \ Get the concept of another not ___ you.

Circuit-3   — Get the concept of others ___ something.
           \ Get the concept of others not ___ something.

C-0/A.T.   — Get the concept of you ___ yourself.
           \ Get the concept of you not ___ yourself.

ROUTE-3E PROCESSING: BASIC EXISTENTIAL PROCEDURE

Basic Terminals (as Sphere-Representations) for Ethics Processing—(1) "YOUR BODY"; (2) "SEX" "CHILDREN" "FAMILY" "HOME"; (3) "WORK" "COMMUNITY" "A 'TYPE' OF PERSON"; (4) "SOCIETY" "HUMAN SPECIES"; (5) "ANIMALS" "NATURE"/"ENVIRONMENT" "PLANET EARTH"; (6) "A 'TYPE' OF OBJECT OR MACHINE" "SOLAR PLANETARY SYSTEMS" "GALAXIES" "PHYSICAL UNIVERSE." Treating higher *Spheres* such as (7) "SPIRITS" *&tc.*; (8) "RELIGION" *&tc.* are also important, especially given the *'religio-mystical'* backgrounds many *Seekers* have before finding the *Pathway* with our Systemology.

Advanced Wizard-Level Applications—this same formula may be applied to upper-level work to handle terminals representative of the *"Arcs of Infinity"* (upper-Alpha *Spheres* beyond "8" on the Standard Model of Beta-Existence for the Human Condition).

  — What *Actions* have you done involving ___ ?
\ What have you *Held-Back* from doing involving ___ ?
  — What *Actions* has another done involving ___ ?[‡]
\ What has another *Held-Back* from doing involving ___ ?

[‡]   Or *"have others"*—based on an agreed upon PCL patter that the *Seeker* understands to mean "circuits other than 1."

— What would you permit others to do involving ___ ?[∞]
\ What have you *Held-Back* others from doing
involving ___ ?

— What could you allow others to find out about you
involving ___ ?[Δ]
\ What have you *Held-Out*[*] on about yourself involving ___ ?

— What could others allow you to safely find out about
themselves involving ___ ?
\ What have others *Held-Out* on about themselves
involving ___ ?

ROUTE-3E: SEARCH AND DISCOVERY ON THE CIRCUITS

Standard and Conceptual methods of *Ethics Processing* usually reveal quite a bit of material to resolve. It may be,
however, that at a certain stage of release (or even at the
very start) some significant attention must be given directly to a "search and discovery" effort. Although no specific instructions are given to restrict its application to *this*
lifetime, there are also no specific instructions given in
Grade-IV for targeting a *Seeker's* "past lives" directly.[∞] [This
is an experimental formula directly distinguishing communication-circuit flows of *Ethics Processing*.]

[∞] Alternative patter to "*permit*" (preferred) includes firstly "*allow*"
and secondly (if needed) "*find acceptable for.*"

[Δ] "*Find out*" implies discovery or a revealing, as opposed to another
version of this: "*What would be acceptable for others to know
about you?*" A *Pilot* may have to work, or rather "*word,*" a PCL
around an individual's acceptance level (reach and understanding)
as discussed prior to simply running a series of command lines out
of the blue. There is an exchange of direct communication during
the setup of each process or series. Lack of such communication
will limit the success rate of our applied philosophy.

[*] This assumes a *Seeker* understands intended systematic meaning of
the phrase "*Hold-Out,*" otherwise an alternative is "*kept hidden.*"

[∞] An exception being the note regarding incidents that do not readily
discharge because they are linked to a larger, stronger, *older*
"chain" requiring a *Seeker* to "scan for" and "spot" a similar type of
incident earlier in "time." This sometimes inspires *Seekers* with a
"*sense*" of something that is only logically connected via a former
incarnation.

NOTE: Energetic discharge and sense of release only takes place if what is discovered is fully confronted "As-It-*Is.*" "Discovery" and "Discharge" processes may be more effective when conducted by a *Professional Pilot* and/or using a mechanical biofeedback device to assist (as in Route-3G).

"Search and Discovery on Circuits" is worded very directly for use by experienced Systemologists. It is originally intended as a *Pilot's* "tool" for accessing layers of significance surrounding *Ethical* fragmentation.

Each circuit is treated separately. The four PCL are run alternately in sequence repeatedly (1-2-3-4; 1-2-3-4) for a single circuit until a *Seeker* has no more readily available answers, they are interested in the discovery process and optimistic or relieved by the results. [If a *Seeker* reaches this point on one PCL of a circuit before the rest, that one part may be omitted from repeated runs.]

This process may be run *Solo* as a personal data-inquiry toward *Self*, but its function is primarily to "root out" information—a list of which should be recorded for later use (in Ethics Processing and/or for *Backtrack*).

Circ-1 — What have you made another *Out-Flow*?
What have you made another *Hold-Out*?
What have you made another *In-Flow*?
What have you made another *Hold-Back*?

Circ-2 — What has another made you *Out-Flow*?
What has another made you *Hold-Out*?
What has another made you *In-Flow*?
What has another made you *Hold-Back*?

Circ-3 — What has another made others *Out-Flow*?
What has another made others *Hold-Out*?
What has another made others *In-Flow*?
What has another made others *Hold-Back*?

Circ-0 — What have you made yourself *Out-Flow*?
What have you made yourself *Hold-Out*?
What have you made yourself *In-Flow*?
What have you made yourself *Hold-Back*?

WIZARD LEVEL-0
IMAGINOMICON PROC. TECHNIQUES
EXTRACTED FROM LIBER-3D

Self-Actualization, as it applies to our *Metahuman* and *Spiritual* "Systemology," is a higher state of *Beingness, exterior* to the *Human Condition*, which includes a true *Self-Honest* realization of, and perception (POV) from, the "I-AM."

ROUTE-180: STEP-1: ESTABLISHING THE ALPHA-SPIRIT

Many who remain suspended within "parameters" of the *Human Condition* cannot *actually* conceive of *Self* as a "Spirit" operating *exterior* to states of "feeling" (sensation) and "thinking" (associative reason), which have far too long substituted actual states of "*Knowingness.*" Even magicians, mystics and priests—with their "astral bodies" and "mental bodies" and "etheric bodies"—are still yet unable to *realize* a *Self* that is not tied to forms and bodies.

"Individuality"—as the true nature of *Self*—is plotted high, **one-to-one** with the Alpha-Spirit, at "7.0" on the (*Zu-line*) Standard Model; even higher than the range of Alpha-Thought, which is the product of the Alpha-Spirit—and, of course, well beyond levels of "association" and "identity." The I-AM—*Self* as Alpha-Spirit—*is* an Individual. It is above any personality-persona-packages and *genetic vehicles* and *forms* that it may later attach to its own considerations of *Beingness*.

Basic methodology and "esoteric exercises" suggested are meant to assist a *Seeker* in more fully *realizing* the *Awareness* of "Spiritual Individuality" as opposed to the "*beta-personality.*" Practice of *Self-Awareness* falls within a subset of the domain of "*Imagination*," which we might refer to as **"POV Processing"** when administered systematically.

The most critical component to operating "out" and *exterior* to *Beta-Existence* is to attain a "crystal clear" certainty and realization—complete reality agreement—that the I-AM, *Self*, is: not the Mind, not the Body (or any *genetic vehicle*), but is commander and operator of these instruments in *Beta-Existence* from a point of true *Spiritual Awareness* that is not directly locatable within the boundaries or parameters of the Physical Universe; it simply operates machinery there. As an individual Alpha-Spirit becomes fragmented by "associative thought," the circuitry of the Mind-System offers POV that make it seem as though the individual *is* confined within those Systems as a point of *Beingness*. But these "implants" do not yield truth.

> In order to get a *realization* that *Self* is apart from— and the superior master to—the *genetic vehicle* as a "body," the Seeker should take time to focus *Awareness* through each part of the body: beginning with the feet and moving up into the head (and including the brain). In the past, mystics referred to these techniques as *"Activating the Light-Body"*—but, what we have found in our Systemology is that the *Awareness* itself act as "Light," not any "body." The Alpha-Spirit operates as an *Awareness* independent of *any* "body"—even a "spiritual" one. Of course, it has had many layers or levels or dimensions of "energetic body" assumed during its experiences through various "Universes"; and the more rigid, solid and condensed the energy-matter of a Universe, the more rigid and solid the *genetic vehicles* are for Life to communicate at that level of *Beta-Existence*.

When *Self* is operating as an *Awareness* "outside" sensory perceptions and energetic rigidity of a "material body," it may, in effect, *look into* the *genetic organism* and view its workings—practice in which will demonstrate that the "I" or *Self* is not identical or identified *as* the "body." For some it is easier to consider that they are operating *exterior* to this Physical Universe, but are "projecting" their *Awareness* to a POV that *is within* another form or "body" to experience a *Beingness*.

"Creativeness Processing" tends to operate best on a gradient scale of reality. A *Seeker* achieves best results by systematically confronting the "whole" in "parts" until they

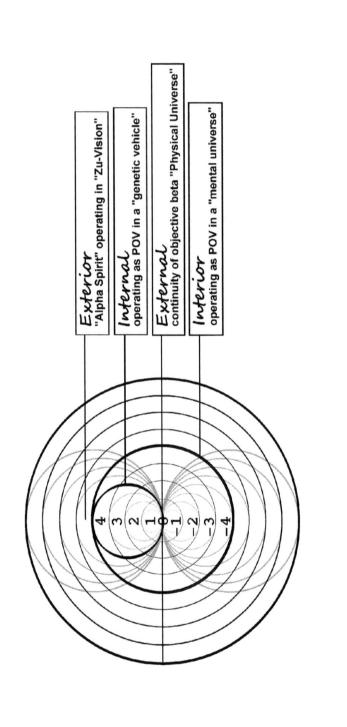

Exterior
"Alpha Spirit" operating in "Zu-Vision"

Internal
operating as POV in a "genetic vehicle"

External
continuity of objective beta "Physical Universe"

Interior
operating as POV in a "mental universe"

are prepared to treat a full realization of the whole. For example, in basic treatment of a "body" using these methods:

> Begin with full directed attention—as *Awareness*—on just the feet (even prior to treating the entire limb), or if that proves challenging at first, just one toe of one foot. Then concentrate that *Awareness* in that location; and using *Creative Ability*, imagine that: if the feet were nonexistent, then *Self* would still continue to exist unchanged as the Alpha-Spirit. Next, consider that they are useful tools for communicating activity when operating a *genetic vehicle* in the Physical Universe, but they are not the "feet" *of* the Spirit; and *Self* is not dependent on the feet of a "body" to act.

It is not the intention of the exercise to lessen or reject the *genetic vehicle.* An individual not getting along well in this lifetime—or experiencing a great deal of pain—is already excessively and compulsively "out of communication" with the "body." The *genetic vehicle* is exactly *that*—a vehicle or instrument or tool that should be cared for like we might any other "possession," but it should not be obsessed over or confused with an "identity" for *Self.*

> The same exercise may be continued with the remainder of the body—the pelvic region (sexual organs), digestive tract, chest, arms, neck, head, &tc.— treating each with the same considerations, and moving off from each with the same realizations, as with the feet. When this is accomplished throughout the whole body, then the *Seeker* may look to consider the "body" as the whole of the *genetic vehicle*, an instrument useful for communication in the Physical Universe, biologically adapted to this *Beta-Existence*; but that *Self*—I-AM; Alpha-Spirit—*is* above and superior, independent and apart, from the *genetic vehicle*, and actually exists *exterior* to it in a "Spiritual Universe."

WIZARD LEVEL PROCESSING: INTRODUCING "ZU-VISION"

Practice of *exterior* "Zu-Vision"—the *Awareness POV* from *Self* independent of a "body" in *Beta-Existence*—ensues until a *Seeker* has an increased *realization* (reality) on the matter. Such practices require "Imagination" and *Creative Ability* for that *realization* to become *actual.* An individual should not invalidate their own experience—or a *Pilot* invalidate a *Seeker*—concerning exactly what is happening within the realm of one's "Imagination" and Personal Universe. An individual *"imagines"* the potentiality of something until it is *realized*, from which it may then be *actual* to themselves.

A few workable premises were discovered for our Systemology scattered throughout history—pieces waiting to be picked up and assembled into foundations for a new level of *"Metahuman"* understanding. Although more precise and systematic applications of our philosophy and spiritual techniques have since developed, we read of similar suggestions for practical exercises by *William Walker Atkinson (1862-1932)*—a pioneer of American 'New Thought' over a century ago. In his esoteric library of arcane teachings:—

> "Let the **Neophyte**, in imagination, leave the physical body and gaze upon the latter. A little mental practice will enable one to do this in imagination, thus bringing fully to mind the realization that it is possible for the *Self* to leave the body and dwell apart from it. When the mind has once grasped this possibility, the body will ever after be recognized as merely a physical machine, sheath or covering, of the *Self*—and one will never again commit the folly of identifying the 'I' with the physical body.

> "Then let the Neophyte imagine themselves leaving behind their physical body, until, as Holmes says: '...thou at length are free, leaving thine outgrown shell by life's unresting sea.' Let them then consider themselves as occupying other and different bodies, one at a time, in different phases of life and condition, in different ages, &tc. This will bring about the realization that *Self* is something higher and indepe-

ndent of the particular physical shell or machine that it is now using, and which it may have at one time considered identical with itself. Then will the particular body occupied seem, in reality, to be *'my body'* instead of *'I'* or *Me*."

EXPERIMENT: MENTAL ASSIST TO THE GENETIC VEHICLE

Where one does find persistent difficulties in managing the *genetic vehicle*—or some reoccurring psycho-somatic or triggered condition—the Mind-System "short-circuits" energetic communication flows to locations of the "body" that are injured. Being a composite system, that "part" of the *genetic vehicle* is treated unaffectionately by the "automated" network—and this causes the *pings* and *pains* of life to continue being *created* as they are, until *Self* resumes control and responsibility for command of the "body."

When a particular part of the *genetic vehicle* has been injured or pains us, we "prefer" to *not* "think" about it—or put any *Awareness* on to that region of the "body" because it "hurts." An individual can go as far as to "damn" and "curse" that part of their "body"—even succumbing to lower levels of physical mutilation—all simply to avoid actually *confronting* that part of a "body." A better approach is to "imagine" *Mental Image* copies (or create Self-Determined *facsimiles*) of that "part" within the vicinity of the "part." This reestablishes that the "part" exists and that there is no "mental shortage" of energy passed to the "terminal." As a "Route-0" application of *Communication Processing*: an individual might even *imagine* literal spoken communications between *Self* and that "part," complete with *"Hello's"* (greetings) and acknowledgments.

INTRODUCING "SYSTEMOLOGY PROCEDURE 1-8-0"

"Systemology Procedure 1-8-0" remains the primary experimental *route out*, if completely actualized—even should we later discover more direct or effective means of achieving similar *realizations*. This first began in the 1990's, when reading from *Atkinson's* arcane teachings:—

"Let the Neophyte meditate upon the great Ocean of Life in which the individual entities are but focal Centers of Consciousness and Force. Let them picture themselves, in imagination, as being an actual Center, with all the Universe revolving around them; see themselves as the pivot around which the Universe moves—the Central Sun around which the infinite world and planets circle in their cosmic flight. Let them feel themselves to be the focal Center of the Cosmos.

"And this is indeed, in accordance with the centuries of old occult axiom, which informs us that 'the Cosmos is infinite—its circumference is nowhere—its center is everywhere.' Let the Neophyte lose all thought of the outside world in this meditation—let them regard it as totally unmanifest if they like—but see *Self* in Actual Existence and in Full Power. Let them realize 'I-AM' to the fullest extent of their power of imagination and conception."

Development of *'Systemology Procedure 1-8-0'* began with the various routes for which it was named for—though it is also named for the compass-direction of our *Pathway*, meaning: 180-degrees (*back the way we came*). "Liber-2B" included directions for one route: "Proc. 180, Route-1" (*SP-2B-8A*) exactly as given below. This was originally intended to move *Awareness* "out" from the *genetic vehicle* to personally experience one's impressions of *each* "Sphere of Existence"—along the "Zu-line"—on their approach to *Infinity*.

"Proc. 180, Route 8" is given in the "*Creative Ability Training*" ("CAT"), emphasizing its ultimate destination: the "Infinity of Nothingness"—directly experiencing the "Infinity of Nothingness" in all directions.

The third and final tested demonstration is "Proc. 180, Route 0," whereby an individual directs their *Beingness* as an Alpha-Command to any point in space-time for any Universe—though it is generally practiced with local planets of the local solar system first. This would include *Processing Command Lines* (PCLs) such as "*Be* outside the body" or "*Be* above the Earth" and other similar practices that effectively prepare an individual to operate independent of the *genetic vehicle* (in "*Zu-Vision*").

The three routes of "Systemology Procedure 180" are:

(1) Self-Awareness;
(8) Nothingness; and
(0) Beingness.

For reference purposes, the procedural instructions for "*Systemology 1-8-0, Route-1*" are given below exactly as they first appear in the text "*Crystal Clear.*" This same formula can be applied for each of the "*Spheres of Existence.*"[*]

—IMAGINE your Awareness as outside and *exterior* to the body.
—FOCUS your *Awareness* on the *Eighth Sphere* of *Infinity*.
—IMAGINE the *Infinity* of *Nothingness* extending out "infinitely" on all sides as a great Ocean of Cosmic Consciousness.
—FOCUS your *Awareness* from *Self* as a singular focal point of individuated consciousness in the center of the *Infinite Ocean*.
—SENSE that the *Nothingness-Space* all around you is rising up as tides and wave-actions of invisible motion; its abyssal stillness broken by the singular point that is *You*.
—SENSE that as you press your *Awareness* against the *Nothingness*, there is no resistance, there is no sensation —no feeling of any kind.
—IMAGINE your totality of *Awareness* as the singular focal point of *Infinity*—then REALIZE that the waves you see crashing up against you and rippling into *Infinity* are an extension of your every thought, will and action.
—REALIZE that you are the *Alpha Spirit*; that "wave peak" in an otherwise *Infinity of Nothingness* stretching out within and back off all that was, is and ever will.

---

[*] 1) Self; 2) Home; 3) Groups; 4) Humanity; 5) Life on Earth; 6) The Physical Universe; 7) The Spiritual Existence; and 8) Infinity.

214 – *Wizard Level-0*

—REALIZE that your conscious *Awareness* as "I", your direction of WILL as *Alpha Spirit*, and the "central wave peak" born out of *Infinity* are all the same pure individuated ZU—are all *One; Infinity; None.*

—WILL yourself to project *Awareness* ahead of you and see an extension of this ZU as your projection of Identity extending infinitely in front of you—all the way to the *zero-point-continuity* of existence—and back to *Infinity.*

—REPEAT this several times, IMAGINING this ZU as a *Clear Light* radiant extension from *Self*, directed across *Infinity* to *Zero-point* and back to *Infinity;* then REALIZE that you are dissolving and wiping out all *fragmentation* from the channel as you direct the *Clear Light.*

—REPEAT this several times, until you feel confidant in your current results for this cycle of work.

—RECALL the instance you decided to start this present *session*—get a sense of the Intention you *Willed* to begin the session.

—REALIZE that your *beta-Awareness* and the true WILL of the Alpha Spirit are One continuous stream and that the *Self* is superior to, and master of, the *genetic vehicle;* End the session.

Apart from the *Infinity of Nothingness*, the *Self* exists as a point or unit of *Spiritual Awareness* as the "I-AM" amidst that *Sea of Infinity*. All else is Universes—or what some have called "dimensions"—and we typically *know* them by their "space" and "forms" existing against a background matrix, which is itself backed by *Nothingness*. So, the Alpha-Spirit *creates* and *experiences* a "World of Lights" no matter what level of condensation those *spots* and *points* may manifest as.

A MEDITATION: "MENTAL IMAGERY AS IMPRINTING"

Mental Imagery is always *generated* with energy created by *Self*, even when it is a "response" to some external stimulus and/or created using automatic-mechanisms and "filter-screens"—such as the information received through "eyes" of a *genetic vehicle* and then broadcast as an "image" in the *"Mind's Eye"* (as it used to be called; and as people generally are likely to understand it at first), which is then viewed by *Self*. But all that is actually taking place is an encounter with the *forms* and *colors* of an "impression."

These "impressions" give our directed *Awareness* "cues" of an objective Physical Universe (*beta-existence*)—qualities of light, color and form, which make up the visual *facets* of the images we register as our "view" of an "external" environment. These varying "qualities" are treated as *facets* of the experience in "systematic processing"—each *facet* representing some type of recognizable energy or potential perception that can be recorded. All of the significance and meaning—all of the data for reasoning and future evaluation—is entirely *Self*-generated and maintained as an experience. But the truth is that the considerations of the *imagery* are completely up to an individual to determine; as theosophical philosopher, *J.J. Van der Leeuw*, even suggests:—

> "We, as it were, clothe the nakedness of the unknown reality with the image produced in our consciousness. The same facts, which are true for the sense of vision, hold good for our perception through any of the senses; thus there is no question of 'should' but in our consciousness, no question of 'taste' or 'smell' but in our consciousness, no question of 'hardness' or 'softness', of 'heaviness' or 'lightness' but in our consciousness; our entire world-image is an image arising on our consciousness because of the action on that consciousness by some 'unknown reality'."

We address this directly in with the systematic procedure **'Bell, Book and Candle'** treated at great length in *"Liber-2D"* —a procedure included in the "Creative Ability Training" (CAT). The "objective" Physical Universe is the external other-determined *beta*-force impressing action, that *Van der Leeuw* refers to as the "mysterious unknown reality"— because to an individual operating at low-levels of *Beta-Awareness* or even fixed within the *Human Condition* at all, an "outside world" is continuously hungry for *attention*. It prompts compulsive *looking* and *validation* by maintaining itself as a Mystery.

The **physiology** and sensory perception of the *genetic vehicle* incites "internal" stimulation of a type that registers "familiar" enough to seem as though *it* is actually happening *to* the Alpha-Spirit, when it is only happening in *beta-existence*. *Van der Leeuw* goes on from earlier:—

> "It is the peculiar relation in which we stand to our own body, the intimate link we have with it and which we do not have with regard to any other object in the outer world, which makes us feel that we know all about its reality. We have an *inside* feeling of our body which we do not have in regard to a stone or a tree, our body appears to us as part of ourselves and we forget that it is as much part of that *outer* world as the tree or the stone, and that our perception of it as a visible and tangible object takes place in just the same way as our perception of the tree or of the stone. Even the *inner* feeling we have of our body is but a variety of sense-perception which exists for our body alone..."

We come to the *realization*: all perceptions of an objective reality are *Self-created* or generated based on impressions or suggestions from participation (reality agreement) with a Universe—regardless of what considerations or assignments of value are given to those perceptions.

Some will find it incredibly difficult to have any "reality" on what is *Imagined* and *Created* as *Mental Imagery* within one's own 'Personal Universe'. But!—even when dealing with the more condensed "concrete solidity" of the Physical Universe, *Self* as the Alpha-Spirit is still interacting with *fields* and *screens* and treating the "reality" communicated as *Mental Imagery*. In either case, the individual, as a *Spiritual Awareness*, is interacting from a point *exterior* to the projected images of a holographic-reality that appear viewable on the "*screen*" of perception and are treated as "experience."

This would all just be simple intellectual curiosities to ponder in our "free time" were it not for how detrimental these truths are to the *Human Experience* and liberation of the *Spirit* back to its higher states.

Van der Leeuw reminds us with a clear message:—

"When an event takes place in this world of reality, there is produced, in the consciousness of each creature concerned, an *Awareness*, or *mental image*, which is the event as we see it. Unreality or illusion never resides in the event, or the thing in itself, nor even in my interpretation of it, which is true enough *for me*, but in the fact that I take my interpretation to be the thing in itself—**exacting** to it the stature of an absolute and independent reality.

"The illusion or unreality is neither in the thing itself, nor in the image produced in my consciousness by that thing—but in my conception of the image in my consciousness as the thing in itself; as an object existing independent of my consciousness. We can see the way we have to go: we must withdraw ourselves from the enticing images of our own production and turn towards that center through which the production of our world image takes place—*Self* as a unit of *Awareness*."

We are quite close to completing a final leg on the current cycle of the spiral-like *Spiritual Timeline*. Generally by the end of such cycles of action, everything equals everything else and a Universe collapses into yet one more level of condensation. If we allow identification of *Beingness* to get much lower, there is less likelihood for an individual to get themselves *through and out* again.

Effective systematic processing should include an increased *Awareness* along with the ability to clearly **differentiate**—rather than associate and categorize—the qualities of *energies* and *forms* and Universes encountered.

First we *clear* the *slate*; then we can truly *create*.

POV PROCESSING: PERSONALITY-PACKAGES AND PHASES

Just as Universes condense as we perceive lower and lower levels of existence, working our way back up through the *Gates* requires increasingly greater degrees of personal refinement. Metaphorically speaking, an individual is essentially purging additional layers of low-level artificiality with each *Grade* and *Gate*. Only energy-matter of a specific type or frequency is manifest at each tier of the *Pathway*—and behind each *Gateway to Infinity*.

> An individual is allowed to carry less and less "mass"—even "mental mass"—along with them at each level of ascent. It is the "mass"—the rigidly fixed "resistance" on the *Zu-line*—that keeps an individual's POV or sense of *Beingness* suspended by the low-level "gravity" and tethered to a locatable mass that "forces" can act upon.

Processing may also be applied to scanning and locating the characteristics inherent in the "personality package" or "identity phase" that a *Seeker* is "wearing" as a "**player**" in this "game." This may or may not be inherently part of the "goals and roles" implanted prior to *this* "lifetime." At first, *facets* of a "personality package" (a "role") or "Identity-Phase" (representative of a "specific person") may be more difficult to identify and analyze. It is often easier to first locate facets of a "role" because they are more widely understood "**archetypes**" with socially educated definitions. For example: a mother, a father, a teacher, a priest, a lawyer, a politician—these are all "roles" that have certain attributes, characteristics or *facets* "associated" with them as a consideration. When we speak of "Identity-Phases," we mean more specifically the attributes, characteristics or *facets* "associated" with a *specific* individual: their beliefs, the way they talk, certain phrases they say, the mannerisms and behaviors—even physical ailments can be assimilated from persons we know and have assumed the "phase" of.

Alternating PCLs may be used to separate identifications. This continues until a *Seeker* comes to the *realization* that

the role is simply a reality agreement; the specific iden-
tity/person (from their past) is not actually present; and
none of these have anything to do with the true individual
Self, which lies at the center, which has been *looking* out
through a lens or POV that is artificial to the Alpha-Spirit.

A: —How are you similar to ___ ?

B: —How are you different from ___ ?

Self-Directing POV is simply a matter of *attention* as *Awareness*. Systematic processing is used to uncover "where" (or
on "what") *attention* is compulsively fixed; and in the case
of confusions and energetic dispersals, "where" (or on
"what") it is unable to be concentrated or fixed upon by
command and determination of *Self*.

Deepak Chopra, in his own training of Wizards, states:—

"The wizard sees themselves everywhere they look,
because their sight is innocent; unclouded by judgments, labels and definitions.

A wizard still knows they have a self-image, but is
not distracted by such either. All these things are
seen against the backdrop of the totality, the whole
context of life—where our worldview is also a looking glass.

"The 'I' is your singular point-of-view. In innocence, this point-of-view is pure, like a clear lens;
but without innocence, the focus is extremely distorting. If you think you know something—including yourself—you are actually seeing your own
judgments and labels.

"The simplest words we use to describe each other
—such as *friend, family, stranger*—are loaded with
judgments. The enormous gulf between *friend* and
stranger, for example, is filled with interpretations.
A friend is treated one way; an enemy, another.
Even if we do not bring these judgments to the surface, they cloud our vision like dust obscuring a
lens."

When we are dealing with POV, we are treating the same fundamentals as *Creation*, which is *Being—Beingness*, "to be." This contrasts greatly with conditions of *beta-exist-ence*, wherein individuals are forced to engage in "motion" or "effort" to accomplish similar results in the Physical Universe. When a *Seeker* operates "*Proc. 180, Route-8*" and "*Proc. 180, Route-0*" there is no sense of movement; and no effort is necessary. The Alpha-Spirit says "*Be*" and it *is so*.

An individual has spent most of their spiritual existence *operating* or *occupying* various POV, none of which are the actual perspective of the "**undefiled** Self" as Alpha-Spirit. Now, it is true that any POV can be assumed by *Self* as dir-ected attention—but the standard-issue *Human Condition* is quite "fixed" (or entrapped) in POV exclusively *interior* to "beta-existence" (and confined to a *genetic vehicle*), already consistently reinforced, validated and agreed to, by exper-ience of "internal sensation" prompted by an "external" Physical Universe.

Expanded version:

A: —Recall a time when you were ___ .

B: —Identify someone who is ___ . (*use answer below*)

C: —Find a time someone said you were like ___ .

Alternatively, a *Seeker* might "spot a time" (they) "decided to be like *so-and-so*." Sometimes the first step of increasing a *Seeker's* handling of POV is to get them to recognize—or *realize*—the POV they are compulsively occupying or '*look-ing through*'.

A MEDITATION: "HANDLING SPACE AND CREATION"

When considering a *beta-existence* restricted to dense masses, symbolic objects, physical "efforts" and a neces-sity to destroy, fragment or transmute Physical Universe energy-matter in order to "create," it should come as little surprise that a *beta*-fragmented individual carries many of these same considerations about *Self* being identified *one-to-one* with conditions of *beta-existence*. An individual finds great difficulty in exercising "freedom of the spirit" when they are tied to a mortal POV. Actual conditions for an Alpha-Spirit are independent of the Physical Universe—and any effective regimen for rehabilitating *Actualized Awareness* to a point beyond the "Mind" ("MCC" or "**Master Control Center**") must include full *realization* of *Self* independent of lower-level considerations.

> An Alpha-Spirit essentially has infinite potential and ability to *Create*, and it continues to exercise this quality of its nature all the way down the line— whether it knowingly commands such, or unknowingly and compulsively doing so "on automatic."

In one's personal universe, there are no concerns of "where" energy comes from in order to *Create*, because the Alpha-Spirit needs only to "consider" or "postulate" for something *to be.* Similar to "internal" experience of the Human Mind, the subjective *reality* of an individual's personal universe is as *real* to the individual as they *realize* it; and that is all the consideration necessary for *Self* to cause something to *be* what it *is* for *Self.*

Rather than eternally confront an *Infinity of Nothingness*, the Alpha-Spirit turned around the "other way" and became very interested in the business of "pictures."—which our materials tend to generalize as "*Mental Images*"—even if they are higher-level "facsimile copies" an individual began to collect and experience in *Alpha-Existence.* This even begins prior to formal solidification of a *Human* "Mind-System" implanted like a circuit-board to key-in various types of *Imprints* and additional *coding.*

> The Alpha-Spirit is an individual *Spiritual Beingness* (I-AM)—an epicentric unit of *Awareness*—described in Hermetic/Mesopotamian interpretations ("*Tablets of Destiny*") as:
>
> > a *consciousness* that exists independently from *action/motion* and *form/substance.*

Where we have an *Awareness* observing *forms* in *action*, we have perception of "manifestation." An individual copies and stores an *impression* of all information perceived about the environment. This develops the more permanent "*Spiritual Timeline*" (of registry) carried by an individual from one lifetime incarnation to another. After cumulatively collected "memory" is crystallized, an individual can begin falsely *identifying* it one-to-one with *Self.*

Mental Imagery treated in our previous material is of the type referred to as an "*Imprint.*" In some ways, an *Imprint* could be any experience which makes an "impression" on recordings kept by *Self.* We are most concerned with those that significantly "impinge upon," "hang up" or "stick" an individual—and units of attention somewhere on their "*Spiritual Timeline.*"

There are many *imprints* an individual doesn't want to confront or handle; but rather than "uncreate," "destroy" or postulate them out of existence, their creation is misappropriated to another "source" and hidden away from view, yet still active and compulsively created.

An Alpha-Spirit becomes "effect of their own cause" as they lose control and **relinquish** responsibility of *created* and *copied* (mirrored, facsimile) *Mental Images.*

Rather than take responsibility for continuing creation and ownership (*create*), properly managing it (*control*) and letting it go (*destroy*), a person will often "blame" (attribute responsibility to) someone or something *else* for its creation. They hold onto it permanently as a "rare" or "unique" thing to "have"—something of value they can use to later evaluate their present environment or use on a circuit. This not only makes it more solid, but more difficult to manage. As a compulsive creation, an individual is lending to it their own energies for sustenance. This is handled better by an individual who carries no *masses* with them, allowing for unlimited *Self-directed* energy to simply *Create* whatever they want to "see" or "know" without holding a POV in suspension indefinitely.

A MEDITATION: "RESPONSIBILITY FOR VIEWPOINTS"

When regarding a *Point-of-View* (POV) as "remote,"
it is important to specify "remote from *what.*"

In most instances, we found intended implications concerned "remote from the POV of a body." This serves to increase considerations that the individual *Awareness* as "I-
AM"-*Self* could be separated from a *genetic vehicle*—although they were usually still fixated on the "Mind" or a
"mortal body." Today, this all seems like obvious truth to
us; but, the only reason there is a truth here in any regard,
is because:

the POV maintained from within a "body" (or "head")
is *already* "remote" from the actual existence of
the Alpha-Spirit that is doing the "*viewing.*"
A POV is a "point" *from which* "to view."

At each major tier or gradient (or *Gate*), there is a significant quality or a certain type of "*Barrier*" that *Self* is imposing on *itself* by its own considerations and the relative
"space" occupied by the recordings and energetic *masses*
still compulsively carried forth.

Managing "points" is similar to handling a *Seeker's* "presence" in session—particularly objective techniques where
a *Pilot* directs a *Seeker* to make contact (communicate) with
the immediate environment. One reason is to get directed
Awareness "present" and the other, which is related, is:

to establish that the "points" in one's environment
are actually "safe" to both "look at" *and* "view from."

An Alpha-Spirit does not like to *knowingly* leave its
attentions on a space that is considered unsafe (or
containing "cues" from *facets* that are considered
unsafe by fragmented associative reasoning)—but,
if there is a strong enough impression, it does so
unknowingly anyway, leaving part of its *Awareness*
there to hold that *image* in suspension so as not to
completely "turn its back" on something that *might*
"get" them. They don't destroy the creation, as they
should. They keep a facsimile-copy of it in existence

with a big warning sign that says: "Must Never Duplicate"—but there it is, maintained continuously created with entangled energy all the while.

Willingness—and therefore, ability—to locate and access a particular Universe collapses for an individual when all possible extant POV are intolerable or deemed unsafe.

In most instances, the key consideration is "*betrayal*." The certainty of what is safe to *view*, and acceptable points to *view from* reduces. An individual is less able when they are less willing; and less willing when they are uncertain in ability.

Systematic processing supplements training routes. It is a means for an individual to practice *Self-Determinism* and alternating "viewpoints." This effectively free up tendencies and considerations operating on "automatic." We use objective techniques involving "corners" or "points" that *anchor* the *space* of a room, because they are considered "determined" and "owned" by something separate from *Self*.

An individual operating in *beta-existence* starts to believe they cannot be responsible for (or create) *Space*, because it all seems to be already "determined" for them. We are erroneously told that even the "ideas" have all been thought of before and thus *belong* to someone else.

Fragmentation exists when an individual considers that they would be "nothing" or "not" if they weren't *identified* with some "thing"—and, of course, at the Physical Universe level of *beta-existence*, the identification is with "objects" (solid masses). Therefore, one objective of *Wizard Level-0* is to detach an individual from compulsive POVs of the *genetic vehicle* they "think" they are. This is systematically accomplished by introducing viewpoint "shifts" into a secondary alternate POV and then practicing alternation between them on one's own *Self-Determination*.

An individual *can* assume a POV from within a *genetic vehicle*, but when one *knows* they are willingly doing so, they also know they have freedom and ability to shift to other POV independent of any body. Since occupation of the *Human Condition* POV is generally "enforced" and "implanted," the Alpha-Spirit forgets considerations that its own true nature is located *exterior* to this *beta-existence*.

POV PROCESSING/PRACTICE: LOCATIONAL VIEWPOINTS

When practicing POV techniques, it is preferable to shift to a POV that is not dependent on any type of form or body, astral or otherwise, in which to maintain existence as a "point." Tolerance can be increased by applying "*creativeness processing*" methods that treat 'points' and 'spots' in space. In the past, practitioners have preferred to work with "astral bodies" because it still provides a "sense" that they *have* something.

To remedy this, practice *Self-directing* a POV-alternation between shifting "into" and "out of" an *imagined body*. The primary difference is that processing treats a *form* that the individual *knows* they are *creating*, can take a responsibility for, and then stop creating (and dissolve) it when the exercise is completed. Ultimately, a *Seeker* desires to be free of compulsively identifying with one or another 'bodies'.

The generally accepted belief that an individual *must* be occupying a POV exclusively *interior* to a Mind-Body in order to operate that *genetic vehicle* is quite false. *All* of the potential POV are actually "remote" from existence of *Self*, therefore an Alpha-Spirit could maintain a POV "just outside" the Mind-Body system and still very adequately operate it independent from an *Identity with Self*, just as one might operate a marionette puppet.

The premise of "*Zu-Vision*" is not introduced prior to "Wizard Level" work. Earlier materials focused on *Seekers* reducing energetic intensity of the "field" created and automated by circuitry of the Mind-Body system for "*Beta-Defragmentation*." Such circuitry is often created and/or reinforced when an individual is "keyed-in" or fixed to those *interior* considerations—and this "electric field" seems to also have "magnetic" qualities to it. While an individual *does* have a natural ability to "get out" on command, there is also a tendency to "snap in" again with the sensation of some force of impact. The sense of "pull" or "gravity" can accumulate and decrease willingness and ability to knowingly *Self-direct* "getting out" *again*.

Years ago at the Systemology Society we began to experiment with basic techniques inspired by an obscure volume of German mysticism. Therein, "transference of consciousness" is described—where:

> an initiate practices imagining their POV "going inside" solid masses separate from the *genetic vehicle*.

Original methods seemed to emphasize one direction of flow, and we can improve this for our practices:

> using alternation—"going in" *and* "going out" —with repetition and fluidity.

Our experiments demonstrated that better results could be earned initially by selecting large masses, which one is familiar with but that are not in the immediate vicinity—which returned us to our original tests with "a mountain" (one which the individual is not already sitting on).

Practice of "Locational POV" may be *Self-processed* or *Piloted*. When *Piloted*, the *Pilot* is not to evaluate significances or invalidate results. Whatever is happening in a *Seeker's* perception of reality *is* what is happening *for them*. To ensure proper continuation of processing (and to keep the *Seeker's* attention "on the mark"), a *Pilot* may follow up a "Route-0" or "*creativeness processing*" PCL series with: "Did you?" But this is only to be certain a *Pilot* remains in communication with a *Seeker* during their subjective use of imagination. It is never asked with skepticism. So long as the *Seeker* says "Yes," a *Pilot* should only respond with an acknowledgments that the message was received.

—Imagine being above (*a mountain*) looking down on it.
—Imagine your POV moving in *to* it.
\ Imagine your POV moving out *from* it.

When this has been practiced with efficiency, a *Seeker* may apply the more advanced version to various locations.

—Be near (*or above*) ___ .
—Be inside of ___ (*it*).
\ Be outside of ___ (*it*).
—Be at the center ___ (*it*).
\ Be outside ___ (*it*).
—Be on the surface ___ (*it*).
\ Be above ___ (*it*).

> This may be practiced with eyes closed and by imagining a "secondary POV" independent of the *genetic vehicle.* By establishing a new viewpoint, a *Seeker* is not demanding themselves to reach much higher-level goals: completely separating from a compulsive POV within the "body." Certainty and skill for that will follow greater actualized success.

The extended "A.T." version (included above for reference) is also applied to upper-route Wizard Grades to direct *Actualized Awareness* to various POV in the Universe—and beyond it—on command. It is based on a popular meditation technique appearing in **Eastern** Mysticism concerning "journeying to other planets."

An Alpha-Spirit is also certainly able to maintain circuits with multiple POV simultaneously and shift its *Awareness* fluidly among them.

> Once an individual has certainty on the basic technique, expansion includes practice maintaining multiple POV. With the above example, a *Seeker* "anchors" the POV they are using above "the mountain" and holds it there; then begins alternating attention:
>
> between an "imagined POV" with eyes closed and the POV maintained by the *genetic vehicle* with eyes open
>
> —making that the "secondary POV" is held stable in the imagination, so when one closes their eyes they are immediately assuming this other viewpoint.

As an additional gradient of practice, a *Seeker* can develop enough perception with this experience to simultaneously "*look*" through both POV. It will be noticed, of course, that perceptions of the *genetic vehicle* POV are considerably "louder" than a "secondary" one. All an individual needs to do, even with eyes open, is increase the attention that is directed to the "secondary POV" to keep it from completely fading out. "Alternating Locational POV" may be incorporated into an individual's regular "*Creativity Session*" regimen, since certainty on this ability can always be increased—and is critical for upper-level development.

CREATIVE ABILITY PROCESSING: CREATION OF SPACE

Creation and handling of *Space*...

| begins with a *point* in which to consider that Space *is*. |

When the mystic says that "space extends infinitely in all directions," it assumes an **epicentral** *point* in which to "view" *out from* into "Space." We can also consider that there are specialized points—such as we treat in geometry—that define "boundaries" of a dimensional plane of space.

| The concept of distance and time enters in when there is more than one existing *point* to consider. |

To truly *create* energy, matter and various forms, there must be space for them to exist in.

The Alpha-Spirit has forgotten its ability to create and handle space—relying on an existence of *genetic vehicles* and the Physical Universe in which to *have* any sense of space. Many treat the concept of Space (and Universes) as a *spherical* nature—such as a mystic or magician that "casts circles" or *imagines* a "shield-like sphere" surrounding their ritual area. However, our experiments show:

| —easier and more effective, in basic practice, to represent six directions of a three-dimensional space with a "cube." |

As a demonstration, this basic idea can be put into practice as an extension of the previous technique. Rather than use "a mountain" as it exists within the Physical Universe (*beta*), this time we want to actually *imagine* "a mountain" within one's own "Personal Universe." This is "practiced with imagination" by:

A: first *creating* and defining dimensions of "space"; and

B: then *creating* the masses and objects within.

An individual *could* just close their eyes and *"Imagine"* certain forms that they perceive, which satisfy written directions for techniques (or from a *Pilot*)—but, if greater attention is given to the *creation* of *space* the *form* exists in, than greater certainty on actual *Creative Ability* can be earned.

"Imaginative" work increases *realizations* so that an individual's *Awareness* can even receive *actual perception.*

Rather than closing your eyes and "recalling" an actual mountain from memory in order to duplicate a scene, this time we want to *create* fixed dimensions of finite *space* in our Personal Universe for which to *imagine* "a mountain" of our own unique design.

"Creation of space" is dependent on an individual's ability to perceive a *"point."* The following technique applies basic steps to create a "cube of space." Once an individual has a sense of this, a more direct method is simply to *Imagine* the eight points to form a cube and *Create* it as a single-step. However, it is more important that an *Seeker* has absolute certainty on their *creation* of each point as fully as possible —holding a "point" still enough to perceive it solidly.

—Imagine a *point* that is independent of *beta-existence.*
—Imagine a *line* stretches to a second *point.*
—Imagine those two *points* extend *lines* upward to another two *points.*
—Imagine these four *points* connected by *lines* form a *square.*
—Imagine another set of four *points* connected as a second *square.*
—Imagine lines connecting the *squares* to form a *cube.*
—Imagine that this *cube* is pure *space.*

Once there is effective certainty on *"Creation of Space,"* an individual can go on to *Imagine* creation of "a mountain" *inside* the "cube." This is why it is important to *create* a large enough space to work in.

Effective "*creativeness processing*," requires an individual make certain the imagery *created* is not a *reactionary imprint*, or *mental image* that spontaneously surfaces into view. For example: at the mention of the word "*mountain*." This is ensured by "throwing away" any "pictures" that "come to Mind"—and then further, *creating* changes in whatever is *imagined*. For example: reforming and adjusting the shape and color (and other *facets*) until it is absolutely certain that *Self* is fully responsible for the *creation* of every detail of the imagery.

As an individual applies these techniques, a realization may occur that equally applies to the structure of POV in every Universe. There is a fixed or "anchored" POV in place that maintains *creation* of space and form. Meanwhile the "secondary POV" may still be directed "in to" and "out of" the object. As an additional step, the POV is alternated between the "copied beta-mountain" (from a previous technique) and the "uniquely created mountain" (from this one). For best results, rather than simply flashing between the two scenes each time, use POV to *actually look* at some detail or *facet* that is interesting, acceptable and/or safe to look at.

The exercise relates the idea that:—

> The POV of a *Spiritual Being* as a unit of *Awareness*, can: *create* dimensional boundary points to define a space; *create* forms to view by condensing points in that space; shift its POV to be any point in a form or point in space, while maintaining POV on *creation* of forms and space.

We are most concerned with what can be managed within an individual's own "*created space*"; and even the very "*creation-of-space*" for a "Personal Universe." It is far better to train and practice our brand of "Wizardcraft" in a dimension of "personal space" independent of Physical Universe reality agreements.

The previous techniques are intended to direct attention toward realizations that: the Alpha-Spirit, as a "point" of *Awareness*, can *create* space and forms within it using one POV and then experience it with another. This defies many commonly held beliefs about *beta-existence* and yet is a simple truth in Alpha-Existence.

In practice, an hour or more spent developing total certainty on *creation* of a single "point" is more significant for ongoing development (progress) than considering a whole "cube" vaguely with only a slight perception on its reality.

> The *"point"* is an interesting fundamental encountered by a Seeker during the *Creation-of Space*; because the *"point"* represents *no-dimension* and *no-mass* and thus closely resembles the nature of the Alpha Spirit's own existence.

It takes *two* "points" to create a line (segment) and a single *'spatial dimension'*. This makes the "point" an effective tool (in systematically processing) to "reach" higher states. Holding the concept of a "point" by itself runs an individual very close on having to confront "non-motion" and "a true static"; comparable to experiences on the *"Spiritual Timeline"* that an Alpha-Spirit had difficulties with prior. Hence, our Systemological compass points toward a *180-* degree turnabout regarding condensation of Universes and restriction of our considerations of *Beingness.*

A MEDITATION: "THE RESPONSIBILITY FOR CREATION"

> Total *Actualized Awareness* and full *Creative Ability* is hindered only by "automated circuitry" and "mental machinery" that an Alpha-Spirit formerly *created* (or *copied,* then *compulsively creates unknowingly*) to manage control of all these functions.

Our ongoing solution is to *knowingly* take responsibility and control over whatever is compulsively *unknowingly* or reactively happening automatically.

> For example, the natural tendency is to put in *"effort"* to "stop" (destroy) what is taking place outside personal control and determination; but a more eff-

232 – Wizard Level-0

ective method of regaining control is to "change" what is happening or make it happen more strongly. An individual might create their "point" with structural intent of no mass or dimension, yet it takes on characteristics on its own; perhaps of a "spot" by expanding its size, or flashing as a light rather than remaining a static point.

A static point, whether as a point "anchoring" corners of *created space* or a point within space, should be able to be fixed in a location and suspended from motion. In either case we have "other-determined" actions affecting the basic command postulate directed to hold a single "point" still. If it's faintly flicking in and out of *Awareness* or flashing, the individual can intend for it do so strongly and more boldly. If it won't remain still, the course or direction it travels can be changed. If it keeps moving in on the body, give it a little "knock" (with an intention) the other way back toward its intended location, rather than giving in to withdrawing your POV backward.

Anything that impinges on a specific/fixed "postulate-of-creation" can be systematically put under control of *Self* using gradients of *change* to increase or decrease what is already happening, even if it seems contrary to the original intent. A fast moving *image* or *point* can be more easily *changed* to go faster before there is enough certainty to slow it and hold it still.

Once there is certainty on creating and viewing "out in front" (of their POV), the next applicable gradient is *creating* eight points around the individual's own POV—so as *to be* the only existential-point of *Awareness* within the 'cube' of *created space* that is otherwise intended as "empty" of *creations* and *imagery*.

Responsibility for "*Creation-of-Space*" increases with certainty of command and control of it; hence remaining at "*Cause*" throughout the cycle-of-creation—including discard, dissolve or destruction—when an individual intends to no longer create it and has not intended on it to persist compulsively on some automatic-circuit of creation (because we now know that *Self* contributes to that as well).

Placing attention on "corners" of space, as suggested in the *Creative Ability Training*, this can be done while remaining stationary within the *created-space*. An individual can also rotate their view to inspect the boundaries as well. To further increase certainty on the *creation* and its contents (or lack thereof), the individual can go *look* from other POV to see that it is empty and simultaneously determine the level of control, responsibility and ability. For example, unlike points that define the dimensions of this space, the individual's POV *can* be relocated, such as from one corner to the next and *look* inward at the space. A *realization* should become increasingly actualized that: *Self* completely owns and is totally responsible for this independently created personal space.

Practicing, imagining and eventually establishing a POV in a *created-space* of one's own Personal Universe is an objective goal for *Wizard Level-0*; not only for its function, but to increase subjective certainty or personal reality that:

> *Space* can exist independent of the *Physical Universe* and experiencing existence of exterior Universes depends on an *Exterior POV* and not a *genetic vehicle* in *beta-existence*. I-AM is an *Alpha Spirit* existing independent of any body and any universe other than its original *Alpha-Existence* as a unit of *Awareness* with unlimited Creative Ability.

Actualization *follows* Realization. Only when the I-AM-*Self* (Alpha-Spirit) is certain enough that there is *somewhere to be* existing outside of this *beta-existence,* is there enough willingness and determinism to break ties that have long fixed one's attention exclusively on existence in this Physical Universe. The range of *Actualized Awareness* under full control of the Alpha-Spirit is fairly unlimited in ability to direct its POV and locate itself in existence, but logically: an individual must first *realize* that a destination exists for them to actually be there—particularly one that is *exterior* to this Universe.

WIZARD LEVEL-0
CREATIVE ABILITY TRAINING ("CAT")
TECH REPORT #R011-C
EXCERPTED FROM LIBER-011

BACKGROUND
The project director accumulated a large collection of esoteric exercises and 'New Thought' techniques over a 25-year period. These were then tested by members of the Systemology Society and evaluated for their relevance to Grade-IV 'end-goals'. A precise study of 'background theory' is not necessary for the exercises to be effective.

DEVELOPMENTAL RESEARCH
After two years of intensive experimentation with innumerable "basic techniques" by many Seekers around the world reporting their results to the Systemology Society, surprisingly few exercises survived our rigorous testing and scrutiny for inclusion in this training primer. Some versions of these exercises have appeared in previous Mardukite and Systemology publications; others may bare striking resemblance to 'mystical' and/or 'occult' techniques found elsewhere among 6,000 years of esoteric lore.

APPLICATION
A Seeker will notice that as they develop greater degrees of Creative Ability, these 'exercises' may be repeated with cumulatively better results. These 'exercises' are approached on a gradient scale of 'success' that relatively extends to Infinity. An individual will get a 'sense' of their own present ability, which admittedly, can always be expressed 'stronger,' 'longer' or 'clearer' with additional practice.

RECORD-KEEPING
Recordable data (for training purposes) is virtually identical to traditional 'Systematic Processing Sessions', including: the session environment (location, weather, day

of the week, &tc.); your apparent condition (a personal **Beta-Awareness** or Emotimeter evaluation)[*] at the start and end; the specific exercises or techniques applied; the duration of time spent on each exercise and the entire testing session; energy handling (clarity of the operation, certainty of success, new realizations); the material objects encountered and other 'body phenomenon' (solid forms, imagery, physical/emotional reactions, discomfort or 'pings' sensed from the genetic vehicle).

COMPLETE INSTRUCTIONS
Even if an exercise seems 'familiar', pay particular attention to specific wording of directions for each application, treating each step in its own unit of time (separate from previous exercises). This regimen may be Self-Administered or 'Piloted'. In either case, to provide lasting 'gains', it is necessary to focus validation on what an individual is able to do, rather than 'exercising' in the direction of failure and shortcomings.

We have found it more effective for beginners to cycle through as many of the basic steps of each exercise as possible during a single 'creative training session' —because, when starting out, Seekers are likely to 'try' too intensely on particulars of an exercise, in exclusion to others, straining for a specific result or effect to occur. No effort should be applied; a Seeker should simply emphasize validating what they can do with each cycle.

Although relay of these 'exercises' is quite casual here (emphasizing light practice to encourage accumulating greater certainty), actual realizations and stable gains develop only by pushing through whatever fragmentation appears during practice —discomfort, **somatic** 'pings', intrusive thoughts, reactive images, various emotional responses. Only by working through these to the height of personal certainty and clarity are they useful tools for de-

---

[*] See "*Crystal Clear: Handbook for Seekers*"; also available in the complete Grade-III 'Master Edition' anthology, "*The Systemology Handbook.*"

fragmenting such automatic (obsessive or compulsive) phenomenon.

At first, a Seeker may only be able to focus for a few minutes on the more basic steps of each exercise cycle, realizing it to the extent that present Actualized Awareness and attention allows —even if the extent of 'success' is a vague sense of certainty. As the individual continues their studies and practice (increasing their understanding, willingness and ability) the results become more vivid, certainty is stronger, greater realizations provide for higher 'ledges' of Actualization, and personal development relevant to approaching upper-level 'Gateways to Infinity' is demonstrably more apparent.

As an individual works toward Spiritual (or 'Alpha') Actualization (emphasized for 'Wizard-Level' Systemology) any one of these exercises produces increasingly better results the longer its clarity may be held. It is not unreasonable, as an individual advances, to eventually apply 30, 60 or even 120 continuous minutes (an entire two-hour '**creativeness** session') toward a single exercise with increasing cumulative results.

Each section represents a specialized cycle, building upon previous cycles. Even after greater certainty is established on a particular cycle: for each new creativeness session, an individual should start at the beginning ("#1") and move through each, however briefly, before going to the next.

There are no 'short cuts' to getting through and out from the trappings of this Beta-Existence; our Systemology is the most direct path we can access and best chance humanity has had toward its own Ascension, for at least 6,000 years.

ADDITIONAL NOTICES
Before proceeding take factual note that the directives for this training regimen do not include personal intention (or commands) for a creation or image 'to persist'.

 * Any 'masses' Imagined or Copied (and any Mental Ima-

ges "manufactured") in these exercises and systematic processing should be handled by (**Alpha Thought**) consideration or command postulate, either: discarded, reduced down to a ball to toss away, dissolved to nothing, treated as being given away —or even pushed into the body from time to time to satisfy the illusion of replenishing energy (though all energy is actually manufactured by the 'Unlimited Self' when necessary).

The 'Alpha-Spirit' is a god-like artist with unlimited 'Creative Ability', access to limitless ink and pad of unending paper at their disposal. But over time, it became increasingly fixed on its one track of compulsive creation. Once we can rehabilitate SELF with certainty of its own 'Creative Ability' again —only then might an individual be convinced enough to finally tear off that top sheet of paper and regain the freedom of its true 'Spiritual Beingness'.

—#1—
PRESENCE: ENVIRONMENTAL SECURITY
• Look around your environment and spot objects that are acceptable—that you don't mind being present.
• Look around your environment and find objects that you wouldn't mind having.
• Look around your environment and spot locations where you are not.
• Look around your environment and notice persons that are not present; objects that are not present; animals that are not present; locations that are not present; times and incidents that are not happening.

—#2—
MENTAL IMAGERY: TURNING ON PICTURES
• Recall an actual event that has happened. When was it? Where was it? Who was there? What is its duration? Imagine the scenery. Notice as many facets of perception as you can—time of day, sensations, touch, weather, humidity, objects, brightness, smells, tastes, sounds, communications, dialogue, emotions of others, personal emotions, gestures, body positions, motion, personal movement, &tc.

• Repeat the above step several times (with eyes closed if it is easier); recalling, imagining and looking at times/ events which are acceptable to view, noticing all the details and facets—for example: when you saw something beautiful; when you heard something you enjoyed; when you smelled something pleasant, &tc.

• Continue until a clearer perception of Mental Imagery is realized.

:: Persistent Blackness/No Images—Imagine a duplicate of the blackness in the same space as the one you're looking at. Make a copy of it beside it. Make another copy. And another. Several more. Push the copies together and compress into nothing. Make eight more copies; then push them together and throw it away. Make eight more copies; push them together and then push them into the body. Continue this step until the compulsively generated blackness is under your control and you can perceive imagined or recalled images.

—#3A—

PRESENCE: BETA-EXISTENCE SPACE-TIME

• Select two walls in a room with a clear path to walk between them. Start in the center facing one wall and get the sense that you are making the body perform these actions: Look at that wall; Walk over to that wall; Touch that wall; Turn around. Repeat the actions numerous times between both walls, each time giving the same attention to each action as if it's the first time.

• For advanced practice, perform the previous step as directed without moving the body from the center of the room and with eyes closed. Perform it again using Imagination and Self-directed attention to alternate your Awareness between the two walls and touch them (with your Awareness). Then, repeat the actions, focusing on getting an actual sense of the perception of touching the wall. If this doesn't happen right away, just imagine the feel of the wall.

—#3B—

PRESENCE: SPATIAL CORNER-POINTS

• Eyes closed, sitting near the center of a room—Reach up with Awareness and locate an upper corner-point in back of the room. Then find the second upper-corner. Focus all Awareness on these back two corner-points without thinking anything else. Keep all attention on these corner-points.

• To take a step further as an advanced practice, during a separate creative session, perform the same procedure treating all four back corner-points.

• This exercise can be extended to include all eight corner-points defining a room. This demonstrates basic principles behind the "imagined" or "spiritual" version of this exercise called "Creation-of-Space."

—#4A—

FACSIMILE-COPIES: "WHAT'RE YOU LOOKING AT?"

• Eyes closed. What are you looking at? Imagine another copy just like it. Make another copy next to it. And several more. Then compress them all together into a ball and discard or toss away.

• Eyes open. Spot an object in the environment. Imagine a duplicate or copy of it right beside it. Spot another object and repeat. Continue to do this with various objects.

• With eyes closed, get a sense of looking at the objects in the environment. Imagine a duplicate or copy beside each, one by one.

• With eyes closed, while indoors, get a sense of looking at objects outside the environment/room/building; and imagine a duplicate or copy beside each.

• Practice each of the above—but imagining a perfect duplicate of the object, making it in the same space, using the same energy-mass; then consider that the object is there again; then make a perfect duplicate; then consider the original object is there again. Alternate repeatedly between the original object and the duplicate.

:: Persistent Images/Imprints—Imagine a duplicate of the image in the same space as the one you're looking at.

Make a copy of it beside it. Make another copy. And another. Several more. Jam the copies together into a ball and compress into nothing. Make eight more copies; then jam them together into a ball and toss it away. Make eight more copies; jam them together into a ball and push them into the body. Continue this step until the compulsively generated image is under your control.

—#4B—
FACSIMILE-COPIES: IDENTIFICATION & BODIES
• Eyes closed. Imagine a duplicate (identical copy) of your presently owned Human body out in front of you. Make a copy next to it. And another. And several more. When you have eight or so, push them together into a ball and collapse it into nothing. Imagine another duplicate. Make a copy next to it. And many more copies; then push them together into a ball and toss it away. Continue this step until you feel comfortable in creating bodies.

–Imagine a duplicate of your present body as ideal and healthy; then unmake it. Make it again; then unmake it. Alternate repeatedly.

–Looking into a mirror. Get the sense that there is "something there"; then get the sense there is "nothing there." Alternate these considerations repeatedly.

• Eyes closed. Imagine a busy or crowded place, mall, depot or street corner. Place your point-of-view in a fixed location; then look around and spot objects, motions and people in this scenery. Practice this for multiple locations (preferably until an increase in actual perception).

–Choose the location you like best from the previous step to use for the remaining cycle of exercises; Imagine making a facsimile-copy of your present Human body to use as a point-of-view; then unmake the body and remain looking as an Awareness. Alternate repeatedly.

• Perform the previous step, but this time: Imagine an identical copy of the body out in front of you, using a point-of-view outside the body to look around the location; then use a point-of-view from inside the body to look around the location. Alternate viewpoints repeatedly.

–Perform the previous step, but this time adding: Get the sense of other persons acknowledging your presence when they are near or walking by (even if they don't look at the body).

• Select a basic solid object (pyramid, cone, cube, sphere, &tc.); Imagine using the "object" as your body to practice each previous step of this locational-cycle of exercises; making and unmaking, alternating viewpoints, spotting other objects, noticing motions and persons, and receiving acknowledgment ("hellos") for your presence. Now add to this cycle: unmaking the body and point-of-view in one spot, then making it again at other spots in the location. Get a sense of moving that body like a "playing piece."

–As before; Imagine using a duplicate copy of your present body.

–As before; Imagine use of an elderly body.

–As before; Imagine use of a child body.

–As before; Imagine using a body of a different gender.

–As before; Imagine using a body that appears strong.

–As before; Imagine using a body that appears wise.

–As before; Imagine using a sparkly cloud of silvery-white energy for a body with small golden balls for eyes.

–As before; using only the point-of-view as an Awareness with nothing added as a body.

—#4C—

FACSIMILE-COPIES: MACHINERY AND BODIES

• Select an object that has a basic mechanical function "to produce a flow." (This may be best practiced with a "sink" or "water-spigot" until there is an independent reality on electricity and basic motions.)

–With eyes open. Look at the mechanical-object in its "off" condition and imagine an identical duplicate beside it. Look between the two and spot any differences, adjusting your created duplicate to match the original. Continue until satisfied with the certainty of duplication.

–Turn the mechanical-object "on" and look at it in this condition, noting the motion and getting a sense of the energy-flow driving it. Adjust your imagined duplicate to match this in every way, noting the motion and getting a sense of the energy-flow involved.

• For advancing these steps, with eyes closed; use an object not present.

• Select a mechanical-object that has a basic "motor" function. (This may be best practiced with an "electric fan" until there is an independent reality on generators and engines.)

–Apply the previous basic steps for imagining duplicate machinery; this time giving particular attention to its internal mechanics: at basic, a circuit or energy flow that drives or propels the spinning motion of the blades and is started and stopped by a switch. As it runs (is "on") get a sense of the internal mechanics and match this energy and motion in your duplicate.

• For additional practice: use more complex machines; use machinery not present; use electronic devices. A basic study in physical mechanics on "how things work" is of benefit.

• Eyes closed. Imagine being a "motor-vehicle"; create the machine, the internal mechanics, and get the sense of identifying with it as a body. Establish a point-of-view from the car, while maintaining a sense of the energy and motion mechanically operating inside of it.

• For advancing this step further, move your point-of-view through each mechanical system of the vehicle as you imagine it running: steering, brakes, the engine, transmission, &tc. (to the best of your reality on these systems). Get a sense for how it operates from the inside.

• Apply basic directions for using a solid object in locational-cycle exercises (#4B), this time using a vehicle (such as a car) for a body. Run the whole cycle using the vehicle: everything from "making and unmaking" to considerations as a "playing piece."

• Imagine the creation and unmaking of various machinery, devices, motors, vehicles, engines, generators, and power plants. Imagine as much detail in your creations as you can.

–Additionally; Imagine being various machinery. Alternate your point-of-view between inside and outside various vehicles and machines.

• Imagine the creation and unmaking of various personal "mental machinery": devices that inform you of things, so you don't have to know; devices that react for you, so you don't have to remember; devices that show impressions of what things are, so you don't have to look; devices that make your creations invisible as soon as you imagine them; devices that turn mental images into dark screens and black clouds when you try to remember them; devices that make mental images for you, so you don't have to create. Consider other mental mechanism that could be created.

–Additionally; Imagine being various mental machinery. Alternate your point-of-view between inside and outside various mental machinery.

• Eyes open, outdoors, public area. Spot a person that is standing or sitting for a while (like at a bus-stop). Imagine the creation of an identical duplicate copy beside them. As in previous steps; look between the two and spot any differences, adjusting your duplicate to match.

–Additionally; if the person leaves your view during practice, simply select another. If they change positions or spots in the area, adjust your duplicate copy to match the motion. Practice this step with several persons.

• Once certainty is established with the previous step: use the step to duplicate a person; this time giving particular attention to copying the internal parts of that body (bones, organs, muscle, &tc.) and get a sense of the **organic** systems functioning inside (as with the previous exercise on machines).

–Additionally; apply this step to duplicate a moving person, copying the motion in your duplicate. Get a sense of how the internal organic machinery drive various motors and systems during the motion. Practice this step with several persons. Practice this step repeatedly.

—#5A—

CONTROL: "WHAT IS THAT BODY DOING?"
• Get the sense of you making the body do "what it's do-ing." Get the sense of making the body sit in a chair. Get the sense that you're making that body hold a book, &tc.
• Get the sense that you are behind the body, controlling its movement by strings or beams.
• Decide when to lift a finger of the body and then do so, imagining its control by a string. Decide when to lower it and then do so. Practice this on other movable parts of the body.
• Decide to conduct some activity (walk outdoors, &tc.) and focus Awareness behind the body's head. Expand your POV to encompass the entire space around the body. Move the body around, still using its eyes, but imagine con-trolling the body from behind it.
• Perform the previous step, emphasizing attention on the presser (push) and tractor (pull) energy beams directed to control movement of the body.
  :: Compulsions/Ticks and Twitches—Consider a behavior that the body does compulsively on its own. Now decide to do this on your own determinism and you do so. Decide to stop and you do so. Start it again and decide to increase/exaggerate the action; then you do so. Decide to decrease the action and you do it. Decide to stop again and do it. Repeated this cycle until the behavior is under better control.

—#5B—

PRESENCE: DISTANCE & CONNECTEDNESS
• Eyes open. Spot two objects and notice the differences between them; then note the distance between them. Then get a sense of the space between them.
• With eyes closed, repeat the above step.
• Eyes open. Look around and spot an object that you wouldn't mind connected to you. Get the sense of making that object connect to you. Then get the sense that it is separate from you. Alternate. Determine how you could make it connect. Then consider in what ways it is different

from you.

• With eyes closed, repeat the above step.

• Eyes open. Spot an object. Decide that you will walk over to the object and do so. Decide that you will reach out and touch the object and do so. Decide that you will let go of the object and do so.

• With eyes closed, repeat the above step by extending your Awareness.

• Walking outdoors; get the sense of being stationary and moving space around you, then get the sense of moving through space.

• Eyes open, then eyes closed. Indoors and outdoors; spot two objects and notice the distances between the objects and you. Then get a sense of the space between them and you.

• Perform the above step using three objects.

• Look around and spot something that is still; then spot something that is in motion. Alternate repeatedly.

• Eyes closed, repeat the above step, using a point-of-view from spaces or locations where you are not.

—#6—

ALTERNATION: "BELL, BOOK & CANDLE"

• Select a small simple object (such as a "bell, book or candle") that is easily moved. Locate two spots. Move the object uniformly back and forth between these exact two spots at a consistent speed. Reach and let go for every spot change, leaving the object in precisely the same position at each spot for a moment.

• Select two small dissimilar objects (such as a "bell, book or candle") that are easily moved. Locate two spots (on a table). Place an object in each spot. Pick up "Object-1" and look at it. Notice its weight, its feel and its appearance. Get the sense of you making it more solid. Put it back in the same exact spot and position. Pick up "Object-2" and look at it. Notice its weight, its feel and its appearance. Get the sense of you making it more solid. Put it back in the same exact spot and position. Alternate this step between the two objects, each time treated as the first time.

• Continue the previous step until there is no compulsion toward automatic actions or responses, no fluctuation in attention and no desire to "leave" the exercise.

• For advanced practice, perform the physical version of the previous step, then close your eyes and imagine six walls forming a room that is not located in the Physical Universe. Imagine two tables or pedestals in the room. Imagine "Object-1" is on one table; hold it still and make it more solid. Imagine "Object-2" is on the other table; hold it still and make it more solid. Imagine "Object-1" floating up in the air; get a sense of its weight, its feel and its appearance; then have it float back down. Imagine "Object-2" floating up in the air; get a sense of its weight, its feel and its appearance; then have it float back down. Alternate as described above.

• Continue the previous step until there is increased perception of actual solidity and weight (in addition to imagined).

—#7—
ALTERNATION (POV): AWARENESS OF SPOTS
• Eyes open. Locate a spot on the body, decide to reach out and touch it, then do so. Decide when to let go and do so. Find another spot on the body, and repeat the step. And again.

• With eyes closed, repeat the above step.

• Locate a spot in space, decide to move the body and touch it, then do so. Decide when to let go and do so. Find another spot in space, and repeat the step. And again.

• With eyes closed, repeat the above step.

• Locate a spot on the floor, decide to move the body over it, then do so. Find another spot on the floor, and repeat the step. And again.

• With eyes closed and without moving the body, repeat the above step.

• Locate two spots on the floor, decide to move the body over one, then walk toward it. Before reaching the spot, decide to change your mind and move the body over the other one instead. Find another two spots on the floor, and repeat the step. And again.

• With eyes closed and without moving the body, repeat the above step, relocating your Awareness-POV.

• Locate three points in the body; direct all attention on these three points in the body. Locate three points in space; direct all attention on these three points in space. Alternate these repeatedly—three points in the body; three points in space.

• With eyes closed, perform the above step; rapidly and re- peatedly.

• Continue until there is perception separate from a body.

—#8—

PROCEDURE 1-8-0, ISSUE #4, ROUTE-8

• Eyes closed. Imagine you are extending your Awareness, reaching through the entire Physical Universe, as far as you can imagine. Now reach a little further beyond and outside of all dimensional space and find the Nothingness. Hold your point-of-view on the Nothingness, without thinking or imagining anything else.

–Extend your reach out on the right side, getting a cer- tainty of the Nothingness.

–Extend your reach out on the left side, getting a cer- tainty of the Nothingness.

–Repeat the previous step for each direction; reaching in front, reaching behind, reaching above, reaching below.

–Extend your reach out to the right and left simultan- eously, holding the perception of Nothingness in both dir- ections.

–Repeat the previous step for each direction-pair: in front of and behind you; then above and below you.

–Extend your reach out on all six sides of you at once, maintaining a certainty of Nothingness in all directions.

• To take a step further, alternate between this point-of- view (on Nothingness) with eyes closed and the point-of- view toward the Physical Universe with eyes open. Look around each time and orient Self to the environment.

• Alternate getting full perception of Nothingness and full perception of the Physical Universe.

SYSTEMOLOGY
TECHNICAL
DICTIONARY

THE COMPLETE SYSTEMOLOGY TECHNICAL DICTIONARY (VERSION 5.0)

—A—

A-for-A (one-to-one) : an expression meaning that what we say, write, represent, think or symbolize is a direct and perfect reflection or duplication of the actual aspect or thing—that "A" is for, means and is equivalent to "A" and not "a" or "q" or "!"; in the relay of communication, the message or particle is sent and perfectly duplicated in form and meaning when received.

aberration : a departure from what is right; in chromatic light science, the failure of a mirror, lens or refracting surface to produce an exact *"one-to-one"* or *"A-for-A"* duplication between an object and its image; a deviation from, or distortion in, what is true or right or straight; in *NexGen Systemology*, a term to describe *fragmentation* as it applies to an individual, which causes them to "stray" form the *Pathway*.

abreaction (abreactive therapy) : the "burn off" or "purging" or "discharge" of "unconscious" (reactive response) as applied to early 20th century German psychology, from *abreagieren*, meaning "coming down" from a release or expression of a repressed or forgotten emotion; in *NexGen Systemology*, fully "resurfacing" traumatic past experiences consciously (on one's own determinism) in order to purge them of their emotional excess (or "charge"); also *"Route-1"* and *"catharsis."*

acid-test : a metaphor refers to a chemical process of applying harsh nitric acid to a golden substance (sample) to determine its genuineness; in *NexGen Systemology*, an extreme conclusive process to determine the reality, genuineness or truth of a substance, material, particle or piece of information.

acknowledgment : a response-communication establishing that an immediately former communication was properly received, duplicated and understood; the formal acceptance and/or recognition of a communication or presence.

activating event : an incident or occurrence that automatically stimulates a conscious or unrecognized reminder or 'ping' from an earlier *imprinting incident* recorded on one's own personal timeline as an emotionally charged and encoded memory; an incident or instance when thought systems are activated to determine the consequence or significance of an activity, motion or event—often demonstrated as *Activating Event → Belief Systems → Consideration*.

actualization : to make actual, not just potential; to bring into full solid Reality; to realize fully in *Awareness* as a "thing."

affinity : the apparent and energetic *relationship* between substances or bodies; the degree of *attraction* or repulsion between things based on natural forces; the *similitude* of frequencies or waveforms; the degree of *interconnection* between systems.

agreement (reality) : unanimity of opinion of what is "thought" to be known; an accepted arrangement of how things are; things we consider as "real" or as an "is" of "reality"; a *consensus* of what is real as made by standard-issue (common) participants; what an individual contributes to or accepts as "real"; in *NexGen Systemology*, a synonym for "*reality.*"

allegorical : a representation of the abstract, metaphysical or "spiritual" using physical or concrete forms.

alpha : the first, primary, basic, superior or beginning of some form; in *NexGen Systemology*, referring to the state of existence operating on spiritual archetypes and postulates, will and intention "exterior" to the low-level condensation and solidarity of energy and matter as the 'physical universe'.

alpha control center (ACC) : the highest relay point of *Beingness* for an individuated *Alpha-Spirit*, *Self* or "I-

AM"; in *NexGen Systemology*—a point of spiritual separation of ZU at (7.0) from the *Infinity of Nothingness* (8.0); the truest actualization of *Identity*; the highest *Self-directed* relay of *Alpha-Self* as an *Identity-Continuum*, operating in an *alpha-existence* (or "Spiritual Universe"–AN) to *determine* "Alpha Thought" (6.0) and WILL-*Intention* (5.0) *exterior* to the "Physical Universe"–(KI); the "wave-peak" of "I" emerging as individuated consciousness from *Infinity*.

alpha-spirit : a "spiritual" *Life*-form; the "true" *Self* or I-AM; the *individual*; the spiritual (*alpha*) *Self* that is animating the (*beta*) physical body or "*genetic vehicle*" using a continuous *Lifeline* of spiritual ("*ZU*") energy; an individual spiritual (*alpha*) entity possessing no physical mass or measurable waveform (motion) in the Physical Universe as itself, so it animates the (*beta*) physical body or "*genetic vehicle*" as a catalyst to experience *Self*-determined causality in effect within the *Physical Universe*; a singular unit or point of *Spiritual Awareness* that is *Aware* that it is *Aware*.

alpha thought : the highest spiritual *Self-determination* over creation and existence exercised by an Alpha-Spirit; the Alpha range of pure *Creative Ability* based on direct postulates and considerations of *Beingness*; spiritual qualities comparable to "thought" but originating in Alpha-existence (at "6.0") independently superior to a *beta-anchored* Mind-System, although an Alpha-Spirit may use Will ("5.0") to carry the intentions of a postulate or consideration ("6.0") to the Master Control Center ("4.0").

amplitude : the quality of being *ample*; the size or amount of energy that is demonstrated in a *wave*. In the case of audio waves, we associate amplitude with "volume." It is not a statement about the frequencies of waves, only how "loud" they are—to what extent they are or may be projected (or audible).

AN : an ancient "Sumerian" cuneiform sign for Heaven or "God"; in *Mardukite Zuism and Systemology* designating the *'spiritual zone'* (or *'Alpha Existence'*); the *Spiritual Universe*—comprised of spiritual matter and spiritual energy; a direction of motion toward spiritual *Infinity*, away from or superior to the physical (*'KI'*); the spiritual condition of existence providing for our primary *Alpha* state as an individual *Identity* or *I-AM-Self* which interacts and experiences *Awareness* of a *beta* state in the *Physical Universe* (*'KI'*) as *Life*.

anathema : a thing or person to be detested, loathed or avoided; a thing or person accursed or despised such as to wish damnation or "divine punishment" upon.

anchor (conceptual) : a stable point in space; a fixed point used to hold or stabilize a spatial existence of other points; a spatial point that fixes the parameters of dimensional orientation, such as the corner-points of a solid object in relation to other points in space; in *Nex-Gen Systemology*, "beta-anchored" is an expression used to describe the fixed orientation of a viewpoint from Self in relation to all possible spatial points in *beta-existence* ("physical universe"), or else the existential points that fix the operation of the "body" within the space-time of *beta-existence*.

Ancient Mystery School : the original arcane source of all esoteric knowledge on Earth, concentrated between the Middle East and modern-day Turkey and Transylvania c. 6000 B.C. and then dispersing south (Mesopotamia), west (Europe) and east (Asia) from that location.

antinomian : a term applied to *Gnostics* (popularized by Martin Luther during the Christian reformation) denoting a rejection of formal religious morals and dogma —decreed, written and interpreted by humanity—as a true pathway to Ascension (some elements appear in all forms of religious protest and reformation but as an extreme, would be considered spirto-religious rebellious punkdom by some modern standards, but it should be understood that it does follow a higher ethic, such as Mardukite Utilitarianism.

apotheosis : from the *Greek* word, meaning *"to deify"*; the highest point or apex (for example, of "true knowledge" and "true experience"); an ultimate development of; a glorified or "deified" *ideal*, such as is a quality of *godhood*.

apparent : visibly exposed to sight; evident rather than actual, as presumed by Observation; readily perceived, especially by the senses.

a-priori : from "cause" to "effect"; from a general application to a particular instance; existing in the mind prior to, and independent of experience or observation; validity based on consideration and deduction rather than experience.

archetype : a "first form" or ideal conceptual model of some aspect; the ultimate prototype of a form on which all other conceptions are based.

ascension : actualized *Awareness* elevated to the point of true "spiritual existence" exterior to *beta existence*. An "Ascended Master" is one who has returned to an incarnation on Earth as an inherently *Enlightened One*, demonstrable in their actions—they have the ability to *Self-direct* the "Spirit" as *Self*, just as we are treating the "Mind" and "Body" at this current grade of instruction; previously treated in *Moroii ad Vitam* as a state of Beingness after *First Death*, experienced by an *etheric body*, which is able to maintain consciousness as a personal identity continuum with the same *Self-directed* control and communication of Will-Intention that is exercised, actualized and developed deliberately during one's present incarnation.

assessment : an analysis or synthesis of collected information, usually about a person or group, in relation to an *assessment scale*.

assessment scale : an official assignment of graded/gradient numeric values correlated to specific tiers with individual preassigned meanings.

associative knowledge : significance or meaning of a

facet or aspect assigned to (or considered to have) a direct relationship with another facet; to connect or relate ideas or facets of existence with one another; a reactive-response image, emotion or conception that is suggested by (or directly accompanies) something other than itself; in traditional systems logic, an equivalency of significance or meaning between facets or sets that are grouped together, such as in *(a + b) + c = a + (b + c)*; in Nex-Gen Systemology, erroneous associative knowledge is assignment of the same value to all facets or parts considered as related (even when they are not actually so), such as in *a = a, b = a, c = a* and so forth without distinction.

assumption : the act of taking or gathering to one's Self; taking possession of, receive or behold.

attenergy : *NexGen Systemological NewSpeak* for "attention energies"; the flow of consciousness "energy" that is directed as "attention"; semantic recognition of an axiom from the *Arcane Tablets* that states: "energy flows where attention goes."

attention : active use of *Awareness* toward a specific aspect or thing; the act of "attending" with the presence of *Self*; a direction of focus or concentration of *Awareness* along a particular channel or conduit or toward a particular terminal node or communication termination point; the Self-directed concentration of personal energy as a combination of observation, thought-waves and consideration; focused application of *Self-Directed Awareness*.

authoritarian : knowledge as truth, boundaries and freedoms dictated to an individual by a perceived, regulated or enforced "authority."

auto-suggestion (self-hypnosis) : auto-conditioning; self-programming; delivering directed affirmations or statements repeatedly to *Self* in order to condition a change in behavior or beliefs; any *Self-directed* technique intended to generate a specific "*post-hypnotic suggestion.*"

awareness : the highest sense of-and-as Self in knowing and being as I-AM (the *Alpha-Spirit*); the extent of be-ingness directed as a POV experienced by Self as knowingness.

axiom : a fundamental truism of a knowledge system, esp. *logic*; all *maxims* are also *axioms*; knowledge state-ments that require no proof because their truth is self-evident; an established law or systematic principle used as a *premise* on which to base greater conclusions of truth.

—B—

Babylonian : the ancient Mesopotamian civilization that evolved from *Sumer*; inception point for systematiz-ation of civic society and religion.

Back-Scan : to apply Awareness, *Zu-Vision* or "Al-pha-Sight" (*exterior* to the *Human Condition*) and *resurface* impressions for recreating *Mental Imagery* of the *Backtrack* within one's own Personal Universe and treat with Wizard-Level (*Grade-V+*) methodology.

Backtrack : to retrace one's steps or go back to an early point in a sequence; an applied spiritual philosophy within *Metahuman Systemology* "*Wizard Grades*" re-garding continuous existence of an individual's "*Spiritual Timeline*" through all lifetime-incarnations; the course that is already laid behind us; a methodology of systematic processing methods developed to assist in revealing "hidden" *Mental Images* and *Imprints* from one's past and reclaim attention-energies "left behind" with them by increasing ability to manage and control personal energy mechanisms fixed to their continuous automated creation.

band : a division or group; in *NexGen Systemology*, a division or set of frequencies on the ZU-line that are tuned closely together and referred to as a group.

BAT (Beta-Awareness Test) : a method of *psychomet-ric evaluation* developed for *Mardukite Systemology* to determine a "basic" or "average" state of personal *beta-Awareness*; first developed for the text *"Crystal Clear."*

"bell, book & candle" : three dissimilar objects that are kept accessible during a processing session (the book is often a copy of *The Systemology Handbook* or a hard-cover copy of *The Tablets of Destiny* with the dust-jacket removed if it is less distracting that way); a term meant to indicate a Pilot's "objective processing kit" of objects generally present in the session room (accessible on a shelf, table or pedestal stands); in *NexGen Systemology,* the name of an objective processing philosophy pertaining to command of personal reality; historically, a formal ritual used by the Roman Catholic church to ce-remonially declare an individual "guilty of the most heinous sins" as "excommunicated (to hold no further communications with) by anathema"—whereby a *bell* is rung, a *holy book* is closed and all *candles* are snuffed out—thus we therapeutically use the same symbolism historically representing religious fragmentation for modern systematic defragmentation purposes.

beta (awareness) : all consciousness activity (*"Awareness"*) in the "Physical Universe" (KI) or else *beta-existence*; *Awareness* within the range of the *genetic-body*, including material thoughts, emotional responses and physical motors; personal *Awareness* of physical energy and physical matter moving through physical space and experienced as "time"; the *Awareness* held by *Self* that is restricted to a physical organic *Lifeform* or *"genetic vehicle"* in which it experiences causality in the *Physical Universe*.

beta (existence) : all manifestation in the "Physical Universe" (KI); the "Physical" state of existence con-sisting of vibrations of physical energy and physical matter moving through physical space and experienced as "time"; the conditions of *Awareness* for the *Al-pha-spirit* (*Self*) as a physical organic *Lifeform* or *"genetic vehicle"* in which it experiences causality in the *Physical Universe*.

beta-defragmentation : toward a state of *Self-Honesty* in regards to handling experience of the "Physical Universe" (*beta-existence*); an applied spiritual philosophy (or technology) of Self-Actualization originally described in the text "*Crystal Clear*" (*Liber-2B*), building upon theories from "*Systemology: The Original Thesis*."

biological unconsciousness : the organism independent of the sentient *Awareness* of the *Self* to direct it; states induced by severe injury and anesthesia.

biomagnetic/biofeedback : a measurable effect, such as a change in electrical resistance, that is produced by thoughts, emotions and physical behaviors which generate specific 'neurotransmitters' and biochemical reactions in the brain, body and across the skin surface.

—C—

cacophony : dissonant, turbulent, harsh and/or discordant sound or noise.

calcified : in nature, to calcify is to harden like stone from calcium and lime deposits; in philosophic applications, refers to a state of hardened fixed bone-like inflexibility; a condition change to rigidly solid.

capable : the actual capacity for potential ability.

CAT / "Creative Ability Test" : a method of increasing personal freedom and unlimited creative potential of the Alpha-Spirit (Self) independent and exterior to conditions and reality agreements with beta-existence; a Wizard-Level training regimen first developed for the Grade-IV text "*Imaginomicon*" (*Liber-3D*).

catalog / catalogue : a systematic list of knowledge or record of data.

catalyst : something that causes action between two systems or aspects, but which itself is unaffected as a variable of this energy communication; a medium or intermediary channel.

catharsis / cathartic processing : from the Greek root

meaning "pure" or "perfect"; Gnostic practices of "consolamentum" where an individual removes distorting/fragmented emotional charges and encoding from a personal energy flow/circuit connected or associated with some terminal, mass, thing, *&tc.*; in *NexGen Systemology*, the emptying out or discharge of emotional stores; also "*abreaction*" or "*Route-1.*"

causative : as being the cause; to be at cause.

chakra : an archaic Sanskrit term for "wheel" or "spinning circle" used in *Eastern* wisdom traditions, spiritual systems and mysticism; a concept retained in NexGen Systemology to indicate etheric concentrations of energy into wheel-mechanisms that process *ZU* energy at specific frequencies along the *ZU-line*, of which the *Human Condition* is reportedly attached *seven* at various degrees as connected to the Gate symbolism.

channel : a specific stream, course, current, direction or route; to form or cut a groove or ridge or otherwise guide along a specific course; a direct path; an artificial aqueduct created to connect two water bodies or water or make travel possible.

charge : to fill or furnish with a quality; to supply with energy; to lay a command upon; in *NexGen Systemology*—to imbue with intention; to overspread with emotion; application of *Self-directed (WILL)* "intention" toward an emotional manifestation in beta-existence; personal energy stores and significances entwined as fragmentation in mental images, reactive-response encoding and intellectual (and/or) programmed beliefs; in traditional mysticism, to intentionally fix an energetic resonance to meet some degree, or to bring a specific concentration of energy that is transferred to a focal point, such as an object or space.

circuit : a circular path or loop; a closed-path within a system that allows a flow; a pattern or action or wave movement that follows a specific route or potential path only; in *NexGen Systemology*, "*communication processing*" pertaining to a specific flow of energy or information along a channel; *see* also *"feedback loop."*

Circuit-1 : in *Grade-IV* "communication processing" (introduced in *Metahuman Destinations* as *Route-3*), the flow of energy and information connected to outflow, what *Self* has expressed, projected outwardly or done.

Circuit-2 : in *Grade-IV* "communication processing" (introduced in *Metahuman Destinations* as *Route-3*), the flow of energy and information connected to inflow, what "others" have done to *Self,* what it has received inwardly or had *happen to.*

Circuit-3 : in *Grade-IV* "communication processing" (introduced in *Metahuman Destinations* as *Route-3*), the flow of energy and information connected to cross-flows, what *Self* has witnessed of others (or another) projecting or doing toward others (or another).

Circuit-0 : a more advanced concept introduced to *Grade-IV* "communication processing" (as listed on SOP-2C in *Metahuman Destinations* for "*Pre-A.T*" or "*Route-0*" applications), which targets *'postulates'* and *'considerations'* generated and stored by *Self* for *Self* and the direction, energy or flows representing what *Self* "does" for and/or to *Self.* This circuit is treated further in *Wizard Level* work,

chronologically : concerning or pertaining to "time"; to treat as "units" of "time" ; to sequence a series of events or information with regard to the order it happened or originated (in time).

clockwork : rigidly fixed gear-like systems that operate mechanically and directly upon one another to function; a "clockwork universe theory" is a "closed-system design" popular in Newtonian Physics attributes all actions of energy-matter in space-time as reactions in accordance with a "Divine Decree" or fixed design that functions like a "clock-mechanism" and does not account for the "Observer."

code (ethics) : an outline of *ethical* standards regarding social participation and acceptable behavior; not generally enforced as *law* itself, but a standard that reasonable individuals are actualized (or civil) enough to *Self-Determine* (by choice) their own following (or adherence) if it is *right* and *good*; shared reality agreements that promote optimum conditions of continued existence ("SURVIVAL" in *Beta-existence*; "CREATION" in *Alpha*) for the highest affected "Sphere of Existence" (on the *Standard Model*).

codification : process of collecting, analyzing and then arranging knowledge in a standardized and more accessible systematic form, often by subject, theme or some other designation.

collapsing a wave : also, "*wave-function collapse*"; in *Quantum Physics*, the concept that an Observer is "collapsing" the wave-function to something "definite" by measuring it; defining or calculating a wave-function or interaction of potential interactions by an Observation; in *NexGen Systemology*, when a wave of potentiality or possibility because a finite fixed form; Consciousness or *Awareness* "collapses" a wave-function of energy-matter as a necessary "third" Principle of Apparent Manifestation (first described in "*Tablets of Destiny*"); potentiality as a wave is collapsed into an apparent "*is*", the energy of which is freed up in systematic processing by "*flattening*" a "collapsed" wave back into its state of potentiality.

command : in *Metahuman Systemology*, responsibility and ability of Self (I-AM) as operating from its ideal "exterior" *Point-of-View* as Alpha Spirit; to direct communication for control of the *genetic vehicle* and Mind-Body connection that is perfectly duplicated from a source-point to a receipt-point along the ZU-line.

command line : see "*processing command line*" (PCL).

common knowledge (game theory) : facts that all "players" know, and they know that all other "players" also know—such as the very structure of the "game" being played.

communication : successful transmission of information, data, energy (&tc.) along a message line, with a reception of feedback; an energetic flow of intention to cause an effect (or duplication) at a distance; the personal energy moved or acted upon by will or else 'selective directed attention'; the 'messenger action' used to transmit and receive energy across a medium; also relay of energy, a message or signal—or even locating a personal POV (viewpoint) for the Self—along the *ZU-line*.

communication (circuit) processing : a methodology of Grade-IV Metahuman Systemology that emphasizes analysis of all Mind-System energy flows (information) transmitted and stored along circuits of a channel toward some terminal, thing or concept, particularly: what Self has out-flowed, what Self has in-flowed, and the cross-flows that Self has observed; also *"Route-3"*

compulsion : a failure to be responsible for the dynamics of control—starting, stopping or altering—on a particular channel of communication and/or regarding a particular terminal in existence; an energetic flow with the appearance of being 'stuck' on the action it is already doing or by the control of some automatic mechanism.

computing device : a calculator or modern computer; a mechanism that performs specific functions, particularly input, output and storage of data/information.

concept : a high-frequency thought-wave representing an "idea" which persists because it is not restricted to a unique space-time; an abstract or tangible "idea" formed in the "Mind" or *imagined* as a means of understanding, usually including associated "Mental Images"; a seemingly timeless collective thought-theme (or subject) that entangles together facets of many events or incidents, not just a single significant one.

conceptual processing : a Wizard-Level methodology introduced intermittently throughout materials of Metahuman Systemology that emphasizes fully "getting the sense of" (or "contacting the idea of") a particular condition as prompted by a PCL and on one's own determination; a systematic practice-drill regarding considerations and postulates (Alpha Thought) regarding various reality agreements; a *Route-0* variant employing *Creativeness* and *Imagination* for systematic processing; also *Route-0E* when used for *Ethics Processing.*

condense (condensation) : the transition of vapor to liquid; denoting a change in state to a more substantial or solid condition; leading to a more compact or solid form.

condition : an apparent or existing state; circumstances, situations and variable dynamics affecting the order and function of a system; a series of interconnected requirements, barriers and allowances that must be met; in "contemporary language," bringing a thing toward a specific, desired or intentional new state (such as in "conditioning"), though to minimize confusion about the word "condition" in our literature, *NexGen Systemology* treats "contemporary conditioning" concepts as imprinting, encoding and programming.

conflict : the opposition of two forces of similar magnitude along the same channel or competing for the same terminal; the inability to duplicate another POV; a thought, intention or communication that is met with an opposing counter-thought or counter-intention that generates an energetic cluster.

confront : to come around in front of; to be in the presence of; to stand in front of, or in the face of; to meet "face-to-face" or "face-up-to"; additionally, in *NexGen Systemology*, to fully tolerate or acceptably withstand an encounter with a particular manifestation or encounter.

consciousness : the energetic flow of *Awareness*; the Principle System of *Awareness* that is spiritual in nature, which demonstrates potential interaction with all degrees of the Physical Universe; the *Beingness* component of our existence in *Spirit*; the Principle System of *Awareness* as *Spirit* that directs action in the Mind-System.

consensual (consensus) : formed or existing simply by consent—by general or mutual agreement; permitted, approved or agreed upon by majority of opinion; knowingly agreed upon unanimously by all concerned; to be in agreement on the objective universe and/or a course of action therein.

consideration : careful analytical reflection of all aspects; deliberation; determining the significance of a "thing" in relation to similarity or dissimilarity to other "things"; evaluation of facts and importance of certain facts; thorough examination of all aspects related to, or important for, making a decision; the analysis of consequences and estimation of significance when making decisions; in *NexGen Systemology*, the postulate or Alpha-Thought that defines the state of beingness for what something "*is.*"

continuity : being a continuous whole; a complete whole or "total round of"; the balance of the equation ["–120" + "120" = "0" *&tc.*]; an apparent unbroken interconnected coherent whole; also, as applied to Universes in *NexGen Systemology*, the lowest base consideration of space-time or commonly shared level of energy-matter apparent in an existence, or else the lowest degree of solidity or condensation whereby all mass that exists is identifiable or communicable with all other mass that exists; represented as "0" on the *Standard Model* for the Physical Universe (*beta-existence*), a level of existence that is below Human emotion, comparable to the solidity of "rocks" and "walls" and "inert bodies."

continuum : a continuous enduring uninterrupted sequence or condition; observing all gradients on a *spectrum*; measuring quantitative variation with gradual transition on a spectrum without demonstrating discontinuity or separate parts.

control (general) : the ability to start, change or start some action or flow of energy; the capacity to originate, change or stop some mode of human behavior by some implication, physical or psychological means to ensure compliance (voluntarily or involuntarily).

control (systems) : communication relayed from an operative center or organizational cluster, which incites new activity elsewhere in a system (or along the *ZU-line*).

correlate : a relationship between two or more aspects, parts or systems.

correspondence : a direct relationship or correlation; see also "*associative knowledge.*"

Cosmic History : the entire continuous *Spiritual Timeline* of all existence, starting with the *Infinity of Nothingness* and individuation of Self and its Home Universe, running through various Games Universes and ultimately leading to condensation and solidification of this Physical Universe experienced in present-time.

Cosmic Law : the "Law" of Nature (or the Physical Universe); the "Law" governing cosmic ordering; often called "Natural Law" in sciences and philosophies that attempt to codify or systematize it.

cosmology : a systematic philosophy defining origins and structure of an apparent Universe.

Cosmos : archaic term for the "Physical Universe"; semantically implies chaos brought into order; in *NexGen Systemology*, can also include considerations of "Universes" experienced previously as a *beta-existence*.

counter-productive : contrary to the greater or original purpose or intention; in *NexGen Systemology*, anything which brings *Life* away from its sustainable goal or position of *Infinite Existence*.

crash-coursed : a very intense or steep delivery of education over a very brief time period, usually applied to bring a student "up-to-speed" or "up-to-date" for receiving and understanding newer or cumulatively more advanced material.

266 – Technical Dictionary

creative ability test : see "*CAT.*"

creativeness processing : a *systematic processing* methodology introduced in *Grade-IV Metahuman Systemology* (*Wizard Level-0*) that emphasizes personal use of "*Imagination,*" or else "creative ability" of Self and freeing considerations of the Alpha-Spirit to *Be* or *Create* anything within its Personal Universe, independent of reality agreements with beta-existence; also "*Route-0.*"

Crossing the Abyss : to enter the spiritual or metaphysical unknown in "Self-annihilation" to purify the Self and "return to the Source."

Crystal Clear : the second professional publication of Mardukite Systemology, released publicly in December 2019; the second professional text in Grade-III Mardukite Systemology, released as "*Liber-2B*" and reissued in the Grade-III Master Edition "*Systemology Handbook*"; contains fundamental theory of "*Beta-Defragmentation*" and "*Route-2*" systematic processing methodology.

cuneiform : the oldest extant writing system at the inception of modern civilization in Mesopotamia; a system of wedge-shaped script inscribed on clay tablets with a reed pen, allowing advancements in record keeping and communication no longer restricted to more literal graphic representations or pictures.

cuneiform signs : the cuneiform script, as used in ancient Mesopotamia, is not represented in a linear alphabet of "letters," but by a systematic use of basic word "signs" that are combined to form more complex word "signs"—each sign represented a "sound" more than it did a letter, such as "ab," "ad", "ba", "da" *&tc.*

—D—

data-set : the total accumulation of knowledge used to base Reality.

dead-memories : outdated/inadequate/erroneous data.

defragmentation : the *reparation* of wholeness; collecting all dispersed parts to reform an original whole; a process of removing "*fragmentation*" in data or knowledge to provide a clear understanding; applying techniques and processes that promote a *holistic* interconnected *alpha* state, favoring observational *Awareness* of continuity in all spiritual and physical systems; in *NexGen Systemology*, a "*Seeker*" achieving an actualized state of basic "*Self-Honest Awareness*" is said to be *beta-defragmented*, whereas *Alpha-defragmentation* is the rehabilitation of the *creative ability*, managing the *Spiritual Timeline* and the POV of *Self* as Alpha-Spirit (I-AM); see also "*Beta-defragmentation.*"

degree : a physical or conceptual *unit* (or point) defining the variation present relative to a *scale* above and below it; any stage or extent to which something *is* in relation to other possible positions within a *set* of "*parameters*"; a point within a specific range or spectrum; in *NexGen Systemology*, a *Seeker's* potential energy variations or fluctuations in thought, emotional reaction and physical perception are all treated as "*degrees.*"

demographics : segments of the population uniquely identified, whether real or representative; targeting a specific portion of the population, such as for marketing or statistics.

destiny : what is set down, made firm, standard, or stands fixed as a constant end; the absolute *destination* regardless of whatever course is traveled; in *NexGen Systemology*, the "*destiny*" of the "*Human Spirit*" (or "*Alpha Spirit*") is infinite existence—"*Immortality.*"

dichotomy : a division into two parts, types or kinds.

differential : the quantitative value difference between two forces, motions, pressures or degrees.

differentiation : an apparent difference between aspects or concepts.

discernment : to perceive, distinguish and/or differentiate experience into true knowledge.

displace : to compel to leave; to move or replace something with something else in its place or space.

dissonance : discordance; out of step; out of phase; disharmonious; the "differential" between the way things are and the way things are experienced; cognitive dissonance could be demonstrated as A = abc, or C = A, the duplication of truth/communication is not A-for-A.

dogma : religious doctrines or opinion-based beliefs (data-set) treated socially as fact, especially regarding "divinity" or "God" (the common "Human" interpretation of the "domain" of Infinity) represented by the "Eighth Sphere" on our original Standard Model of Systemology; religiously defined values, taboos and ethical standards emphasized by cultural/religious socialization and mythographic beliefs (even above any observable causal effects, logical sequences or verifiable proofs).

dramatization / dramatize : a vivid display or performance as if rehearsed for a "play" (on stage); a *'circuit'* recording *'imprinted'* in the past and, once restimulated by a facet of the environment, the individual "replays" it as through reacting to it in the present (and identifying that reality as present reality); acts, actions and observable behaviors that demonstrate identification with a particular character type, "phase" or personality program; a motivated sequence-chain, implant series or imprinted cycle of actions—usually irrational or counter-survival—repeated by an individual as it had previously happened to them; a reoccurring or reactively triggered out-flow, communication or action that indicates an individual "occupying" a particular *'Point-of-View'* (*POV*)—typically fixed to a specific (past) identification (identity) that is space-time locatable (meaning a point where significant *Attenergy*—enough to compulsively create and maintain a POV—is "stuck" or "hung up" on the *BackTrack*).

dross : prime material; specifically waste-matter or refuse; the discarded remains collected together.

dynamic (systems) : a principle or fixed system which demonstrates its *'variations'* in activity (or output) only in constant relation to variables or fluctuation of interrelated systems; a standard principle, function, process or system that exhibits *'variations'* and change simultaneously with all connected systems; each *'Sphere of Existence'* is a dynamic system, systematically affecting (supporting) and affected (supported) by other *'Spheres'* (which are also dynamic systems).

—E—

Eastern traditions : the evolution of the *Ancient Mystery School* east of its origins, primarily the Asian continent, or what is archaically referred to as "oriental."

echelon : a level or rung on a ladder; a rank or level of command.

eclipse : to cast a shadow or darken; to block out or obscure a comparison.

EDA : "electro-dermal activity"; see also *GSR-Meter.*

electro-psychometer ("E-meter") : see *GSR-Meter.*

elocution : the skillful use of clearly directed and expressive speech; the expert demonstration of articulation, pronunciation and dictation to express a message.

emotional encoding : the readable substance/material (data) of *'imprints'*; associations of sensory experience with an *imprint*; perceptions of our environment that receive an *emotional charge*, which form or reinforce facets of an *imprint*; perceptions recorded and stored as an *imprint* within the "emotional range" of energetic manifestation; the formation of an energetic store or charge on a channel that fixes emotional responses as a mechanistic automation, which is carried on in an individual's *Spiritual Timeline* (or personal continuum of existence).

enact : to make happen; to bring into action; to make part of an act.

encompassing : to form a circle around, surround or envelop around.

end point : the moment when the goal of a process has been achieved and to continue on with it will be detrimental to the gains; the finality of a process when the *Seeker* has achieved their optimum state from the current cycle (whether or not they run through it again at a later date with a different level of *Awareness* or knowledge base doesn't change the fact that it has flattened the standing wave

energetic exchange : communicated transmission of energetically encoded "information" between fields, forces or source-points that share some degree of interconnectivity; the event of "waves" acting upon each other like a force, flowing in regard to their proximity, range, frequency and amplitude.

energy signatures : a distinctive pattern of energetic action.

enforcement : the act of compelling or putting (effort) into force; to compel or impose obedience by force; to impress strongly with applications of stress to demand agreement or validation; the lowest-level of direct control by physical effort or threat of punishment; a low-level method of control in the absence of true communication.

engineering : the *Self-directed* actions and efforts to utilize knowledge (observed causality/science), maths (calculations/quantification) and logic (axioms/formulas) to understand, design or manifest a solid structure, machine, mechanism, engine or system; as *"Reality Engineering"* in *NexGen Systemology*—intentional *Self-directed* adjustment of existing Reality conditions; the application of total *Self-determinism* in *Self-Honesty* to change apparent Reality using fundamentals of *Systemology* and *Cosmic Law*.

entanglement : tangled together; intertwined and enmeshed systems; in *NexGen Systemology*, a reference to the interrelation of all particles as waves at a higher point of connectivity than is apparent, since wave-functions only "collapse" when someone is *Observing*, or doing the measuring, evaluating, &tc.

entropy : the reduction of organized physical systems back into chaos-continuity when their integrity is measured against space over time; reduction toward a zero-point.

epicenter : the point from which shock-waves travel.

epistemology : a school of philosophy focused on the truth of knowledge and knowledge of truth; theories regarding validity and truth inherent in any structure of knowledge and reason; the original "school of philosophy" from which all other "disciplines" were derived; the study of knowing how to know knowledge, reason and truth.

erroneous : inaccurate; incorrect; containing error.

esoteric : hidden; secret; knowledge understood by a select few.

etching : to cut, bite or corrode with acid to produce a pattern.

ethics : an intellectual philosophy concerning *rightness* and *wrongness* based on "logic" and "reason" (rationale) combined with observable consequences and tendencies of action or conduct; formal name for a "moral philosophy" (study of moral choices); in ancient times, originally treated *one-to-one* with "Cosmic Law" regarding *causation*, *order* and *sequence*; an objective (Universal) philosophy of *rightness* and *wrongness*, treated separate from culture-specific (subjective/relative) considerations, such as *morals* and *dogma*; in *NexGen Systemology* (*Grade-IV Metahuman Systemology*), a dynamic philosophy (applying "logic-and-reason") to understand the nature of "reality agreements" concerning *rightness* and *wrongness*, then treating the most optimum conditions of continued existence ("SURVIVAL" in *Beta-existence*; "CREATION" in *Alpha*) for the highest affected "Sphere of Existence" (on the *Standard Model*).

ethics processing : a *systematic processing* methodology introduced for bridging *Grade-IV Metahuman Systemology* (*Wizard Level-0*) with *Grade-V Spiritual Systemology* (*Wizard Level-1*) that emphasizes personal realization of *"Ethics"* and increased ability and responsibility to confront the "rightness" and "wrongness" of past actions (on the Backtrack), including defragmentation of *"Harmful Acts"* (as *Imprinting Incidents*) and any corresponding *"Hold-Backs"* and *"Hold-Outs"* (which reduce *Actualized Awareness* and prompt an individual to *withdraw* their *reach*); also *"Route-3E."*

etymology : the origins of "words" and their development.

evaluate : to determine, assign or fix a set value, amount or meaning.

exacting : a demanding rigid effort to draw forth from.

executable : the supreme authoritative ability to carry out according to design.

existence : the *state* or fact of *apparent manifestation*; the resulting combination of the Principles of Manifestation: consciousness, motion and substance; continued *survival*; that which independently exists; the *'Prime Directive'* and sole purpose of all manifestation or Reality; the highest common intended motivation driving any *"Thing"* or *Life*.

existential : pertaining to existence, or some aspect or condition of existence.

exoteric : public knowledge or common understanding; the level of understanding and *Knowing* maintained by the "masses"; how a thing is generally understood "by all" or the opposite of *esoteric*.

experiential data : accumulated reference points we

store as memory concerning our "experience" with Reality.

exponent : a person that is a critical example of something.

extant : in existence; existing.

exterior : outside of; on the outside; in *NexGen Systemology*, we mean specifically the POV of *Self* that is *'outside of'* the *Human Condition,* free of the physical and mental trappings of the Physical Universe; a metahuman range of consideration; see also *'Zu-Vision'*.

external : a force coming from outside; information received from outside sources; in *NexGen Systemology*, the objective *'Physical Universe'* existence, or *beta-existence*, that the Physical Body or *genetic vehicle* is essentially *anchored* to for its considerations of locational space-time as a dimension or POV.

extrapolate : to make an estimate of the "value" outside of the perceivable range.

extropy : *NexGen Systemology NewSpeak*—the reduction of organized spiritual systems back into a singularity of Infinity when their integrity is measured against space over time; reduction toward an infinitate; the opposite of *entropy*.

—F—

facets : an aspect, an apparent phase; one of many faces of something; a cut surface on a gem or crystal; in *NexGen Systemology*—a single perception or aspect of a memory or "*Imprint*"; any one of many ways in which a memory is recorded; perceptions associated with a painful emotional (sensation) experience and "*imprinted*" onto a metaphoric lens through which to view future similar experiences; other secondary terminals that are associated with a particular terminal, painful event or experience of loss, and which may exhibit the same encoded significance as the activating event.

faculties : abilities of the mind (individual) inherent or developed.

fallacy : a deceptive, misleading, erroneous and/or false beliefs; unsound logic; persuasions, invalidation or enforcement of Reality agreements based on authority, sympathy, bandwagon/mob mentality, vanity, ambiguity, suppression of information, and/or presentation of false dichotomies.

fate : what is brought to light or actualized as experience; the actual *course* taken to reach an end, charted end, or final *destination*; in *NexGen Systemology*, the *'fate'* of a *'Human Spirit'* (or *'Alpha Spirit'*) is determined by the choice of course taken to experience *Life*.

feedback loop : a complete and continuous circuit flow of energy or information directed as an output from a source to a target which is altered and return back to the source as an input; in *General Systemology*—the continuous process where outputs of a system are routed back as inputs to complete a circuit or loop, which may be closed or connected to other systems/circuits; in *NexGen Systemology*—the continuous process where directed *Life* energy and *Awareness* is sent back to *Self* as experience, understanding and memory to complete an energetic circuit as a loop.

flattening a wave : see *"process-out"* for definition; also see *"collapsing a wave."*

flow : movement across (or through) a channel (or conduit); a direction of active energetic motion typically distinguished as either an *in-flow*, *out-flow* or *cross-flow*.

fodder : food, esp. for cattle; the raw material used to create.

forgive(ness) : to let go of resentment (against an offender, source of *Harmful-Act*) or give up emotional (energetic) turbulence connected to inclinations to punish; a legal pardon; to intentionally "overlook" (as opposed to "forget") the repayment of a debt or sense of something owed.

fractal : a wave-curve, geometric figure, form or pattern, with each part representative of the same characteristics as the whole; any baseline, sequence or pattern where the 'whole' is found in the 'parts' and the 'parts' contain the 'whole'; a pattern that reoccurs similarly at various scales/levels on a continuous whole; a subset of a Euclidean space explored in higher-level academic mathematics, in which fractal dimensions are found to exceed topological ones; in NexGen Systemology, a "fractal-like" description is used specifically for a pattern or form that has a reoccurring nature without regard to what level or scale it is manifest upon. Examples include the formation of crystals, tree-like patterns, the comparison of atoms to solar systems to galaxies, &tc.

fragmentation : breaking into parts and scattering the pieces; the *fractioning* of wholeness or the *fracture* of a holistic interconnected *alpha* state, favoring observational *Awareness* of perceived connectivity between parts; *discontinuity*; separation of a totality into parts; in *NexGen Systemology*, a person outside a state of *Self-Honesty* is said to be *fragmented*.

—G—

game : a strategic situation where a "player's" power of choice is employed or affected; a parameter or condition defined by purposes, freedoms and barriers (rules).

game theory : a mathematical theory of logic pertaining to strategies of maximizing gains and minimizing loses within prescribed boundaries and freedoms; a field of knowledge widely applied to human problem solving and decision-making; the application of true knowledge and logic to deduce the correct course of action given all variables and interplay of dynamic systems; logical study of decision making where "players" make choices that affect (the interests) of other "players"; an intellectual study of conflict and cooperation.

general systemology ("systematology") : a methodo-

logy of analysis and evaluation regarding the systems—
their design and function; organizing systems of interrelated information-processing in order to perform a given
function or pattern of functions.

genetic memory : the evolutionary, cellular and genetic
(DNA) "memory" encoded into a *genetic vehicle* or *living organism* during its progression and duplication
(reproduction) over millions (or billions) of years on
Earth; in *NexGen Systemology*—the past-life Earth-
memory carried in the genetic makeup of an organism
(*genetic vehicle*) that is *independent of any* actual "spiritual memory" maintained by the *Alpha Spirit*
themselves, from its own previous lifetimes on Earth
and elsewhere using other *genetic vehicles* with no direct evolutionary connection to the current physical form
in use.

genetic-vehicle : a physical *Life*-form; the physical
(*beta*) body that is animated/controlled by the (*Alpha*)
Spirit using a continuous *Lifeline* (ZU); a physical
(*beta*) organic receptacle and catalyst for the (*Alpha*)
Self to operate "causes" and experience "effects" within
the *Physical Universe*.

gifted : attributing a special quality or ability; having
exceptionally high intelligence or mental faculties.

gnosis : a *Greek* word meaning knowledge, but specifically "true knowledge"; the highest echelon of "true
knowledge" accessible (or attained) only by mystical or
spiritual faculties whereby actualized realizations are
achieved independent of specialized education.

Gnostics : a name meaning "having knowledge" in
Greek language (see also *gnosis*); an early sect of Judeo-
Christian mysticism from the 1st Century AD emphasizing true knowledge by *Self-Honest* experience of
metahuman and spiritual states of beingness, emphasizing defragmentation of "illusion" and overcoming of
material "deception"; an esoteric proto-Systemology organization disbanded by the Roman Church as heretical.

godhood : a divine character or condition; "divinity."

gradient : a degree of partitioned ascent or descent along some scale, elevation or incline; "higher" and "lower" values in relation to one another.

GSR-Meters ("galvanic skin response"–"electropsy-chometer") : a *biofeedback* device used for measuring electrical resistance (in "Ohms") of the skin surface; one of many parts used in a polygraph system; a highly sensitive "Ohm-meter" with variable range, set points and amplification used to monitor electrical fluctuations of the skin surface.

—H—

harmful-act : a counter-survival mode of behavior or action (esp. that causes harm to one of more *Spheres of Existence*)—or—an overtly aggressive (hostile and/or destructive) action against an individual or any other *Sphere of Existence*; in *Utilitarian Systemology*—a shortsighted (serves fewest/lowest *Spheres of Existence*) intentional overtly harmful action to resolve a perceived problem; a revision of the rule for standard *Utilitarian-ism* for Systemology to distinguish actions which provide the least benefit to the least number of *Spheres of Existence*, or else the greatest harm to the greatest number of *Spheres of Existence*; in *moral philosophy*— an action which can be experienced by few and/or which one would not be willing to experience for them-selves (*theft, slander, rape, &tc*); an iniquity or iniquitous act.

help : to assist survival of; aid continuing optimum suc-cess.

heralded : proclaimed ahead of or prior to; officially announced.

hold-back : withheld communications (esp. actions) such as "*Hold-Outs*"; intentional (or automatic) with-drawal (as opposed to reach); Self-restraint (which may eventually be enforced or automated); not reaching, acting or expressing, when one should be; an ability that is now restrained (on automatic) due to inability to withhold it on Self-determinism alone.

hold-outs : in photography, the numerous snapshots/pictures withheld from the final display or professional presentation of the event; withheld communications; in Utilitarian Systemology—energetic withdrawal and communication breaks with a *"terminal"* and its *Sphere of Existence* as a result of a *"Harmful-Act"*; unspoken or undiscovered (hidden, covert) actions that an individual withholds communications of, fearing punishment or endangerment of *Self-preservation* (*First Sphere*); the act of hiding (or keeping hidden) the truth of a *"Harmful-Act"*; a refusal to communicate with a *Pilot*; also *"Hold-Back."*

holistic : the examination of interconnected systems as encompassing something greater than the *sum* of their "parts."

Homo Novus : literally, the "new man"; the "newly elevated man" or "known man" in ancient Rome; the man who "knows (only) through himself"; in NexGen Systemology—the next spiritual and intellectual evolution of *homo sapiens* (the "modern Human Condition"), which is signified by a demonstration of higher faculties of *Self-Actualization* and clear *Awareness*.

Homo Sapiens Sapiens : the present standard-issue Human Condition; the *hominid* species and genetic-line on Earth that received modification, programming and conditioning by the *Anunnaki* race of *Alpha-Spirits*, of which early alterations contributed to various upgrades (changes) to the genetic-line, beginning approximately 450,000 years ago (*ya*) when the *Anunnaki* first appear on Earth; a species for the Human Condition on Earth that resulted from many specific *Anunnaki* "genetic" and "cultural" *interventions* at certain points of significant advancement—specifically (but not limited to) *circa* 300,000 *ya*, 200,000 *ya*, 40,000 *ya*, and 8,000 *ya*; a species of the Human Condition set for replacement by

Homo Novus.

hostile-motivation : an *imprint* of a counter-survival action (or *"Harmful-Act"*) committed by another against Self, stored as data to justify future actions (retaliation, *&tc.*); any *Sphere of Existence* (though usually an individual) receiving the effect of a *"Harmful-Act"*; an *imprint* used to rationalize "motivation" or "justification" for committing a *"Harmful-Act"*; in systematic *games theory*—the *modus operandi* concerning "payback," "revenge" and "tit-for-tat."

hot button : something that triggers or incites an intense emotional reaction instantaneously; in *NexGen Systemology*—a slang term denoting a highly reactive *channel*, heavily *charged* with a long chain of cumulative *emotional imprinting*, typically (but not necessarily) connected to a significant or "primary" *implant*; a nontechnical label, first applied during *Grade-IV Professional Piloting "Flight School"* research sessions of Spring-Summer 2020, to indicate specific circuits, channels or terminals that cause a *Seeker* to immediately react with intense emotional responses, whether in general, directed to the *Pilot*, or even at effectiveness of processing.

Human Condition : a standard default state of Human experience that is generally accepted to be the extent of its potential identity (*beingness*)—currently treated as *Homo Sapiens Sapiens,* but which is scheduled for replacement by *Homo Novus.*

humanistic psychology : a field of academic psychology approaching a holistic emphasis on *Self-Actualization* as an individual's most basic motivation; early key figures from the 20th century include: Carl Rogers, Abraham Maslow, L. Ron Hubbard, William Walker Atkinson, Deepak Chopra and Timothy Leary (to name a few).

hypothetical : operating under the assumption a certain aspect actual "is."

—I—

identification : the association of *identity* to a thing; a label or fixed data-set associated to what a thing is; association "equals" a thing, the "equals" being key; an equality of all things in a group, for example, an "apple" identified with all other "apples"; the reduction of "I-AM"-*Self* from a *Spiritual Beingness* to an "identity" of some form.

identity : the collection of energy and matter—including memory—across a "*Spiritual Timeline*" that we consider as "I" of *Self*, but the "I" is an individual and not an identification with anything other than *Self* as *Alpha-Spirit*.

identity-system : the application of the *ZU-line* as "I"— the continuous expression of *Self* as *Awareness* across a "*Spiritual Timeline*"; see "*identity*."

illuminated : to supply with light so as to make visible or comprehensible.

imagination : the ability to create *mental imagery* in one's Personal Universe at will and change or alter it as desired; the ability to create, change and dissolve mental images on command or as an act of will; to create a mental image or have associated imagery displayed (or "conjured") in the mind that may or may not be treated as real (or memory recall) and may or may not accurately duplicate objective reality; to employ *Creative Abilities* of the Spirit that are independent of reality agreements with beta-existence.

Imaginomicon : the fourth professional publication of Mardukite Systemology, released publicly in mid- 2021; the second professional text in Grade-IV Metahuman Systemology, released as "*Liber-3D*"; contains fundamental theory of "*Spiritual Ability*" and "*Route-0*" systematic processing methodology.

immersion : plunged or sunk into; wholly surrounded by.

imperative : a high-level authoritarian command; a command triggering urgency and necessity of a certain goal or directive; see also "*Spheres of Existence*" and "*Prime Directive.*"

implant : to graft or surgically insert; to establish firmly by setting into; to instill or install a direct command or consideration in consciousness (Mind-System, &tc.); a mechanical device inserted beneath the surface/skin; in *Metahuman Systemology*, an "energetic mechanism" (linked to an Alpha-Spirit) composing a circuit-network and systematic array of energetic receptors underlying and filter-screening communication channels between the Mind-System and *Self*; an energetic construct installed upon entry of a Universe; similar to a platen or matrix or circuit-board, where each part records a specific type or quality of *emotionally encoded imprints* and other "heavily charged" *Mental Images* that are "impressed" by future encounters; a basic platform on which certain *imprints* and *Mental Images* are encoded (keyed-in) and stored (often beneath the surface of "knowing" or *Awareness* for that individual, although an implanted "command" toward certain inclinations or behavioral tendencies may be visibly observable.

imprint : to strongly impress, stamp, mark (or outline) onto a softer 'impressible' substance; to mark with pressure onto a surface; in *NexGen Systemology*, the term is used to indicate permanent Reality impressions marked by frequencies, energies or interactions experienced during periods of emotional distress, pain, unconsciousness, loss, enforcement, or something antagonistic to physical (personal) survival, all of which are are stored with other reactive response-mechanisms at lower-levels of *Awareness* as opposed to the active memory database and proactive processing center of the Mind; an experiential "memory-set" that may later resurface—be triggered or stimulated artificially—as Reality, of which similar responses will be engaged automatically; holographic-like imagery "stamped" onto consciousness as composed of energetic *facets* tied to the "snap-shot" of an experience.

imprinting incident : the first or original event instance communicated and *emotionally encoded* onto an individual's *"Spiritual Timeline"* (recorded memory from all lifetimes), which formed a permanent impression that is later used to mechanistically treat future contact on that channel; the first or original occurrence of some particular *facet* or mental image related to a certain type of *encoded response*, such as pain and discomfort, losses and victimization, and even the acts that we have taken against others along the Spiritual Timeline of our existence that caused them to also be *Imprinted*.

inadvertent : an unintended (knowingly) result caused by low-Awareness actions; applying effort (enacting change) outside Self-Honesty, leading to negligent oversights with harmful outcomes.

incarnation : a present, living or concrete form of some thing, idea or beingness; an individual lifetime or lifecycle from birth/creation to death/destruction independent of other lifetimes or cycles.

inception : the beginning, start, origin or outset.

incite : to urge on or cause; instigate; prove or stimulate into action.

indefinable : without a clear definition being currently presented.

individual : a person, lifeform, human entity or creature; a *Seeker* or potential *Seeker* is often referred to as an "individual" within Mardukite Zuism and Systemology materials.

infinite existence : "immortality."

infinitude : being infinite; quantity or quality of *Infinity*.

inhibited : withheld, held-back, discouraged or repressed from some state.

iniquities : wickedness or wicked acts ("sinful" in religious use); literal etymology, "that which is not equal";

synonymous with *Harmful-Acts.*

"in phase" : see *"phase alignment."*

insistence : repeated use of a communicated energy into a form that demands acknowledgment, is more difficult to avoid or ignore.

institution : a social standard or organizational group responsible for promoting some system or aspect in society.

intention : the directed application of Will; to intend (have "in Mind") or signify (give "significance" to) for or toward a particular purpose; in *NexGen Systemology* (from the *Standard Model*)—the spiritual activity at WILL (5.0) directed by an *Alpha Spirit* (7.0); the application of WILL as "Cause" from a higher order of Alpha Thought and consideration (6.0), which then may continue to relay communications as an "effect" in the universe.

inter-dimensional : systems that are interconnected or correlated between the Physical Universe and the Spiritual Universe—or between "dimension states" observably identified as "physical," "emotional," "psychological" and "spiritual." The only point of true interconnectivity that we can systematically determine is called *"Life"* or the POV of *Self.*

interior : inside of; on the inside; in *NexGen Systemology*, we mean specifically the POV of *Self* that is fixed to the *'internal' Human Condition,* including the *Reactive Control Center* (RCC) and Mind-System or *Master Control Center* (MCC); within *beta-existence*.

intermediate : a distinct point between two points; actions between two points.

internal : a force coming from inside; information received from inside sources; in *NexGen Systemology*, the objective *'Physical Universe'* experience of *beta-existence* that is associated with the Physical Body or *genetic vehicle* and its POV regarding sensation and perception; from inside the body; within the body.

interrogation : obtaining specific information through responses to questions, such as in 'systematic processing' and other forms of two-way communication.

invalidate : decrease the level or degree or *agreement* as Reality.

invest : spend on; give or devote something in exchange for a beneficial result; to endow with.

—**J**—

justice : observable social actions (or consequential re-action) and predetermined civic (legal) processes employed in a society or group to uphold or enforce their reality agreements concerning *"law"*; a civic authority and administrative body responsible for carrying out practical/physical responses and penalties; the words, *"just," "justice"* and *"justification,"* all stem from the Latin *"jus"* (meaning *"morally right," "law, in accordance with"* and *"lawful"*) or *"iustus"* (expressing what is "true," "proper," "up-right" and "justified").

—**K**—

"kNow" : a creative spelling and use of semantics for *"know"* and *"now"* to indicate the state of present-time actualized "Awareness" as Self (Alpha-Spirit), developed for fun dual-meaning messages made by early Mardukite Systemologists in 2008-9, such as "Live in the kNow" or "Be in the kNow"—and even "Drown in the kNow" (parodying a song featuring Matisyahu, by electronic music duo, *Crystal Method*).

knowledge : clear personal processing of informed understanding; information (data) that is actualized as effectively workable understanding; a demonstrable understanding on which we may 'set' our *Awareness*—or literally a "know-ledge."

KI : an ancient cuneiform sign designating the *'physical zone'*; the *Physical Universe*—comprised of physical matter and physical energy in action across space and observed as time; a direction of motion toward material *Continuity,* away from or subordinate to the Spiritual (*'AN'*); the physical condition of existence providing for our *beta* state of *Awareness* experienced (and interacted with) as an individual *Lifeform* from our primary Alpha state of Identity or *I-AM-Self* in the *Spiritual Universe* (*'AN'*).

kinetic : pertaining to the energy of physical motion and movement.

—L—

law : a formal codified outline (or list) of *ethical* standards regarding social participation and acceptable behavior, like a "*code,*" except that it *is* enforced by civic consequences (or even "*Cosmic Law*") when not adhered to, usually with punishment coming either by the group (exclusively) or by involvement with an "outside party" or societal (legal) authority; a predictable sequence of naturally occurring events that will consistently repeat under the right conditions (such as "*Cosmic Law*" or "*Natural Law*").

learned : highly educated; possessing significant knowledge.

level : a physical or conceptual *tier* (or plane) relative to a *scale* above and below it; a significant *gradient* observable as a *foundation* (or surface) built upon and subsequent to other levels of a totality or whole; a *set* of "*parameters*" with respect to other such *sets* along a *continuum*; in *NexGen Systemology,* a *Seeker's* understanding, *Awareness* as *Self* and the formal grades of material/instruction are all treated as "*levels.*"

Liber-One : First published in October 2019 as "*The Tablets of Destiny: Using Ancient Wisdom to Unlock Human Potential*" by Joshua Free; republished in the complete *Grade-III* anthology, "*The Systemology Handbook*"; revised in August 2022 as "*The Tablets of Destiny (Revelation): How Long-Lost Anunnaki Wisdom*

Can Change the Fate of Humanity."

Liber-Two : First published in October 2020 as "*Metahuman Destinations: Piloting the Course to Homo Novus*" by Joshua Free; an anthology of the *Grade-IV* "Professional Piloting Course," containing revised materials from *Liber-2C*, *Liber-2D* and (most of) *Liber-3C*; republished in the complete *Grade-IV* anthology, "*The Metahuman Systemology Handbook.*"

Liber-Three : see "*Liber-3E.*"

Liber-2B : First published in December 2019 as "*Crystal Clear: The Self-Actualization Manual & Guide to Total Awareness*" by Joshua Free; republished in the complete *Grade-III* anthology, "*The Systemology Handbook*"; revised in April 2022 as "*Crystal Clear (Handbook for Seekers): Achieve Self-Actualization and Spiritual Ascension in This Lifetime.*"

Liber-2C : First published in April 2020 as "*Communication and Control of Energy & Power: The Magic of Will & Intention (Volume One)*" by Joshua Free; revision republished as an integral part of the *Grade-IV* "Professional Piloting Course," in October 2020 within "*Metahuman Destinations*" (*Liber-Two*); republished in the complete *Grade-IV* anthology, "*The Metahuman Systemology Handbook.*"

Liber-2D : First published in June 2020 as "*Command of the Mind-Body Connection: The Magic of Will & Intention" (Volume Two)*" by Joshua Free; revision republished as an integral part of the *Grade-IV* "Professional Piloting Course," in October 2020 within "*Metahuman Destinations*" (*Liber-Two*); republished in the complete *Grade-IV* anthology, "*The Metahuman Systemology Handbook.*"

Liber-3C : First published in July 2020 as "*Now You Know: The Truth About Universes & How You Got Stuck in One*" by Joshua Free; a discourse in the *Grade-IV* Metahuman Systemology series; a revision of one part republished in October 2020 within the "*Profess-*

ional Piloting Course" manual, "*Metahuman Destinations*" (*Liber-Two*), a revision of the remaining part republished in June 2021 within the "*Imaginomicon*" (*Liber-3D*); republished in the complete *Grade-IV* anthology, "*The Metahuman Systemology Handbook.*"

Liber-3D : First published in June 2021 as "*Imaginomicon: The Gateway to Higher Universes (A Grimoire for the Human Spirit)*" by Joshua Free; a manual completing the *Grade-IV* (Metahuman Systemology) professional series with a treatment of "Wizard Level-0"; revised in June 2022 as "*Imaginomicon (Revised Edition): Approaching Gateways to Higher Universes (A New Grimoire for the Human Spirit)*"; republished in the complete *Grade-IV* anthology, "*The Metahuman Systemology Handbook.*"

Liber-3E (Liber-Three) : First published in April 2022 as "*The Way of the Wizard: Utilitarian Systemology (A New Metahuman Ethic)*" by Joshua Free; a professional manual bridging *Grade-IV* (Metahuman Systemology, *Wizard Level-0*) with *Grade-V* (Spiritual Systemology, *Wizard Level-1*); republished in the complete *Grade-IV* anthology, "*The Metahuman Systemology Handbook.*"

localized : brought together and confined to a particular place.

logic : philosophical science of correct *reasoning*.

logic equations : using symbols and basic mathematical logic to establish the validity of statements or to see how a variable within a system will change the result; a basic demonstration of proportion or relationship between variables in a system.

logistics : pertaining to the movement or transportation between locations.

—**M**—

macrocosmic : taking examples and system demonstrations at one level and applying them as a larger demonstration of a relatively higher level or unseen di-

288 – Technical Dictionary

mension.

malefactor : a person that knowingly commits *Harmful-Acts*; a source of frequent turbulence and destruction on a system.

manifestation : something brought into existence.

Marduk : founder of Babylonia; patron Anunnaki "god" of Babylon.

Mardukite Zuism : a Mesopotamian-themed (Babylonian-oriented) religious philosophy and tradition applying the spiritual technology based on *Arcane Tablets* in combination with "Tech" from *NexGen Systemology*; first developed in the New Age underground by Joshua Free in 2008 and realized publicly in 2009 with the formal establishment of the *Mardukite Chamberlains*. The text *"Tablets of Destiny"* is a crossover from Mardukite Zuism (and Mesopotamian Neopaganism) toward higher spiritual applications of Systemology.

Master-Control-Center (MCC) : a perfect computing device to the extent of the information received from "lower levels" of sensory experience/perception; the proactive communication system of the *"Mind"*; a relay point of active *Awareness* along the Identity's *ZU-line*, which is responsible for maintaining basic *Self-Honest Clarity* of *Knowingness* as a *seat of consciousness* between the *Alpha-Spirit* and the secondary *"Reactive Control Center"* of a *Lifeform* in *beta existence*; the Mind-center for an *Alpha-Spirit* to actualize cause in the *beta existence*; the analytical *Self-Determined* Mind-center of an *Alpha-Spirit used* to project *Will* toward the genetic body; the point of contact between *Spiritual Systems* and the *beta existence*; presumably the *"Third Eye"* of a being connected directly to the *I-AM-Self*, which is responsible for *determining* Reality at any time; in *NexGen Systemology*, this is plotted at (4.0) on the continuity model of the *ZU-line*.

"Master Grades" : literary materials by Joshua Free

(written between 1995 and 2019) revised and compiled for the "Mardukite Academy of Systemology" instructional grades—"Route of Magick & Mysticism" (*Grade I, Part A*), "Route of Druidism & Dragon Legacy" (*Grade I, Part D*), "Route of Mesopotamian Mysteries" (Grade II) and "Route of Mardukite Systemology" or "Pathway to Self-Honesty" (*Grade III*).

maxim : the greatest or highest *premise* of a paradigm or particular literary *treatment*; a concise rule for conducting action or treating some subject; the most relevant "proverbial adage" applicable.

MCC : see "*Master-Control-Center.*"

mental image : a subjectively experienced "picture" created and imagined into being by the Alpha-Spirit (or at lower levels, one of its automated mechanisms) that includes all perceptible *facets* of totally immersive scene, which may be forms originated by an individual, or a "facsimile-copy" ("snap-shot") of something seen or encountered; a duplication of wave-forms in one's Personal Universe as a "picture" that mirror an "external" Universe experience, such as an *Imprint*.

Mesopotamia : land between Tigris and Euphrates River; modern-day Iraq; the primary setting for ancient *Sumerian* and *Babylonian* traditions thousands of years ago, including activities and records of the *Anunnaki.*

metahumanism : an applied philosophy of *transhumanism* with an emphasis on "spiritual technologies" as opposed to "external" ones; a new state or evolution of the *Human Condition* achievable on planet Earth, rooted in *Self-Honesty*, whereby individuals are operating *exterior* to considerations that are fixed exclusively to the *genetic vehicle* (Human Body) and independent of the *emotional encoding* and *associative programming* typical of the present standard-issue *Human Condition.*

Metahuman Destinations : the third professional publication of Mardukite Systemology, released publicly in

October 2020; the first professional text in Grade-IV Metahuman Systemology, released as *"Liber-Two"* and containing materials from *Liber-2C, Liber-2D* and *Liber-3C*; contains fundamental theory of *"Professional Piloting"* and *"Route-3"* systematic processing methodology. Reissued as two volumes in 2022.

meter : a device used to measure; see *GSR-Meter.*

methodology : a complete system of applications, methods, principles and rules to compose a *'systematic'* paradigm as a "whole"—esp. a field of philosophy or science.

"mind's eye" : following semantics of archaic esoterica, the point where "mental pictures" (and senses) are generated that define what an individual believes they are experiencing in present time; activities or phenomenon described in archaic esoterica as the "Third-Eye" (or actualized MCC) where the *Alpha-Spirit* directly interacts with the organic *genetic vehicle* in *beta-existence*; in the semantics of basic Mardukite Zuism and Hermetic Philosophy, *Self-directed* activity on the plane of "mental consciousness" between "spiritual consciousness" of the *Alpha-Spirit* and "physical/emotional consciousness" of the *genetic vehicle*; *NexGen* 'slang' used to describe "consciousness activity" *Self-directed* by an actualized WILL.

misappropriated : put into use incorrectly; to apply ineffectively or as unintended by design or definition.

missed hold-out : an individual's *Hold-Out* that someone else nearly found out about, or which leaves the individual wondering if they did actually find out or not; undisclosed event when someone else's behavior or speech restimulates emotional-response-reactions ("worry" *&tc.*) about potential discovery of a withheld *Harmful-Act* or *Hold-Out*; in *systematic processing*, a Seeker's "held-out" (hidden) data that they expect to be discovered during a *session*, but which is *missed* by the Pilot.

morals : widely held culturally conditioned (socially learned) ethical standards of conduct used to "judge" *rightness* from *wrongness* of an individual's character, personality or actions (which may or may not be intellectually and emotionally influenced by "local" religious customs, taboos and *dogma*; basic social reality agreements determining "proper conduct" and "right actions" (behavior) based on civic *laws*, social *codes* and religious *doctrines* of a particular society or group and its own cultural experiences of *Reality*.

motor functions : internal mechanisms that allow a body to move.

—N—

Nabu : the *Anunnaki* "god of wisdom, writing and knowledge" for Babylonian (Mardukite) Tradition.

negligible : so small or trifle that it may be disregarded.

neophyte : a beginning initiate or novice to a particular sect or methodology; novitiate or entry-level grade of training, study and practice of an esoteric order or mystical lodge (fellowship).

neurotransmitter : a chemical substance released at a physiological level (of the genetic vehicle) that bridges communication of energetic transmission between the *Mind-Body* systems, using the "nervous system" of the physical body; biochemical amino acids and peptides (neuropeptides), hormones, &tc.

NexGen Systemology : a modern tradition of applied religious philosophy and spiritual technology based on *Arcane Tablets* in combination with "*general systemology*" and "*games theory*" developed in the New Age underground by Joshua Free in 2011 as an advanced futurist extension of the "*Mardukite Chamberlains*"; also referred to as "*Mardukite Systemology*," "*Metahuman Systemology*" and "*Spiritual Systemology*."

—O—

292 – *Technical Dictionary*

objective : concerning the "external world" and attempts to observe Reality independent of personal "subjective" factors.

occulted / to occult : hidden by or secreted away; to hide something from view; otherwise *occlude*, to shut out, shut in, or block; to *eclipse*, or leave out of view.

one-to-one : see "*A-for-A.*"

optimum : the most favorable or ideal conditions for the best result; the greatest degree of result under specific conditions.

orchestration : to arrange or compose the performance of a system.

organic : as related to a physically living organism or carbon-based life form; energy-matter condensed into form as a focus or POV of Spiritual Life Energy (*ZU*) as it pertains to beta-existence of *this* Physical Universe (*KI*).

oscillation-alternation : a particular type of (or fluctuation) between two relative states, conditions or degrees; a wave-action between two degrees, such as is described in the action of the *pendulum effect*; a flux or wave-like energy in motion, across space, calculable as time; in systematic processing, alternation is the shift between two direction flows on a circuit channel, such as *inflow* and *outflow*, or between two types of processing, such as *objective* and *subjective*; alternation of a POV creates "space."

—P—

pantheism : religious philosophies that observe God as inherent within all aspects of the Physical Universe.

paradigm : an all-encompassing *standard* by which to view the world and *communicate* Reality; a standard model of reality-systems used by the Mind to filter, organize and interpret experience of Reality.

parameters : a defined range of possible variables with

in a model, spectrum or continuum; the extent of communicable reach capable within a system or across a distance; the defined or imposed limitations placed on a system or the functions within a system; the extent to which a Life or "thing" can *be*, *do* or *know* along any channel within the confines of a specific system or spectrum of existence.

paramount : the most important; of utmost importance; "above all else."

participation : being part of the action; affecting the result.

patter : fast-talk; a manner of quickly delivered speech/words, esp. used to persuade or sell something.

patterns (probability patterns) : observation of cycles and tendencies to predict a causal relationship or determine the actual condition or flow of dynamic energy using a holistic systemology to understand Life, Reality and Existence as opposed to isolating or excluding perceived parts as being mutually separate from other perceived parts.

patron god : the most sacred deity of a region or city, of which most temples and religious services are directed; the personal deity of an individual.

PCL : see "*processing command line.*"

perception : internalized processing of data received by the *senses*; to become *Aware of* via the senses.

personality (program) : the total composite picture an individual "identifies" themselves with; the accumulated sum of material and mental mass by which an individual experiences as their timeline; a "beta-personality" is mainly attached to the identity of a particular physical body and the total sum of its own genetic memory in combination with the data stores and pictures maintained by the Alpha Spirit; a "true personality" is the Alpha Spirit as Self completely defragmented of all erroneous limitations and barriers to consideration, belief, manifestation and intention.

perturbation : the deviation from a natural state, fixed motion, or orbit system caused by another external system; disturbing or disquieting the serenity of an existent state; inciting observable apparent action using indirect or outside actions or 'forces'; the introduction of a new element or facet that disturbs equilibrium of a standard system; the "butterfly effect"; in *NexGen Systemology*, *'perturbation'* is a necessary condition for the *ZU-line* to function as a *Standard Model* of actual *'monistic continuity'*—which is a *Lifeforce* singularity expressed along a spectrum with potential interactions at each degree from any source; the influence of a degree in one state by activities of another state that seem independent, but which are actually connected directly at some higher degree, even if not apparently observed.

phase (identification) : in *NexGen Systemology*, a pattern of personality or identity that is assumed as the POV from *Self*; personal identification with artificial "personality packages"; an individual assuming or taking characteristics of another individual (often unknowingly as a response-mechanisms); also *"phase alignment."*

phase alignment or *"in phase"* : to be in synch or mutually synchronized, in step or aligned properly with something else in order to increase the total strength value; in *NexGen Systemology*, alignment or adjustment of *Awareness* with a particular identity, space or time; perfect *defragmentation* would mean being "in phase" as *Self* fully conscious and Aware as an Alpha-Spirit *in* present *space* and *time*, free of synthetic personalities.

philanthropy : charitable; the intention (or programmed desire) to generously provide personal wealth and service to the well-being and continued existence of others.

physics : regarding data obtained by a material science of observable motions, forces and bodies, including their apparent interaction, in the Physical Universe (specific to this *beta-existence*).

physiology : a material science of observable biological functions and mechanics of living organisms, including codification and study of identifiable parts and apparent systematic processes (specific to agreed upon makeup of the *genetic vehicle* for this *beta-existence*).

pilfering : to steal in small quantities; petty theft.

pilot : a professional steersman responsible for healthy functional operation of a ship toward a specific destination; in *NexGen Systemology*, an intensive trained individual qualified to specially apply *Systemology Processing* to assist other *Seekers* on the *Pathway*.

ping : a short, high pitched ring, chime or noise that alerts to the presence of something; in computer systems, a query sent on a network or line to another terminal in order to determine if there is a connection to it; in *NexGen Systemology*, the sudden somatic twinge or pain or discomfort that is felt as a sensation in the body when a particular terminal (lifeform, object, concept) is 'brought to mind' or contacted on a personal communication channel-circuit; the accompanying sensations and mental images that are experienced as an automatic-response to the presence of some channel or terminal.

player (game theory) : an individual that is making decisions in a game and/or is affected by decisions others are making in the game, especially if those other-determined decisions now affect the possible choices.

point-of-view (POV) : a point to view from; an opinion or attitude as expressed from a specific identity-phase; a specific standpoint or vantage-point; a definitive manner of consideration specific to an individual phase or identity; a place or position affording a specific view or vantage; circumstances and programming of an individual that is conducive to a particular response, consideration or belief-set (paradigm); a position (consideration) or place (location) that provides a specific view or perspective (subjective) on experience (of the objective).

postulate : to put forward as truth; to suggest or assume an existence *to be*; to state or affirm the existence of particular conditions; to provide a basis of reasoning and belief; a basic theory accepted as fact; in *NexGen Systemology*, "Alpha-Thought"—the top-most decisions or considerations made by the Alpha-Spirit regarding the "*is-ness*" (what things "are") about energy-matter and space-time.

potentiality : the total "sum" (collective amount) of "latent" (dormant—present but not apparent) capable or possible realizations; used to describe a state or condition of what has not yet manifested, but which can be influenced and predicted based on observed patterns and, if referring to beta-existence, Cosmic Law.

POV : see "*point-of-view*" and/or "*POV Processing.*"

POV processing : a methodology of *Grade-IV Metahuman Systemology* emphasizing systematic processing toward realizations that improve a Seeker's willingness to manage a present POV and associated *phases*, their ability to transfer POVs freely, increased tolerance to experiences (or encounters) with any other viewpoint, and finally, an actualized realization that a POV is not one-to-one with *Beingness* of *Self*; an extension of *creativeness processing* and "Wizard Level" training that systematically handles *Awareness* of "points" and "spots" in space, from which an Alpha-Spirit may place its own viewpoint of a dimension or Universe—also a prerequisite to upper-route practices such as "*Zu-Vision*" and "*Backtrack.*"

precedent : a matter which precedes or goes before another in importance.

precipitate : to actively hasten or quicken into existence.

preconception : to assign values or evaluate a reaction or response to a past "imprint" of something and treat it as present knowledge or experience.

prehistoric : any time before human history is properly

recorded in writing; prior to c. 4000 B.C.

premise : a basis or statement of fact from which conclusions are drawn.

presence : the quality of some thing (energy/matter) being "present" in space-time; personal orientation of *Self* as an *Awareness* (*POV*) located in present space-time (environment) and communicating with extant energy-matter.

prevalent : of wide extent; an extensive or largely accepted aspect or current state.

Prime Directive : a "spiritual" implant program that installs purposes and goals into the personal experience of a Universe, esp. any *Beta-Existence* (whether a 'Games Universe' or a 'Prison Universe'); intellectually treated as the "Universal Imperative" in some schools of moral philosophy; comparable to "Universal Law" or "Cosmic Ordering."

probability : the causal likelihood for something to result, "effect" or manifest in and as a certain way, manner or degree, based on "observed evaluation" of programming and tendencies that follow Cosmic Law.

"process-out" or **"flatten a wave"** : to reduce *emotional encoding* of an *imprint* to zero; to dissolve a *waveform* or *thought-formed* "solid" such as a "*belief*"; to completely run a *process* to its end, thereby *flattening* any previously "*collapsed-waves*" or *fragmentation* that is obstructing the *clear channel* of *Self-Awareness*; also referred to as "processing-out"; to discharge all previously held emotionally encoded imprinting or erroneous programming and beliefs that otherwise fix the free flow (wave) to a particular pattern, solid or concrete "*is*" form.

processing, systematic : the inner-workings or "through-put" result of systems; in *NexGen Systemology*, a methodology of applied spiritual technology used toward personal Self-Actualization; methods of selective directed attention, communicated language and associative imagery that targets an increase in personal control of the human condition.

processing command line (PCL) or **command line** : a directed input; a specific command using highly selective language for *Systemology Processing*; a predetermined directive statement (cause) intended to focus concentrated attention (effect).

projecting awareness : sending out (motion) or radiating "*consciousness*" from *Self* ("I") to another POV.

proportional : having a direct relationship or mutual interaction with.

protest : a response-communication objecting an enforcement or a rejection of a prior communication; an effort to cancel, rewrite or destroy the existence or "isness" (what something "is") of a previous creation or communication; unwillingness to be the Point-of-View of effect or (receipt-point) for a communication.

Proto-Indo-European (PIE) : in Linguistic-Semantic Sciences, a hypothetical single-source Eurasian root language (c.4500 B.C.) demonstrating common origins of many "word-roots" found in European languages.

psychokinesis (PK) / telekinesis : influencing a (physical) system without (physical) interaction; *psychokinesis* from the Greek for 'soul' and 'movement', and *telekinesis* from the Greek for 'at a distance' and 'movement'.

psychometric evaluation : the relative measurement of personal ability, mental (psychological/thought) faculties, and effective processing of information and external stimulus data; a scale used in "applied psychology" to evaluate and predict human behavior.

—**R**—

rationality / reasoning (game theory) : the extent to which a player seeks to play (make decisions, &tc.) in order to maximize the gains (or else survival) achievable within any given game conditions; the ability and willingness of an individual to reach toward conditions that promote the highest level of survival and existence and make the best choices and moves to see the desired goal manifest.

reactive control center (RCC) : the secondary (reactive) communication system of the "*Mind*"; a relay point of *Awareness* along the Identity's *ZU-line*, which is responsible for engaging basic motors, biochemical processes and any *programmed automated responses* of a living *beta* organism; the reactive Mind-Center of a living organism relaying communications of *Awareness* between causal experience of *Physical Systems* and the "*Master Control Center*"; it presumably stores all emotional encoded imprints as fragmentation of "chakra" frequencies of *ZU* (within the range of the "*psychological/emotive systems*" of a being), which it may *react* to as Reality at any time; in *NexGen Systemology*, this is plotted at (2.0) on the continuity model of the *ZU-line*.

reality : see "*agreement.*"

realization : the clear perception of an understanding; a consideration or understanding on what is "actual"; to make "real" or give "reality" to so as to grant a property of "beingness" or "being as it is"; the state or instance of coming to an *Awareness*; in *NexGen Systemology*, "gnosis" or true knowledge achieved during *systematic processing*; achievement of a new (or "higher") cognition, true knowledge or perception of Self; a consideration of reality or assignment of meaning.

receptacle : a device or mechanism designed to contain and store a specific type of aspect or thing; a container meant to receive something.

recursive : repeating by looping back onto itself to form continuity; *ex.* the "Infinity" symbol is recursive.

relative : an apparent point, state or condition treated as distinct from others.

religion : a concise spiritual *paradigm*, set of beliefs and practices regarding "Divinity," "Infinite Beingness"—or else, "God"—as representative symbol of the *Eighth Sphere of Existence* for *Beta-Existence* (or else "Infinity").

relinquish : to give up control, command or possession of.

repetitively : to repeat "over and over" again; or else "repetition."

responsibility : the *ability* to *respond*; the extent of mobilizing *power* and *understanding* an individual maintains as *Awareness* to enact *change*; the proactive ability to *Self-direct* and make decisions independent of an outside authority.

resurface : to return to (or bring up to) the "surface" of that which has previously been submerged; in *NexGen Systemology*—relating specifically to processes where a *Seeker* recalls blocked energy stored covertly as emotional "*imprints*" (by the RCC) so that it may be effectively defragmented from the "*ZU-line*" (by the MCC).

rhetoric : the art, study or skilled craft of using language eloquently (words, writing, speech preparation); expert communication using "words"; effectively using language for persuasive communication.

Route-0 : a specific methodology from *SOP-2C* denoting "*Creativeness Processing*," as described in the text "*Imaginomicon*" (*Liber-3D*).

Route-0E : a specific methodology (expanding on *Route-0* from *Liber-3D*) denoting "*Conceptual Processing*" applied to *Ethics Beta-Defragmentation*, as described in the text "*Way of the Wizard*" (*Liber-Three* or *Liber-3E*).

Route-1 : a specific methodology from *SOP-2C* denoting "*Resurfacing Processing*," as described in the text "*Tablets of Destiny*" (*Liber-One*) as "RR-SP" (and reissued in "*The Systemology Handbook*").

Route-2 : a specific methodology from *SOP-2C* denoting "*Analytical-Recall Processing*," as described in the text "*Crystal Clear*" (*Liber-2B*) as "AR-SP" (and reissued in "*The Systemology Handbook*").

Route-3 : a specific methodology from *SOP-2C* denoting "*Communication-Circuit Processing*," as described in the text "*Metahuman Destinations*" (*Liber-Two*); also the basis for *SOP-2C* routine.

Route-3E : a specific methodology (expanding on *Route-3* from *SOP-2C*) denoting "*Ethics Processing*," as described in the text "*The Way of the Wizard*" (*Liber-Three* or *Liber-3E*); also related to "Standard Procedure R-3E."

—S—

science : a systematized *paradigm* of Knowingness—from the Latin '*scire*', meaning "know"; an empirical and objective understanding of data collected by observation, calculation and logical deduction—and which may usually be used to predict phenomenon or occurrences in the Physical Universe ("*Beta-Existence*").

scions : a descendant or offspring; an offshoot or branch.

Seeker : an individual on the *Pathway to Self-Honesty*; a practitioner of *Mardukite Systemology* or *NexGen Systemology Processing* that is working toward *Spiritual Ascension*.

Self-actualization : bringing the full potential of the Human spirit into Reality; expressing full capabilities and creativeness of the *Alpha-Spirit*.

Self-determinism : the freedom to act, clear of external control or influence; the personal control of Will to direct intention.

Self-evaluation : see "*psychometric evaluation.*"

Self-honesty : the basic or original *alpha* state of *being* and *knowing*; clear and present total *Awareness* of-and-as *Self*, in its most basic and true proactive expression of itself as *Spirit* or *I-AM*—free of artificial attachments, perceptive filters and other emotionally-reactive or mentally-conditioned programming imposed on the human condition by the systematized physical world; the ability to experience existence without judgment.

self-sustained : self-supported; self-sufficient; independent.

semantics : the *meaning* carried in *language* as the *truth* of a "thing" represented, *A-for-A*; the *effect* of language on *thought* activity in the Mind and physical behavior; language as *symbols* used to represent a concept, "thing" or "solid."

semantic-set : the implied meaning behind any groupings of words or symbols used to define a specific paradigm.

sensation : an external stimulus received by internal sense organs (receptors/sensors); sense impressions.

sentient : a living organism with consciousness or intelligence; a "thinking" or "reasoning" being that perceives information from the "senses."

simulacrum : an tangible likeness, image, facsimile or superficial representation that is similar to or resembles someone or something else; in *NexGen Systemology*, any *genetic vehicle* or physical body is considered a reflective "simulacrum" of, and used as a "vessel-shell" by, the *Alpha-Spirit* or *Self* (I-AM), which otherwise maintains no true finite locatable form in *beta-existence*.

sine-wave : the *frequency* and amplitude of a quantified (calculable) *vibration* represented on a graph (graphically) as smooth repetitive *oscillation* of a *waveform*; a *waveform* graphed for demonstration—otherwise represented in *NexGen Systemology* logic equations as 'Wf,' or in mathematics as the *'function of x'* (fx); graphically representing arcs (*parameters*) of a circular *continuity* on a *continuum*; in the *Standard Model of NexGen Systemology*, the actual 'wave vibration' graphically displayed on an otherwise static *ZU-line* (of Infinity) is a *'sine-wave'.*

singularity : in general use, "to be singular," but our working definition suggests the opposite of individuality (contrary to most dictionaries); in upper-level sciences, a "zero-point" where a particular property or attribute is mathematically treated as "infinite" (such as the "black-hole" phenomenon), or else where apparently dissimilar qualities of all existing aspects (or individuals) share a "singular" expression, nature or quality; additionally, in *NexGen Systemology*, a hypothetical zero-point when apparent values of all parts in a Universe are equal to all other parts before it collapses; in *Transhumanism*, a hypothetical "runaway reaction" in technology, when it becomes self-aware, self-propagating, self-upgradable and self-sustainable, and replaces human effort of advancement or even makes continued human existence impossible; also, technological efforts to maintain an artificial immortality of the Human Condition on a digital mainframe.

slate : a hard thin flat surface material used for writing on; a chalk-board, which is a large version of the original wood-framed writing slate, named for the rock-type it was made from.

somatic : specifically pertaining to the physical body, its sensations and response actions or behaviors as separate from a "Mind-System"; also *"pings."*

SOP-2C : *Standard Operating Procedure #2C* or *Systemology Operating Procedure #2C*; a standardized procedural formula introduced in materials for *"Metahuman Destinations"* (*Liber-Two*); a regimen or outline for standard delivery of systematic processing used by *Systemology Pilots* and *Mardukite Ministers*; a procedure outline of systematic processing, which includes applications of *"Route-1," "Route-2," "Route-3"* and *"Route-0"* as taught for *Grade-IV Professional Piloting*.

space : a viewpoint or *Point-of-View* (POV) extended from any point out toward a dimension or dimensions;

the consideration of a point or spot as an *anchor* or *corner* in addition to others, which collectively define parameters of a dimensional plane; the field of energy/matter mass created as a result of communication and control in action and measured as time (wavelength), such as "distance" between points (or peaks on a wave).

spectrum : a broad range or array as a continuous series or sequence; defined parts along a singular continuum; in physics, a gradient arrangement of visible colored bands diffracted in order of their respective wavelengths, such as when passing *White Light* through a *prism*.

Spheres of Existence (dynamic systems) : a series of *eight* concentric circles, rings or spheres (each larger than the former) that is overlaid onto the Standard Model of Beta-Existence to demonstrate the dynamic systems of existence extending out from the POV of Self (often as a "body") at the *First Sphere*; these are given in the basic eightfold systems as: *Self, Home/Family, Groups, Humanity, Life on Earth, Physical Universe, Spiritual Universe* and *Infinity-Divinity.*

spiritual timeline : a continuous stream of moment-to-moment *Mental Images* (or a record of experiences) that defines the "past" of a spiritual being (or *Alpha-Spirit*) and which includes impressions (*imprints, &tc.*) form all life-incarnations and significant spiritual events the being has encountered; in NexGen Systemology, also "*backtrack.*"

standard issue : equally dispensed to all without consideration.

standard model : a fundamental *structure* or symbolic construct used to evaluate a complete *set* in *continuity* relative to itself and variable to all other *dynamic systems* as graphed or calculated by *logic*.

Standard Model, The (systemology) : in *NexGen Systemology*—our existential and cosmological *standard* *model* or cabbalistic model; a *"monistic continuity model"* demonstrating *total system* interconnectivity "above" and "below" observation of any apparent *parameters*; the original presentation of the *ZU-line*, represented as a singular vertical (*y*-axis) waveform in space across dimensional levels or Universes (*Spheres of Existence*) without charting any specific movement across a dimensional time-graph *x*-axis; The Standard Model of Systemology represents the basic workable synthesis of common denominators in models explored throughout Grade-I and Grade-II material.

static : characterized by a fixed or stationary condition; having no apparent change, movement or fluctuation.

stoicism : pertaining to the school of "stoic" philosophy, distinguished by calm mental attitudes, freedom from desire/passion and essentially any emotional fluctuation.

sub-zones : at ranges "below" which we are representing or which is readily observable for current purposes.

successively : what comes after; forward into the future.

succumb : to give way, or give in to, a relatively stronger superior force.

Sumerian : ancient civilization of *Sumer*, founded in Mesopotamia c. 5000 B.C.

superfluous : excessive; unnecessary; needless.

superstition : knowledge accepted without good reason.

surefooted : proceeding surely; not likely to stumble or fall.

symbiotic : pertaining to the closeness, proximity and affinity between two beings that are in mutual communication or maintaining mutually validating interactions.

symbol : a concentrated mass with associated meaning or significance.

sympathy : a sensation, feeling or emotion—of anger, fear, sorrow and/or pity—that is a *personal reaction* to the misfortune and failure of another being.

syntax : from the Greek, "to arrange together"; the semantic meaning that words convey when combined together; the manner in which words are arranged together to provide an understandable meaning, such as following the structure for a sentence.

system : from the Greek, "to set together"; to set or arrange things or data together so as to form an orderly understanding of a "whole"; also a *'method'* or *'methodology'* as an orderly standard of use or application of such data arranged together.

systematization : to arrange into systems; to systematize or make systematic.

Systemology : see *"NexGen Systemology."*

Systemology Procedure 1-8-0 : advanced spiritual technology within our Systemology, which applies a methodology of systematic practice for experiencing: (1) Self-Awareness, (8) Nothingness and (0) Beingness, introduced for "Crystal Clear" but expanded on for *"Imaginomicon"*; *'one-eight-zero'* is included in, but not the same as application *'one-eighty'*—or else the *Beta-Defrag-Intensive* called *"SOP-180"* or *"Systemology-180."*

Systemology-180 : an intensive systematic processing routine employing all *Grade-III*, *Grade-IV* and crossover *Wizard-Level* work to date; the total sum of all effective philosophical and spiritual applications necessary to professionally *Pilot* a *Seeker* to reach a stable point of *Self-Honesty* and basic *Beta-Defragmentation*, as a prerequisite to treating *"Actualized-Ascension Technologies"* (*A.T.*) of upper-level *Wizard Grades*.

systems theory : see *"general systematology"*

—T—

Tablets of Destiny : the first professional publication of Mardukite Systemology, released publicly in October 2019; the first professional text in Grade-III Mardukite

Systemology, released as *"Liber-One"* and reissued in the Grade-III Master Edition *"Systemology Handbook"*; contains fundamental theory of the *"Standard Model"* and *"Route-1"* systematic processing methodology; revised in 2022 as *"The Tablets of Destiny (Revelation)."*

telekinesis : see *"psychokinesis."*

teleological (teleology) : using the end-goal or purpose of something as an explanation of its function (rather than being a function of its cause); example—Aristotle wrote (in his discourse, *"Metaphysics"*) that the intrinsic (inherent or true nature) *telos* of an 'acorn' is to become a fully formed 'oak tree'; the ends are an underlying purpose, not the cause (also known as "final cause"), or else the famous phrase: "the ends justify the means."

terminal (node) : a point, end or mass on a line; a point or connection for closing an electric circuit, such as a post on a battery terminating at each end of its own systematic function; any end point or 'termination' on a line; a point of connectivity with other points; in systems, any point which may be treated as a contact point of interaction; anything that may be distinguished as an 'is' and is therefore a 'termination point' of a system or along a flow-line which may interact with other related systems it shares a line with; a point of interaction with other points.

thought-experiment : from the German, *Gedankenexperiment*; logical *considerations* or mental models used to concisely visualize consequences (cause-effect sequences) within the context of an imaginary or hypothetical scenario; using faculties of the Mind's Eye to *Imagine* things accurately with *considerations* that *have not* already been consciously experienced in *beta-existence*.

thought-form : apparent *manifestation* or existential *realization* of *Thought-waves* as "solids" even when only apparent in Reality-agreements of the Observer; the treatment of *Thought-waves* as permanent *imprints* obscuring *Self-Honest Clarity* of *Awareness* when reinforced by emotional experience as actualized "thought-formed solids" ("*beliefs*") in the Mind; energetic patterns that "surround" the individual.

thought-habit : reoccurring modes of thought or repeated "self-talk"; essentially "self-hypnosis" resulting in a certain state.

thought-wave or **wave-form** : a proactive *Self-directed action* or reactive-response *action* of *consciousness*; the *process* of *thinking* as demonstrated in *wave-form*; the *activity* of *Awareness* within the range of *thought vibrations/frequencies* on the existential *Life-continuum* or *ZU-line*.

threshold : a doorway, gate or entrance point; the degree to which something is to produce an effect within a certain state or condition; the point in which a condition changes from one to the next.

thwarted : to successfully oppose or prevent a purpose from actualizing.

tier : a series of rows or levels, one stacked immediately before or atop another.

time : observation of cycles in action; motion of a particle, energy or wave across space; intervals of action related to other intervals of action as observed in Awareness; a measurable wave-length or frequency in comparison to a static state; the consideration of variations in space.

timeline : plotting out history in a linear (line) model to indicate instances (experiences) or demonstrate changes in state (space) as measured over time; a singular conception of continuation of observed time as marked by event-intervals and changes in energy and matter across space.

tipping point : a definitive "point" when a series of small changes (to a system) are significant enough to be *realized* or *cause* a larger, more significant change; the critical "point" (in a system) beyond which a significant change takes place or is observed; the "point" at which changes that cross a specific "threshold" reach a noticeably new state or development.

transhumanism : a social science and applied philosophy concerning the next evolved state of the *"Human Condition,"*; progress in two potential directions, either "spiritual" technologies advancing *Self* as an "Alpha-Spirit," or the direction of "external"-"physical" technologies that modify or eliminate characteristics of the *Body*; a theme describing contemporary application of material sciences emphasizing only "physical" and "genetic" parts of the *Human* experience, such as brain activity, cell-life extension and space travel; *NexGen Systemology* recently began distinguishing its emphasis on "spiritual technology" as *"metahumanism."*

transmit : to send forth data along some line of communication; to move a point across a distance.

traumatic encoding : information received when the sensory faculties of an organism are "shocked" into learning it as an "emotionally" encoded *Imprint*; a duplicated facsimile-copy or *Mental Image* of severe misfortune, violent threats, pain and coercion, which is then categorized, stored and reactively retrieved based exclusively on its emotional *facets.*

treat / treatment : an act, manner or method of handling or dealing with someone, something or some type of situation; to apply a specific process, procedure or mode of action toward some person, thing or subject; use of a specific substance, regimen or procedure to make an existing condition less severe; also, a written presentation that handles a subject in a specific manner.

turbulence : a quality or state of distortion or disturbance that creates irregularity of a flow or pattern; the quality or state of aberration on a line (such as ragged edges) or the emotional "turbulent feelings" attached to a particular flow or terminal node; a violent, haphazard or disharmonious commotion (such as in the ebb of gusts and lulls of wind action).

—U—

unconscious : a state when *Awareness* as *Self* is removed totally from the equation of *Life* experience, though it continues to be recorded in lower-level response mechanisms (fixed to a simulacrum or genetic vehicle) for later retrieval.

undefiled : to remain intact, untouched or unchanged; to be left in an original "virgin" state.

understanding : a clear 'A-for-A' duplication of a communication as 'knowledge', which may be comprehended and retained with its significance assigned in relation to other 'knowledge' treated as a 'significant understanding'; the "grade" or "level" that a knowledge base is collected and the manner in which the data is organized and evaluated.

Utopian Philosophy : a social philosophy and ethic for (primarily) independent rural (country-dwelling or pagan) living communities that adopt a neo-Utilitarian moral philosophy (as suggested by Systemology) to enhance the "greater happiness" and "Ascension" of all participants.

—V—

validation : reinforcement of agreements or considerations as "real."

vantage : a point, place or position that offers an ideal viewpoint (POV).

Venn diagram : a diagram for symbolic logic using circles to represent sets and their systematic relationship; popularized by logician *John Venn*.

verbatim : precisely reproduced or duplicated communication *one-to-one* or "word"-for-"word" (*'A-for-A'*).

via : literally, "by way of"; from the Latin, meaning "way."

vibration : effects of motion or wave-frequency as applied to any system.

viewpoint : see *"point-of-view" (POV)*.

vizier : a high ranking official; a minister-of-state.

—**W**—

wave-form : see *"sine-wave."*

wave-function collapse : see *"collapsing a wave."*

Western Civilization : modern contemporary culture, ideals, values and technology, particularly of Europe and North America as distinguished by growing urbanization, industrialization, and inspired by a history of rebellion to strong religious and political indoctrination.

will *or* **WILL** (5.0) : in *NexGen Systemology* (from the *Standard Model*), the Alpha-ability at "5.0" of a Spiritual Being (*Alpha Spirit*) at "7.0" to apply *intention* as "Cause" from consideration or Alpha-Thought at "6.0" that is superior to "beta-thoughts" that only manifest as reactive "effects" below "4.0" and *interior* to the *Human Condition*.

willingness : the state of conscious Self-determined ability and interest (directed attention) to *Be*, *Do* or *Have*; a Self-determined consideration to reach, face up to (*confront*) or manage some "mass" or energy; the extent to which an individual considers themselves able to participate, act or communicate along some line, to put attention or intention on the line, or to produce (create) an effect.

—**Z**—

ziggurat : religious temples of ancient Mesopotamia; stepped-pyramids used for spiritual and religious purposes by Sumerians and Babylonians, many of which are presented as seven tiers, levels or terraces representing "Seven Gates" (or "7 Veils") of existence, separating material continuity of the Earth Plane from "Infinity."

ZU : the ancient Sumerian cuneiform sign for the archaic verb—"*to know,*" "*knowingness*" or "*awareness*"; in *Mardukite Zuism and Systemology*, the active energy/matter of the "Spiritual Universe" (AN) experienced as a *Lifeforce* or *consciousness* that imbues living forms extant in the "Physical Universe" (KI); "*Spiritual Life Energy*"; energy demonstrated by the WILL of an actualized *Alpha-Spirit* in the "Spiritual Universe" (AN), which impinges its *Awareness* into the Physical Universe (KI), animating/controlling *Life* for its experience of *beta-existence* along an individual Alpha-Spirit's personal *Identity-continuum*, called a *ZU-line*.

Zu-Line : a theoretical construct in *Mardukite Zuism and Systemology* demonstrating *Spiritual Life Energy* (*ZU*) as a personal individual "continuum" of Awareness interacting with all Spheres of Existence on the Standard Model of Systemology; a spectrum of potential variations and interactions of a monistic continuum or singular *Spiritual Life Energy (ZU)* demonstrated on the Standard Model; an energetic channel of potential POV and "locations" of Beingness, demonstrated in early Systemology materials as an individual Alpha-Spirit's personal *Identity-continuum*, potentially connecting *Awareness (ZU)* of *Self* with "*Infinity*" simultaneous with all points considered in existence; a symbolic demonstration of the "*Life-line*" on which *Awareness (ZU)* extends from the direction of the "Spiritual Universe" (AN) in its true original *alpha state* through an entire possible range of activity resulting in its *beta state* and control of a *genetic-entity* occupying the *Physical Universe (KI)*.

Zu-Vision : the true and basic (*Alpha*) Point-of-View (perspective, POV) maintained by *Self* as *Alpha-Spirit* outside boundaries or considerations of the *Human Condition* "Mind-Systems" and *exterior* to beta-existence reality agreements with the Physical Universe; a POV of Self *as* "a unit of Spiritual Awareness" that exists independent of a "body" and entrapment in a *Human Condition*; "spirit vision" in its truest sense.

WOULD
YOU
LIKE
TO
KNOW
MORE
???

SYSTEMOLOGY
The Pathway to Self-Honesty

A Basic Introduction to Mardukite Systemology

THE WAY INTO THE FUTURE

A Handbook for the New Human

a collection of
writings by
Joshua Free
selected by
James Thomas

Here are the basic answers to what has held Humanity back from achieving its ultimate goals and unlocking the true power of the Spirit and highest state of Knowing and Being.

"*The Way Into The Future*" illuminates the *Pathway* leading to Planet Earth's true "metahuman" destiny. With *excerpts* from "*Tablets of Destiny*," "*Crystal Clear*," "*Systemology—The Original Thesis*" and "*The Power of Zu*." You can help shine clear light on anyone's pathway!

Carefully selected by Mardukite Publications Officer, James Thomas, this critical *collection of eighteen articles, lecture transcripts and reference chapters* by Joshua Free is sure to be not only a treasured part of your personal library, but also the perfect introduction for all friends, family and loved ones.

(*Basic Grade-III Introductory Pocket Anthology*)

SYSTEMOLOGY
The Pathway to Self-Honesty

THE TABLETS
OF DESTINY
REVELATION

How Long-Lost Anunnaki Wisdom Can Change the Fate of Humanity

by Joshua Free

Mardukite Systemology Liber-One

second edition

Discover the origins of the Pathway to Self-Honesty with the book that started it all!

In this newly revised "Revelations" Academy Edition: Rediscover the original system of perfecting the Human Condition on a Pathway that leads to Infinity. Here is a way!—a map to chart spiritual potential and redefine the future of what is means to be human.

A landmark public debut for Grade-III Systemology and the foundation stone for reaching higher and taking back control of your DESTINY!

The revelation of 6,000 year old secrets, providing the tools and wisdom to unlock human potential...

SYSTEMOLOGY
The Pathway to Self-Honesty

CRYSTAL CLEAR
Handbook for Seekers

Achieving
Self-Actualization
& Spiritual Ascension
in This Lifetime

by Joshua Free

Mardukite Systemology
Liber-2B

second edition

Take control of your destiny and chart the first steps
toward your own spiritual evolution.

Realize new potentials of the Human Condition with
a Self-guiding handbook for Self-Processing
toward Self-Actualization in Self-Honesty using actual
techniques and training provided for the coveted
"Mardukite Self-Defragmentation Course Program"
—once only available directly and privately from the
underground International Systemology Society.

Discover the amazing power behind the
applied spiritual technology
used for counseling and advisement in
the Mardukite Zuism tradition.

SYSTEMOLOGY
The Pathway to Self-Honesty

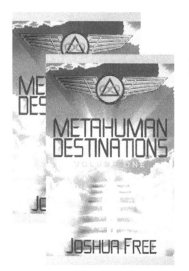

METAHUMAN DESTINATIONS

**The Original 2020
Professional Piloting
Academy Course
for Grade IV**

by Joshua Free

*Mardukite Systemology
Liber-Two (2C,2D,3C)
Revised 2-Volume Set*

available individually

Drawing from the Arcane Tablets and nearly a year of
additional research, experimentation and workshops
since the introduction of applied spiritual technology
and systematic processing methods, Joshua Free
provides the ground-breaking manual for those seeking
to correct—or "defragment"—the conditions that have
trapped viewpoints of the Spirit into programming and
encoding of the Human Condition.

Experience the revolutionary professional course
in advanced spiritual technology for
Mardukite Systemologists to "Pilot" the way to higher
ideals that can free us from the Human Condition
and return ultimate command and control
of creation to the Spirit.

SYSTEMOLOGY
The Gateways to Infinity

IMAGINOMICON

Accessing the Gateway to Higher Universes
A New Grimoire for the Human Spirit

by Joshua Free

*Mardukite Systemology
Grade-IV Metahumanism,
Wizard Level-0, Liber-3D*

revised edition

The Way Out. Hidden for 6,000 Years.
But now we've found the Key.
A grimore to summon and invoke, command and control,
the most powerful spirit to ever exist.
Your Self.

Access beyond physical existence.
Fly free across all Gateways.
Go back to where it all began and reclaim that
personal universe which the *Spirit* once called *"Home."*

Break free from the Matrix;
control the Mind and command the Body
from outside those systems
— because *You* were never "human" —
fully realize what it means to be a *spiritual being,*
then rise up through the Gateways to Higher Universes
and *BE.*

SYS♀EMOLOGY
The Gateway to Infinite Self-Honesty

THE WAY OF THE WIZARD

Utilitarian Systemology

A New Metahuman Ethic

by Joshua Free

Mardukite Systemology Liber-3E

Grade-IV to Grade-V transition bridge

Your ticket off of a Prison Planet...
...and a Pathway leading to Spiritual Ascension!

Accumulated involvement in dangerous situations, states of confusion, unjust destruction and being at the effect end of faulty—or—blatantly false information, all lend to fragmented purposes that may very well be painted to appear "for our own good." Instead they are non-survival or counter-survival oriented, leading us away from routes to achieve "greater heights"—higher, more ideal, states of knowingness and beingness—including the Magic Universe immediately preceding this one.

Here then is a bridge from Grade-IV to Grade-V, the next great frontier of the *Pathway* crossed by participants in the "Freedom From" workshops led by Joshua Free in 2021.

SYS̊TEMOLOGY
The Gateways to Infinity

SYSTEMOLOGY-180
The Fast-Track to Ascension

A Handbook for Pilots

by Joshua Free

*Mardukite Grade-V
Systemology
Liber-180*

*Expert application of
all Grade-III and Grade-IV
training and techniques*

A perfected "metahuman" state for the Human Condition awaits; free of emotional turbulence, societal programming and an ability to be truly Self-Determined from the clear perspective of the actual Self, the Eternal Spirit or "I-AM" Awareness that is back of and beyond this existence—an "Angel" or "god" that has fallen only by its own considerations, by being convinced that it resides locally here on earth within a perishable human shell.

"Systemology-180" presents newly revised instruction from the Mardukite Academy to deliver the fastest results in climbing the Ladder of Ascension. Hundreds of exercises and techniques that progressively free you from bonds of the Human Condition and increase your spiritual horsepower enough to break the chains and attachments to the material world and an existence confined to a material body.

SYSTEMOLOGY
The Gateways to Infinity

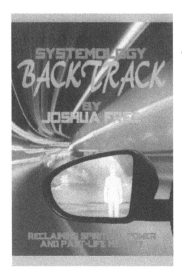

SYSTEMOLOGY:
BACKTRACK

**Reclaiming
Spiritual Power &
Past-Life Memory**

by Joshua Free

*Mardukite Grade-V
Systemology
Liber-4*

*Transcripts of the
original lectures
with diagrams
and glossary*

We are all Spiritual Beings that have known a very long
existence. Even before the evolution of Humans or Earth,
we existed as other forms, in other times and spaces.
We have descended down a very long *track* of potential
Beingness and considerations, a *track* that parallels the
allegory of "Fallen Angels" enticed by mundane bodies;
only to be trapped in them and longing to *Ascend* again.

*What if we could recover the long forgotten Knowingness of our
past existences? What if we could reclaim our true Spiritual power
that we have lost sight of? What if we could actually Backtrack
our descent and return to the Source?*

"*Backtrack*" documents the first advanced course given by
Joshua Free to the Systemology Society for Grade-V.
He candidly introduces the new Wizard-Level subject of
Alpha-Defragmentation to Grade-III and Grade-IV alumni
ready to embark on their next phase of the *Pathway*.

IN A WORLD FULL OF "TENS" BE AN
ELEVEN

THE METAPHYSICS OF STRANGER THINGS

TELEKINESIS, TELEPATHY SYSTEMOLOGY

by Joshua Free

Mardukite Systemology Liber-011

Experimental exploratory edition

Discover the metaphysical truth about the Universe—and maybe even yourself—as we explore what lies beneath the epic saga, *Stranger Things.* You're invited to a world where fantasy, science fiction and horror unite, and games like *Dungeons and Dragons* become reality.

Uncover a world of secret "mind control" projects, just like those at *Hawkins National Laboratory.* Decades of psychedelic experiments among other developmental programs for psychic powers, remote viewing, telekinesis (psychokinesis, PK) and more are revealed. Get an inside look at the operations of a real-life underground organization pursuing the truth about rehabilitating spiritual abilities for an actual "metahuman" evolution on planet Earth.

Premiere edition available in paperback and hardcover!

Commemorating the Mardukite 15th Anniversary!

NECRONOMICON
THE COMPLETE ANUNNAKI BIBLE
(Deluxe Edition Hardcover Anthology)
collected works by Joshua Free

The ultimate masterpiece of Mesopotamian magic, spirituality and history, providing a complete collection—a grand symphony—of the most ancient writings on the planet. The oldest Sumerian and Babylonian records reveal detailed accounts of cosmic history in the Universe and on Earth, the development of human civilization and descriptions of world order. All of this information has been used, since ancient times, to maintain spiritual and physical control of humanity and its systems. It has proved to be the predecessor and foundation of all global scripture-based religious and mystical traditions thereafter. These are the raw materials, unearthed from the underground, which have shaped humanity's beliefs, traditions and existence for thousands of years—right from the heart of the Ancient Near East: Sumer, Babylon and even Egypt...

∞

PUBLISHED BY THE **JOSHUA FREE** IMPRINT REPRESENTING

**The Founding Church of Mardukite Zuism
& Mardukite Academy of Systemology**

mardukite.com

Milton Keynes UK
Ingram Content Group UK Ltd.
UKHW020705220923
429186UK00016B/984